REPORTING QUANTITATIVE RESEARCH IN PSYCHOLOGY

APA Style Products

*Publication Manual of the American Psychological Association,
Sixth Edition*

Concise Rules of APA Style, Sixth Edition

*Reporting Quantitative Research in Psychology: How to Meet APA
Style Journal Article Reporting Standards, Second Edition*
Harris Cooper

*Reporting Qualitative Research in Psychology: How to Meet APA Style
Journal Article Reporting Standards*
Heidi M. Levitt

*Presenting Your Findings: A Practical Guide for Creating Tables,
Sixth Edition*
Adelheid A. M. Nicol and Penny M. Pexman

*Displaying Your Findings: A Practical Guide for Creating Figures,
Posters, and Presentations, Sixth Edition*
Adelheid A. M. Nicol and Penny M. Pexman

Mastering APA Style: Instructor's Resource Guide, Sixth Edition

*Mastering APA Style: Student's Workbook and Training Guide,
Sixth Edition*

APA Style Guide to Electronic References, Sixth Edition

Please visit **http://www.apastyle.org/products/index.aspx** for more
information about APA Style Products or to order.

SECOND EDITION

REPORTING QUANTITATIVE RESEARCH IN PSYCHOLOGY

How to Meet
APA Style Journal
Article Reporting
Standards

HARRIS COOPER

AMERICAN PSYCHOLOGICAL ASSOCIATION
Washington, DC

Published by
American Psychological Association
750 First Street, NE
Washington, DC 20002
www.apa.org

APA Order Department
P.O. Box 92984
Washington, DC 20090-2984
Phone: (800) 374-2721; Direct: (202) 336-5510
Fax: (202) 336-5502; TDD/TTY: (202) 336-6123
Online: http://www.apa.org/pubs/books
E-mail: order@apa.org

In the U.K., Europe, Africa, and the Middle East, copies may be ordered from
Eurospan Group
c/o Turpin Distribution
Pegasus Drive
Stratton Business Park
Biggleswade, Bedfordshire
SG18 8TQ United Kingdom
Phone: +44 (0) 1767 604972
Fax: +44 (0) 1767 601640
Online: https://www.eurospanbookstore.com/apa
E-mail: eurospan@turpin-distribution.com

Typeset in Sabon, Futura, and Universe by Circle Graphics, Inc., Columbia, MD

Printer: Sheridan Books, Chelsea, MI
Cover Designer: Naylor Design, Washington, DC

Library of Congress Cataloging-in-Publication Data

Names: Cooper, Harris M., author. | American Psychological Association.
Title: Reporting quantitative research in psychology : how to meet APA style journal article reporting standards / Harris Cooper.
Other titles: Reporting research in psychology
Description: Second edition. | Washington, DC : American Psychological Association, [2018] | Includes bibliographical references and index.
Identifiers: LCCN 2018003561| ISBN 9781433829376 | ISBN 1433829371
Subjects: LCSH: Psychology—Authorship—Style manuals. | Journalism—Style manuals. | Psychology—Research—Handbooks, manuals, etc. | Report writing—Handbooks, manuals, etc. | Psychological literature—Publishing—Handbooks, manuals, etc.
Classification: LCC BF76.8 .C66 2018 | DDC 150.72/8—dc23 LC record available at https://lccn.loc.gov/2018003561

British Library Cataloguing-in-Publication Data
A CIP record is available from the British Library.

Printed in the United States of America
Second Edition

http://dx.doi.org/10.1037/0000103-000
10 9 8 7 6 5 4 3 2 1

Contents

Acknowledgments

I would like to thank the members of the American Psychological Association Journal Article Reporting Standards (JARS) Working Group for their consent to rework report material for Chapter 1. Also, I thank the members of the JARS Revision Committee. Finally, thanks are extended to Saiying Steenbergen-Hu for providing me with comments on the first edition of this book; to Mary Lynn Skutley and Linda Malnasi McCarter for comments on Chapter 2; and to Art Nezu (on clinical trials), Evan Mayo-Wilson (on nonexperimental designs), and Rex Kline (on structural equation modeling and Bayesian statistics) for feedback on the new revisions to the JARS recommendations.

REPORTING QUANTITATIVE RESEARCH IN PSYCHOLOGY

Reporting Standards for Research in Psychology: Why Do We Need Them? What Might They Be?

Triple-Chocolate Layer Cake

Ingredients:

½ cup cold buttermilk

1 tablespoon instant espresso powder

2 teaspoons vanilla extract

1 cup cake flour

6 tablespoons unsweetened cocoa powder

½ teaspoon salt

¼ teaspoon baking powder

½ teaspoon baking soda

3 large eggs

½ cup unsalted butter, room temperature

Instructions:

Preheat oven. Butter three 8-inch diameter cake pans with 1-inch high sides. Line bottom of three pans. Stir buttermilk, espresso powder, and vanilla until powder dissolves. Sift next five ingredients into large bowl. Add eggs and butter; beat until mixture is thick and smooth. Add buttermilk mixture; beat until light and fluffy. Divide batter among pans. Bake about 20 minutes.

http://dx.doi.org/10.1037/0000103-001

Reporting Quantitative Research in Psychology: How to Meet APA Style Journal Article Reporting Standards, Second Edition, by H. Cooper

Sound tasty? Problem is, I left 1¼ cup of sugar out of the list of ingredients. What would chocolate cake taste like if the recipe left out sugar? And although I told you to preheat the oven, I forgot to say to what temperature (350° F). If I didn't tell you what temperature to set the oven, what are the chances you could follow my recipe and make the cake? (Oops, those 1-inch high pans should have been 1½-inch high; sorry for the mess.)

Why Are Journal Article Reporting Standards Needed?

In many ways, the report of a psychology research project contains a recipe. Without accurate descriptions of the ingredients (the manipulations and measures) and the instructions (research design and implementation), it is impossible for others to replicate what you have done.

Recently, there has been a growing sense in the social and behavioral sciences that the recipes contained in our research reports often do not serve us well. Recognizing this, in 2006 the Publications and Communications Board (P&C Board) of the American Psychological Association (APA) formed a group, the Journal Article Reporting Standards Working Group (JARS Working Group), to look into the issue. The P&C Board wanted to learn about reporting standards that had been developed in fields related to psychology and decide how the issue of reporting standards might be handled in the sixth edition of the *Publication Manual of the American Psychological Association* (APA, 2010; hereinafter referred to as the *Publication Manual*).

The P&C Board asked the JARS Working Group to look at existing reporting standards and adapt them for use by psychology researchers and other behavioral scientists, if this was desirable. The first JARS Working Group was composed of five former editors of APA journals.[1] Then, 7 years later, the P&C Board appointed a working group of seven members to look at JARS, how it had been received by researchers, and how it might be revised and expanded to better meet their needs.[2] At the same time, and because the original JARS Working Group focused exclusively on quantitative research, the P&C Board appointed a separate committee to develop reporting standards for qualitative research.[3] The book you are reading presents the revised reporting standards that came out of the efforts related to quantitative research. A separate volume is dedicated to the reporting standards for qualitative research (Levitt, in press). For ease of exposition, I refer to these reporting standards by the original name, JARS, but you may also see the standards referred to as JARS–Quant to distinguish them from the guidelines for qualitative research (JARS–Qual; Levitt et al., 2018). Both JARS–Quant and JARS–Qual are also referred to as APA Style JARS. Both sets of JARS recommendations are our steps for how to create a good recipe, you might say. Finally, if you are interested in a more in-depth description of why reporting standards are needed, what we found

---

[1]The first JARS Working Group was composed of Mark Appelbaum, Harris Cooper (Chair), Scott Maxwell, Arthur Stone, and Kenneth J. Sher.

[2]The members of the Working Group on Quantitative Research Reporting Standards were Mark Appelbaum (Chair), Harris Cooper, Rex B. Kline, Evan Mayo-Wilson, Arthur M. Nezu, and Stephen M. Rao.

[3]The Working Group on Journal Article Reporting Standards for Qualitative Research members were Heidi M. Levitt (Chair), Michael Bamberg, John W. Creswell, David M. Frost, Ruthellen Josselson, and Carola Suárez-Orozco.

in the literature on this topic, and how the JARS Working Groups went about constructing the standards, see Chapter 9.

What's New in the Revised JARS?

The JARS–Quant Working Group followed the revision process and used the same procedures established by the original JARS Working Group (see Chapter 9). The report of the JARS–Quant Working Group was published in 2018 in *American Psychologist* (Appelbaum et al., 2018).

Most importantly, JARS–Quant now covers types of research that were not included in the original standards. These are included because they often require the reporting of unique features of research that readers need to know in order for the report to be transparent about what was done. Thus, reporting standards for *clinical trials*, or research that evaluates the effects of a health-related therapeutic intervention, were developed by the JARS–Quant Working Group (Chapter 6). Likewise, nonexperimental research—involving perhaps observational, correlational, or historical designs—now have a table with unique reporting standards (Chapter 4), as do studies using longitudinal designs (Chapter 6) and designs that study a single subject or unit (N-of-1; Chapter 6). Studies that are replications of earlier studies (regardless of design) also give rise to reporting issues of their own (Chapter 6). In addition, the revised JARS–Quant sets out reporting standards for two types of statistical analyses: structural equation modeling and Bayesian statistics (Chapter 5). These analyses use procedures and the setting of statistical parameters that go beyond those covered in the general JARS table. Finally, some revisions were made to the original JARS tables to make them clearer and add a few new reporting items that have become commonplace in the past decade.

How to Use the JARS Tables

I present many of the various JARS tables in appendices to the chapters in which they are first discussed. These tables can also be found online (http://www.apastyle.org/jars/index.aspx). In addition, I provide boxes in the text that paraphrase the JARS entries when I discuss that particular material. In some instances, JARS recommendations are repeated in different tables. I won't discuss these twice but will address each recommendation when it first appears and refer you back to that discussion when it appears next.

Table A1.1, in the appendix to this chapter, presents what JARS recommends[4] for information to include in all reports on new quantitative data collections. However, these all-purpose recommendations contain only brief entries regarding (a) the type of research design you employed and (b) your basic statistical analyses. Social and behavioral scientists use many different approaches to these two aspects of methodology. So, there are separate JARS tables in addition to Table A1.1 to cover these. Depending on the research design and analyses you used, you would pick the appropriate set of

---

[4]Of course, JARS is an inanimate object, so it does not actually "recommend" anything. However, I use the active voice for JARS throughout the text for purposes of speedier exposition.

tables to be added to the all-purpose items in Table A1.1. These additional items can be found in the appendices in Chapters 4, 5, 6, and 8. I briefly describe these here to give you the big picture and then add detail in later chapters.

Chapter 2 addresses the material that appears first in a research manuscript. This material includes the title page with an author note; the abstract, which very briefly summarizes the research and its purpose, results, and conclusions; and the introductory section, which sets out the background for the study, why it is important, and what the hypotheses were. Chapter 3 describes the Method section. This is where the sample, measures, and research design are detailed.

Chapter 4 presents the JARS standards for reporting basic research designs. Table A4.1 describes reporting standards for research designs involving a comparison of at least two distinct groups of subjects or participants.[5] The first design covered involves studies with at least one purposive or experimental manipulation and at least one comparison group that gets a different treatment or is treated in the usual way (whatever that may be). What distinguishes this design is that the experimenter has deliberately varied something about the circumstances that different subjects will experience.

Along with Table A4.1, Table A4.2a provides you with items for reporting a group experimental study that used random assignment of subjects to conditions. Alternatively, you would use Table A4.2b to help you report a study that used a purposive manipulation but in which subjects were assigned to conditions using a procedure other than random assignment, such as self-selection or administrative assignment. Thus, depending on how assignment of subjects to conditions was accomplished in your experimental study, you would choose to use Table A4.2a or A4.2b, but not both. The former type of design, involving random assignment, is referred to as an *experiment*, and the latter—the one not employing random assignment—is called a *quasi-experiment*.

Table A4.3 presents the reporting standards (in addition to the all-purpose ones described in Table A1.1) for studies that used no experimental manipulation at all. Examples of these types of studies would be ones that simply observe people's behavior, ask them to complete questionnaires, or use records that already exist. Clearly, if this table is relevant to your study, you would use it rather than Tables A4.1 and A4.2a or A4.2b.

Chapter 5 covers the general reporting requirements for the statistical results of studies with multiple participants in each condition. Also, there are numerous specialized types of statistical analyses that, if they are used, need particular information reported about them. So, in Chapter 5, I include two JARS tables for specialized types of statistical analysis: structural equation modeling (Table A5.1) and Bayesian statistics (Table A5.2).

Chapter 6 covers four additional sets of reporting standards for studies that contain unique design elements. These relate to studies that (a) collect data longitudinally, (b) are meant to be replications of studies that were conducted previously, (c) used only one subject, and/or (d) were clinical trials. Table A6.1 relates to studies that collect longitudinal data—that is, data gathered on more than one occasion. These types of studies are most frequent in developmental psychology, when you want to see how people change over time, or in clinical and health psychology, when you want to see

---

[5]Throughout the text, I use the terms *subjects* and *participants* to refer to the people taking part in a study. Generally, I use *subjects* when referring to studies that involve an experimental manipulation and *participants* when referring to nonexperimental studies.

if the effects of an intervention persist over time. Because Table A6.1 relates to the frequency of collecting data, it covers an aspect of design covered in none of the tables mentioned above but might be relevant to any of them. Therefore, you would use Table A6.1 in addition to the other tables that are relevant to your design. It is needed if, and only if, you collected data on more than one occasion.

Table A6.2 sets out reporting standards for studies that are meant to be replications of earlier studies. Here, the issue of reporting what the differences are between the original study and the study meant to repeat it becomes very important; if the replication doesn't produce the same result as the original study, you need to know how the studies were conducted differently in order to consider why this may have happened. These issues are unique to replication studies. Table A6.2 should be used with any combination of the other tables, depending on the design of the earlier study that is being replicated.

Chapter 6 also covers an additional unique research design, called the N-of-1 or single-case design. It will be of interest if your study was conducted on a single individual or other single unit—for example, a single class or workplace—rather than having multiple subjects in each of the study's conditions. If you did an N-of-1 study, you would complete Table A6.3 along with Table A1.1. Note that the material called for in the introduction and Discussion section in Table A1.1 applies to both types of designs. The material reported in the Method section does as well, including subject characteristics and sampling procedures (in this case, the one individual's demographic characteristics and how he or she was recruited). However, other material in the Method and Results sections would look quite different for a group comparison study and a single-case study, which is why a single-case study needs its own table. For example, in a study with one subject, the intended and achieved sample size is 1. Therefore, power analysis for determining the number of subjects to run is irrelevant for an N-of-1 design. But a complete description of the characteristics of the measures you used in the study is no less important. Similarly, if you examine the entries in Table A1.1 relating to reporting your results, you will see that most are relevant to the N-of-1 design, but they would be reported in a decidedly different way.

When studies evaluate a specific type of experimental intervention, namely, the effects of health interventions, they are called *clinical trials*, and these are also discussed in Chapter 6. Clinical trials can relate to mental health interventions, such as psychotherapy or counseling, or physical health interventions, such as an exercise or dietary program. Clinical trials involve manipulated interventions that are (a) introduced by the experimenters, such as when they recruit subjects to test a new nutrition program, or (b) naturally occurring, such as when a new lunch menu is introduced at a school and researchers are asked to evaluate its effects on student health (e.g., students' weight, frequency of absences because of illness).

An additional set of reporting standards is needed for clinical trials because the amount of detail readers must see about this type of study is greater if they are to adequately understand what transpired in the treatment, what the treatment components were, and what the treatment effects might be. A clinical trial may use random or nonrandom assignment (Table A4.2a or A4.2b), but it always involves an experimental manipulation of the intended treatment. This experimental manipulation can occur in a group design (Table A4.1) or as part of a study with a single subject (Table A6.3). Table A6.4 presents the additional reporting standards for clinical trials. So, if you conducted a clinical trial, you would use Table A6.4 in addition to Table A1.1 (the information included in reports of all new data collections), Table A4.1 (because a clinical trial will always contain a manipulation), and either Table A4.2a or Table A4.2b (depending on how subjects were assigned to conditions). You may also substitute Table A6.3 for Table A4.2a or A4.2b if your clinical trial was conducted on only one subject.

In Chapter 7, I provide the JARS standards for the Discussion section of every study. I also detail those items that should be discussed depending on which type of group research design or specialized strategy for data analyses you used.

Finally, in Chapter 8, Table A8.1 is to be used if you conducted a research synthesis or meta-analysis. These recommendations have a different name, the Meta-Analysis Reporting Standards (MARS). This is a distinct type of research that is meant to identify, summarize, and integrate previous research on a topic rather than to collect new data.

The use of different tables for different research designs and analyses makes it possible to expand JARS even further by adding new tables at a later date.[6] As JARS standards are developed, they can be given different table titles (e.g., JARS now has a table titled "Reporting Standards for Studies With an Experimental Manipulation"; Appelbaum et al., 2018, p. 11) as well as their own subsections within tables (e.g., "Module A: Additional Reporting Standards for Studies Using Random Assignment" and "Module B: Additional Reporting Standard for Studies Using Nonrandom Assignment"; Appelbaum et al., 2018, pp. 11–12). How they are labeled depends on what is needed to fully capture the variations in that research design.

Figure 1.1 provides a flowchart that will help you decide which JARS tables are relevant to your research design. Although it may be daunting to think about the JARS scheme in the abstract, think about a study you know well and work it through the chart. The logic should become apparent to you then.

The Tension Between Complete Reporting and Space Limitations

A thought probably crossed your mind as you examined the entries in the JARS tables: "My goodness! How am I going to fit all of this information into a single report, especially given that the journal I want to submit my paper to has a page limit?" Good question.

There is clearly a tension between transparency in reporting and the space limitations imposed by the print medium. As descriptions of research expand, so does the space needed to report them. However, not everything recommended in JARS (and MARS) needs to go into print. Recent improvements in the capacity of and access to electronic storage of information suggest that this trade-off could someday disappear. For example, APA journals, among others, now make available to authors online archives that can be used to store supplemental materials associated with the articles that appear in

---

[6]The JARS Working Group recognized that our work was incomplete because we included only a few families of research designs. In the future, we hope (and expect) that new tables addressing other research designs will be added to the standards to be used in conjunction with Table A1.1. Also, additional standards could be adopted for any of the parts of a report (see, e.g., Davidson et al., 2003). In future revisions of JARS (and this book), perhaps these will be added.

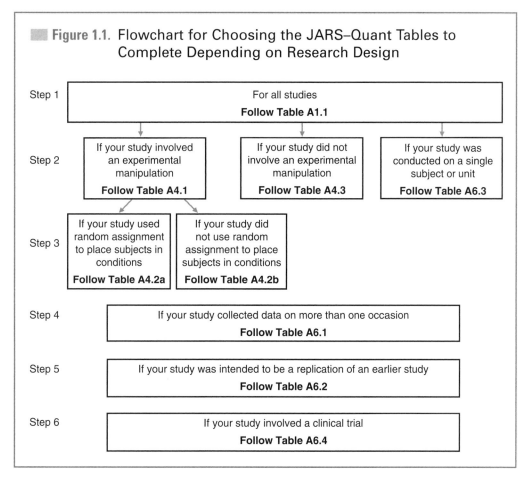

Figure 1.1. Flowchart for Choosing the JARS–Quant Tables to Complete Depending on Research Design

Step 1
For all studies
Follow Table A1.1

Step 2
If your study involved an experimental manipulation
Follow Table A4.1

If your study did not involve an experimental manipulation
Follow Table A4.3

If your study was conducted on a single subject or unit
Follow Table A6.3

Step 3
If your study used random assignment to place subjects in conditions
Follow Table A4.2a

If your study did not use random assignment to place subjects in conditions
Follow Table A4.2b

Step 4
If your study collected data on more than one occasion
Follow Table A6.1

Step 5
If your study was intended to be a replication of an earlier study
Follow Table A6.2

Step 6
If your study involved a clinical trial
Follow Table A6.4

Adapted from "Journal Article Reporting Standards for Quantitative Research in Psychology: The APA Publications and Communications Board Task Force Report," by M. Appelbaum, H. Cooper, R. B. Kline, E. Mayo-Wilson, A. M. Nezu, and S. M. Rao, 2018, *American Psychologist, 73,* p. 5. Copyright 2018 by the American Psychological Association.

print (APA, 2010, pp. 38–40, section 2.13, Appendices and Supplemental Materials). Similarly, it is possible for electronic journals to contain short reports of research with links to websites containing supplemental files.

Therefore, some of the information contained in JARS and MARS might not appear in the published article itself but rather in supplemental materials available online. For example, if the instructions in your investigation were lengthy but critical to understanding what was done, they may be presented verbatim in online supplemental materials. Supplemental materials also might include a flowchart illustrating the flow of participants through the study (see Chapter 5). It might include oversized tables of results (especially those associated with large correlation matrices or with meta-analyses involving many studies), audio or video clips, computer programs, and even primary or supplementary data sets. Of course, you should include these supplemental materials when you submit your report for peer review.

Editors and reviewers can assist you in determining what material is supplemental and what needs to be presented in the article proper. However, *supplemental materials* is probably a misleading term if it gives the impression that the information contained therein is of less importance than that found in the article itself. As JARS suggests, and as I try to argue throughout this book, this information is not less important. In fact, the details of how research has been conducted and what it has found are essential to advance the social sciences. Some of these details are most vital to a more restricted audience—one that wants to know in detail what you did and why and how they, too, might do the same thing—but the information is important nonetheless.

How This Book Can Help You With Your Research

With the above as context, in the chapters that follow I delve more deeply into the individual items you should report that are contained in JARS. As I discuss each item, I try to present a rationale for its inclusion. For some items, the rationale will be fairly obvious, whereas for other items, it may require more explanation; we all know why sugar is important to include in a chocolate cake, but exactly why does the recipe call for baking soda? Then I will give you examples of good and not-so-good ways to present the information called for in JARS.

If you are reading this book as you are writing a research report, the tables that follow not only provide a summary of JARS but also can easily be used as a checklist while you are working. It might also be good to have a copy of the *Publication Manual* handy because I will refer to it frequently.

Appendix 1.1: Journal Article Reporting Standards for All Quantitative Research Designs (JARS–Quant)

▨ **Table A1.1.** Journal Article Reporting Standards for Quantitative Research (JARS–Quant): Information Recommended for Inclusion in Manuscripts That Report New Data Collections Regardless of Research Design

Paper section and topic	Description
Title and title page	
Title	Identify the main variables and theoretical issues under investigation and the relationships between them. Identify the populations studied.
Author note	Provide acknowledgment and explanation of any special circumstances, including <ul><li>Registration information if the study has been registered</li><li>Use of data also appearing in previous publications</li><li>Prior reporting of the fundamental data in dissertations or conference papers</li><li>Sources of funding or other support</li><li>Relationships or affiliations that may be perceived as conflicts of interest</li><li>Previous (or current) affiliation of authors if different from location where study was conducted</li><li>Contact information for the corresponding author</li><li>Additional information of importance to the reader that may not be appropriately included in other sections of the paper.</li></ul>

(table continues)

▨ **Table A1.1.** (*Continued*)

Paper section and topic	Description
Abstract	
Objectives	State the problem under investigation, including • Main hypotheses.
Participants	Describe subjects (animal research) or participants (human research), specifying their pertinent characteristics for this study; in animal research, include genus and species. Participants are described in greater detail in the body of the paper.
Method	Describe the study method, including • Research design (e.g., experiment, observational study) • Sample size • Materials used (e.g., instruments, apparatus) • Outcome measures • Data-gathering procedures, including a brief description of the source of any secondary data. If the study is a secondary data analysis, so indicate.
Findings	Report findings, including effect sizes and confidence intervals or statistical significance levels.
Conclusions	State conclusions, beyond just results, and report the implications or applications.
Introduction	
Problem	State the importance of the problem, including theoretical or practical implications.
Review of relevant scholarship	Provide a succinct review of relevant scholarship, including • Relation to previous work • Differences between the current report and earlier reports if some aspects of this study have been reported on previously.
Hypothesis, aims, and objectives	State specific hypotheses, aims, and objectives, including • Theories or other means used to derive hypotheses • Primary and secondary hypotheses • Other planned analyses. State how hypotheses and research design relate to one another.

■ Table A1.1. (*Continued*)

Paper section and topic	Description
Method	
Inclusion and exclusion	Report inclusion and exclusion criteria, including any restrictions based on demographic characteristics.
Participant characteristics	Report major demographic characteristics (e.g., age, sex, ethnicity, socioeconomic status) and important topic-specific characteristics (e.g., achievement level in studies of educational interventions).
	In the case of animal research, report the genus, species, and strain number or other specific identification, such as the name and location of the supplier and the stock designation. Give the number of animals and the animals' sex, age, weight, physiological condition, genetic modification status, genotype, health–immune status, drug or test naïveté (if known), and previous procedures to which the animal may have been subjected.
Sampling procedures	Describe procedures for selecting participants, including • Sampling method if a systematic sampling plan was implemented • Percentage of sample approached that actually participated • Whether self-selection into the study occurred (either by individuals or by units, such as schools or clinics) Describe settings and locations where data were collected as well as dates of data collection. Describe agreements and payments made to participants. Describe institutional review board agreements, ethical standards met, and safety monitoring.

Sample size, power, and precision	Describe the sample size, power, and precision, including
	• Intended sample size
	• Achieved sample size, if different from intended sample size
	• Determination of sample size, including
	  • Power analysis, or methods used to determine precision of parameter estimates
	  • Explanation of any interim analyses and stopping rules employed.

(*table continues*)

▨ Table A1.1. (*Continued*)

Paper section and topic	Description
Measures and covariates	Define all primary and secondary measures and covariates, including measures collected but not included in this report.
Data collection	Describe methods used to collect data.
Quality of measurements	Describe methods used to enhance the quality of measurements, including • Training and reliability of data collectors • Use of multiple observations.
Instrumentation	Provide information on validated or ad hoc instruments created for individual studies (e.g., psychometric and biometric properties).
Masking	Report whether participants, those administering the experimental manipulations, and those assessing the outcomes were aware of condition assignments. If masking took place, provide statement regarding how it was accomplished and whether and how the success of masking was evaluated.
Psychometrics	Estimate and report reliability coefficients for the scores analyzed (i.e., the researcher's sample), if possible. Provide estimates of convergent and discriminant validity where relevant. Report estimates related to the reliability of measures, including • Interrater reliability for subjectively scored measures and ratings • Test–retest coefficients in longitudinal studies in which the retest interval corresponds to the measurement schedule used in the study • Internal consistency coefficients for composite scales in which these indices are appropriate for understanding the nature of the instruments being used in the study. Report the basic demographic characteristics of other samples if reporting reliability or validity coefficients from those samples, such as those described in test manuals or in the norming information about the instrument.

■ **Table A1.1.** (*Continued*)

Paper section and topic	Description

Conditions and design	State whether conditions were manipulated or naturally observed. Report the type of design consistent with the JARS–Quant tables:
	• Experimental manipulation with participants randomized
	  • Table A4.2a
	• Experimental manipulation without randomization
	  • Table A4.2b
	• Clinical trial with randomization
	  • Table A4.2a and Table A6.4
	• Clinical trial without randomization
	  • Table A4.2b and Table A6.4
	• Nonexperimental design (i.e., no experimental manipulation): observational design, epidemiological design, natural history, and so forth (single-group designs or multiple-group comparisons)
	  • Table A4.3
	• Longitudinal design
	  • Table A6.1
	• Replications
	  • Table A6.2
	• *N*-of-1 studies
	  • Table A6.3
	• Report the common name given to designs not currently covered in JARS–Quant.

Data diagnostics	Describe planned data diagnostics, including • Criteria for post–data collection exclusion of participants, if any • Criteria for deciding when to infer missing data and methods used for imputation of missing data • Definition and processing of statistical outliers • Analyses of data distributions • Data transformations to be used, if any.
Analytic strategy	Describe the analytic strategy for inferential statistics and protection against experiment-wise error for • Primary hypotheses • Secondary hypotheses • Exploratory hypotheses.

(*table continues*)

▨ **Table A1.1.** (*Continued*)

Paper section and topic	Description
Results	
Participant flow	Report the flow of participants, including • Total number of participants in each group at each stage of the study • Flow of participants through each stage of the study (include figure depicting flow when possible; see Figure 5.1).
Recruitment	Provide dates defining the periods of recruitment and repeated measures or follow-up.

Statistics and data analysis	Provide information detailing the statistical and data-analytic methods used, including
	• Missing data
	  • Frequency or percentages of missing data
	  • Empirical evidence and/or theoretical arguments for the causes of data that are missing–for example, missing completely at random, missing at random, or missing not at random
	  • Methods actually used for addressing missing data, if any
	• Description of each primary and secondary outcome, including the total sample and each subgroup, that includes the number of cases, cell means, standard deviations, and other measures that characterize the data used
	• Inferential statistics, including
	  • Results of all inferential tests conducted, including exact p values if null hypothesis statistical testing methods were used, including the minimally sufficient set of statistics (e.g., dfs, mean square [MS] effect, MS error) needed to construct the tests
	  • Effect-size estimates and confidence intervals on estimates that correspond to each inferential test conducted, when possible
	  • Clear differentiation between primary hypotheses and their tests and estimates, secondary hypotheses and their tests and estimates, and exploratory hypotheses and their tests and estimates
	• Complex data analyses—for example, structural equation modeling analyses (see Table A5.1), hierarchical linear models, factor analysis, multivariate analyses, and so forth, including
	  • Details of the models estimated
	  • Associated variance–covariance (or correlation) matrix or matrices

Table A1.1. (*Continued*)

Paper section and topic	Description
	• Identification of the statistical software used to run the analyses (e.g., SAS PROC GLM, particular R library program) • Estimation problems (e.g., failure to converge, bad solution spaces), regression diagnostics, or analytic anomalies that were detected and solutions to those problems • Other data analyses performed, including adjusted analyses, indicating those that were planned and those that were not planned (though not necessarily in the level of detail of primary analyses). Report any problems with statistical assumptions and/or data distributions that could affect the validity of findings.
Discussion	
Support of original hypotheses	Provide a statement of support or nonsupport for all hypotheses, whether primary or secondary, including • Distinction by primary and secondary hypotheses • Discussion of the implications of exploratory analyses in terms of both substantive findings and error rates that may be uncontrolled.
Similarity of results	Discuss similarities and differences between reported results and the work of others.
Interpretation	Provide an interpretation of the results, taking into account • Sources of potential bias and threats to internal and statistical validity • Imprecision of measurement protocols • Overall number of tests or overlap among tests • Adequacy of sample sizes and sampling validity.
Generalizability	Discuss generalizability (external validity) of the findings, taking into account • Target population (sampling validity) • Other contextual issues (setting, measurement, time; ecological validity).
Implications	Discuss implications for future research, programs, or policy.

Note. Tables have been designed to be comprehensive and to apply widely. For any individual report, the author is expected to select the items that apply to the particular study. Adapted from "Journal Article Reporting Standards for Quantitative Research in Psychology: The APA Publications and Communications Board Task Force Report," by M. Appelbaum, H. Cooper, R. B. Kline, E. Mayo-Wilson, A. M. Nezu, and S. M. Rao, 2018, *American Psychologist, 73*, pp. 6–8. Copyright 2018 by the American Psychological Association.

Setting the Stage: Title Page, Abstract, and Introduction

In this chapter, I examine the parts of a research report that set the stage for the description of how the study was carried out and what it found. The title and abstract alert potential readers to whether your study is related to the questions they need to have answered. The introduction section of the report places your work in a broader context and tells the reader why you think your work is important.

Title Page

Title

The title of your report should identify

- the main variables and theoretical issues under investigation,
- the relationships between them, and
- the population under study.

Shakespeare's Juliet pleaded that "a rose by any other name would smell as sweet" (*Romeo and Juliet*, Act 2, Scene 2, lines 43–44). What mattered most to her was not what something was called but rather the characteristics of its fragrance. However, in the reporting of science, a name can matter greatly. The title given to a research report will help (or obscure) readers' understanding of the report's relevance to their needs.

http://dx.doi.org/10.1037/0000103-002
Reporting Quantitative Research in Psychology: How to Meet APA Style Journal Article Reporting Standards, Second Edition, by H. Cooper

When you conduct a computerized search of the literature using PsycINFO, for example, the first thing you must do is choose your search terms. Then, you specify the list of document fields—the parts of the document and document record—the computer should scan to find the terms. In PsycINFO, this list contains many different document fields. Depending on your reference database, the first field listed may be "All Text," but "Title" and "Abstract" are also listed as options. I suspect that these three fields are the most frequently used parameters for searches.

You might ask, "If my audience can search the full document, what difference does it make what terms are in the title?" The fact is that many, if not most, searchers will pass on the full document search. It will lead to the retrieval of too many documents that are not relevant to the question of interest, even if searchers use multiple keywords (and the Boolean command AND) to narrow the search down. For example, if a searcher is looking for research on roses, a full text search would include a study that contained the sentence, "The subjects then rose from their chairs and proceeded into an adjoining room." Wading through all of the document records that include a specified term or terms anywhere in the text can take lots of time better spent otherwise. If terms appear in titles and abstracts, they are more likely to be central to the document content.

Suppose you just wrote a report about a study in which you examined the effects of full-day kindergarten on children's academic achievement and psychological well-being. As you think about an appropriate title, you have a few things to consider. First, you would clearly want the terms *full-day kindergarten*, *academic achievement*, and *psychological well-being* in the title. However, what about specifying the comparison groups (e.g., half-day kindergarten, no kindergarten) against which full-day kindergarten's effects were compared? Also, psychological well-being is a broad construct. It might subsume other constructs, such as happiness, self-confidence, and optimism, and these might have been among the measures you used. You would want readers interested in these narrower constructs to find your report. Therefore, to be fully explanatory, the title might read "Relative Effects of Full-Day Kindergarten Versus Half-Day and No Kindergarten on Children's Academic Achievement and Psychological Well-Being, Including Happiness, Self-Confidence, and Optimism."

This title is about twice the length recommended (12 words) by the *Publication Manual of the American Psychological Association* (6th ed.; APA, 2010, p. 23), so a briefer title is called for, perhaps something like "Effects of Full-Day Kindergarten on Academic Achievement and Psychological Well-Being." Now your title is clear and concise (and contains information about the population of interest) but perhaps not precise. You might worry that searchers using the title alone and looking for studies on children's happiness, self-concept, and/or optimism will miss your report. They will, but that is a trade-off you must make. However, you can minimize the chances your report will be missed by including the additional terms in the abstract. That way, searchers who use this broader level of document screening will find the report.

In picking the terms to include in your title, also consider what other terms might be used in the literature to refer to the same concept. For example, as you looked at the literature on the effects of full-day kindergarten, you might have discovered that some authors called it *all-day kindergarten*. It would be important to ensure that searchers using the term *all-day kindergarten* would retrieve your article. You should not put this alternative term in the title, but you can put it in the abstract, perhaps in parentheses after the first time *full-day kindergarten* is used. In constructing a title (and an abstract), it is important to consider these other labels to ensure that people who search on alternate terms for the same construct will find your report.

Authors are often tempted to think up catchy phrases to include in their titles. When searching was done by hand, this practice might have enticed readers to take a closer look at the article (and perhaps such phrases demonstrated how clever the author was). This practice has been diminishing in recent years. Authors are discovering that extraneous elements in a clever title are a nuisance to them when they conduct computer searches. Today, they want to save others from similar bother; with rare exceptions, clever titles only add to the number of irrelevant documents retrieved. For example, suppose you titled an article "A Rose by Any Other Name Would Smell as Sweet: The Effects of Labels on Subjective Evaluations." The article would be retrieved by searches using the terms *rose*, *smell*, and *sweet*, terms unrelated to your article. Clever is OK if it communicates distinctive qualities of the study not captured elsewhere in the title, but you should be careful to avoid filling search engine results with irrelevant documents.[1]

List of Authors

Under the title on the first page of your manuscript, you list the authors in the order of their relative contribution to the research and research report. This is not mentioned in the Journal Article Reporting Standards (JARS; Appelbaum et al., 2018), perhaps because it is so obvious. This author acknowledgment should also list the complete affiliations of the researchers at the time the study was conducted.

The *Publication Manual* (6th ed.; APA, 2010, pp. 18–19) and the *Ethical Principles of Psychologists and Code of Conduct* (APA Ethics Code; APA, 2017) provide guidance about who should get authorship credit and in what order. I have reproduced the relevant section from the APA Ethics Code in Exhibit 2.1. A more extensive treatment of authorship issues can be found in Cooper (2016).

Author Note

The author note of your report should

- provide registration information about the study, if it was submitted to a research register;
- describe prior use of the data in published articles, dissertation or thesis, and conference presentations;
- acknowledge contributions to your study besides authorship, including sources of funding;
- reveal potential conflicts of interest;
- present the current affiliations of all authors if they are different from when the study was conducted;
- provide contact information for the corresponding author; and
- include any other information of importance to the reader that may not be included elsewhere.

---

[1]Many authors begin their introduction with a quotation. This might be a good way to use the quotation from Ms. Capulet.

▦ **Exhibit 2.1.**

Excerpt From *Ethical Principles of Psychologists and Code of Conduct* Regarding Authorship Credit

8.12 Publication Credit

(a) Psychologists take responsibility and credit, including authorship credit, only for work they have actually performed or to which they have substantially contributed. (See also Standard 8.12b, Publication Credit.)

(b) Principal authorship and other publication credits accurately reflect the relative scientific or professional contributions of the individuals involved, regardless of their relative status. Mere possession of an institutional position, such as department chair, does not justify authorship credit. Minor contributions to the research or to the writing for publications are acknowledged appropriately, such as in footnotes or in an introductory statement.

(c) Except under exceptional circumstances, a student is listed as principal author on any multiple-authored article that is substantially based on the student's doctoral dissertation. Faculty advisors discuss publication credit with students as early as feasible and throughout the research and publication process as appropriate. (See also Standard 8.12b, Publication Credit.)

Note. From *Ethical Principles of Psychologists and Code of Conduct (2002, Amended June 1, 2010 and January 1, 2017)*, by the American Psychological Association, 2017 (http://www.apa.org/ethics/code/index.aspx). Copyright 2017 by the American Psychological Association.

Also on the title page you will put an author note (APA, 2010, pp. 24–25). The first paragraph of an author note contains

■ the study's registration information, if it appears in a research register, and
■ any changes of affiliation if any author now works elsewhere.

In an author note you will list a research register and the number readers will need to find the study if you took the commendable step of submitting your work to a publicly available, searchable database. Research is typically registered before data collection begins. The registered information about the study includes the plans you made for what and how to collect data (called a *research protocol*) before you began conducting the study. These registers alert others to what research is currently under way. This can be very helpful if someone else is considering doing a study similar to your own. It also helps users see how your study methods might have changed from the way you planned them to the way the study was actually carried out. It also makes research easier to find once it is completed in case it is not yet published (or may never be published). You should consider examining relevant study registers for similar research and registering your study before you begin.

The second paragraph of the author note contains information about whether the data in the study

■ were also used in other publications or presentations at conferences or conventions and where these publications can be found and/or
■ were used in a master's thesis or dissertation and where this document can be found.

In the second paragraph, you also disclose the written, public venues through which the data or other unique ideas of your report have appeared previously.[2] Thus, if the study served as all or part of your master's thesis or doctoral dissertation, or if any written version of it is publicly archived (e.g., report to a funding agency), you need to say so in the author note. Such an acknowledgment might read, "This study served as Romeo Montague's doctoral dissertation at Capulet University." Typically, you do not have to report oral presentations of the study at meetings or conferences unless the proceedings of the conference have also appeared in print.

It is critical to acknowledge that your data were previously reported in public documents. If you do not make this acknowledgment, you could be open to a charge of an ethical violation. The APA Ethics Code (APA, 2017) states, "Psychologists do not publish, as original data, data that have been previously published. This does not preclude republishing data when they are accompanied by proper acknowledgment" (Standard 8.13, p. 12). For example, you should disclose in the author note if

- your study includes an analysis of longitudinal data and the first wave of data collection was published previously or
- the data are part of a larger data set, portions of which were published previously.

This acknowledgment should be made whether or not the measures in your new report overlap with measures previously reported. The data still share many things in common with those in the original report—for example, the same participants, data collectors, settings, and timing.

Why is this important? The *Publication Manual* spells this out clearly (6th ed.; APA, 2010, pp. 13–15, section 1.09, Duplicate and Piecemeal Publication of Data). Briefly, duplicate publication can (a) distort the scientific record by making a finding appear to have been replicated when this is not the case, (b) take up space that precludes the publication of other worthy reports, and/or (c) violate copyright laws. Read section 1.09 of the *Publication Manual* carefully. If your course of action is still not clear, contact the editor of the journal you want to submit to and ask for guidance.

A third paragraph of the author note contains

- acknowledgment of people who assisted in conducting the study (e.g., through labor, expertise) but were not contributors in a way that led to authorship,
- sources of funding or other support, and
- any relationships or affiliations that might be perceived as a conflict of interest.

When someone has contributed to the research but not at a level that warrants authorship, acknowledge this person in the author note. Typically, the acknowledgment begins with "We thank [person's name]," followed by a brief description of the nature of the contribution. For example, "We thank Lord Montague for comments on an earlier version of the manuscript," or "We thank Lady Capulet for assistance with statistical analyses."

The second acknowledgment goes to sources of support for the study other than the labor or expertise of an individual. If the study being reported was conducted with

---

[2]APA has teamed up with the Center for Open Science to create PsyArXiv (https://psyarxiv.com/), a website where scholars can post documents—such as working papers, unpublished works, and articles under review (preprints)— making them accessible to other researchers and the public at no cost.

monetary or other forms of material support, acknowledge this in the author note. With regard to funding, some funding agencies require that they be acknowledged in this way; other funding agencies request that they not be acknowledged. Check with your funder before writing your author note. Also include the name of the person to whom the funds were awarded and the award number. This helps readers who want to follow up on the history of your work.[3] Your funder may also request a disclaimer indicating that the research does not reflect the views of the funding organization. The portion of the author note that acknowledges monetary support might read something like this: "This research was supported by Grant 123456 from the Juliet Capulet Foundation to Romeo Montague. However, the research reported does not necessarily reflect the views of the Juliet Capulet Foundation."

Also, sometimes support comes in forms other than money. For example, a shopping mall might have permitted you to set up a table to collect data from shoppers; a community center might have provided a room for interviewing participants; or other researchers might have given you access to equipment, stimulus materials, or measures they used in a previous study. All of these in-kind contributions to the study should be acknowledged with the consent of the provider, of course. Such an acknowledgment might read as follows: "Thanks are extended to Capulet Pharmacy for providing the fragrances used in this study." Of course, you should be careful that the acknowledgment does not reveal anything that might compromise the confidentiality of the participants in your study.

Next in the author note, disclose any possible conflicts of interest. Typically, a conflict of interest involves economic or commercial interests you or your coauthors have in the products or services used or discussed in the report. Again, the *Publication Manual* contains a discussion that will help you decide whether a potential conflict of interest exists (6th ed.; APA, 2010, pp. 17–18, section 1.12, Conflict of Interest). Consult the *Publication Manual* as well as the editor of the journal you are submitting to if questions linger.

In the matters of both previous publication and conflict of interest, I suggest that you err on the side of caution: If you have any concern about either of these issues, say so in the author note when you first submit your article. If your concern is immaterial, it is easier to remove this information later on than to explain its omission if it is later deemed important. Also, when you submit your manuscript to an APA journal (and others as well), you will be asked to verify on a form that you have complied with APA's ethical guidelines and disclosed any potential conflicts of interest.

Your author note might also be the place to provide information that is relevant to how your study was carried out that does not fit anywhere else in the report. This is a catchall suggestion that you will rarely use. It does help emphasize, however, the importance of full disclosure.

A final paragraph of the author note contains information about how to contact the author who has taken responsibility for corresponding with readers who want more information. This information typically includes the mailing and e-mail addresses.

---

[3]In addition to serving as thanks to your funder, notes about your funding sources will help readers interested in your work who are looking for sources of support. Your grant history will help them see who is funding research related to their own.

Abstract

The abstract of your report should provide a concise summary of

- the problem under investigation, including the main hypotheses;
- participants or subjects, specifying their most important characteristics, including, in animal research, their genus and species;
- the study's method, including
    - research design (e.g., experiment, observational study),
    - sample size,
    - materials and any apparatus used (e.g., instruments and apparatus),
    - outcome measures, and
    - data-gathering procedures;
- findings, including effect sizes, confidence intervals, and statistical significance levels; and
- conclusions, implications, and applications.

The *Publication Manual* (6th ed.; APA, 2010, pp. 25–27, section 2.05, Abstract) points out that the abstract to your report "can be the most important single paragraph in an article" (p. 26). I have already noted that the abstract is important because, for many researchers, its content will determine whether your article is retrieved in a computer-assisted literature search. Once retrieved, it is the first thing (perhaps the only thing) about your study that will be read. The *Publication Manual* says the abstract should be dense with information as well as accurate, nonevaluative (i.e., stick to the facts, no judgments), coherent, readable, and concise.

The elements of an abstract called for by JARS are fairly self-explanatory. As examples of good abstracts, I have reproduced in Figure 2.1 two abstracts along with the other material that appears on the first page of a published article for studies from two different areas of psychology. Note first that they both meet the length restrictions of the journals in which they appeared. These restrictions typically range from 150 to 250 words. Note also that the example abstract taken from Bricker et al. (2009) uses five boldface headings to highlight information about the study. The five headings correspond nicely to the information called for in JARS. This type of abstract is called a *structured abstract*, and it is commonly found in the medical sciences. The editors of the journals that APA publishes are free to adopt this style for articles on empirical studies, so it is not surprising, then, that you will see this structured format used frequently in journals like *Health Psychology*. Its purpose is to ensure that authors include the important information in the abstract.

Both example abstracts succinctly describe the problem under investigation. Burgmans et al. (2009) did so in three sentences, whereas Bricker et al. (2009) used just one. Then, each abstract introduces the principal design feature of the study and the important characteristics of the sample of participants. Bricker et al. did not actually mention that their study was a population-based longitudinal study, but this is clear from the title. Burgmans et al. mentioned the important apparatus they used for collecting data (magnetic resonance imaging), whereas Bricker et al. discussed the outcome variables collected by their measures. Each example abstract then presents the major findings. Bricker et al.

Figure 2.1. Examples of Abstracts and Keywords in APA Journals

Neuropsychology
2009, Vol. 23, No. 5, 541–550

© 2009 American Psychological Association
0894-4105/09/$12.00 http://dx.doi.org/10.1037/a0016161

The Prevalence of Cortical Gray Matter Atrophy May Be Overestimated in the Healthy Aging Brain

Saartje Burgmans, Martin P. J. van Boxtel,
Eric F. P. M. Vuurman, Floortje Smeets,
and Ed H. B. M. Gronenschild
Maastricht University

Harry B. M. Uylings
Maastricht University and VU University
Medical Center Amsterdam

Jelle Jolles
Maastricht University and VU University Medical Center Amsterdam

Prevailing opinion holds that normal brain aging is characterized by substantial atrophy of cortical gray matter. However, this conclusion is based on earlier studies whose findings may be influenced by the inclusion of subjects with subclinical cognitive disorders like preclinical dementia. The present magnetic resonance imaging study tested this hypothesis. Cognitively healthy subjects (M age = 72 years, range = 52–82 years) who remained cognitively stable over a 3-year period were compared with subjects with significant cognitive decline. Subjects who developed dementia within 6 years after the scan session were excluded. The gray matter volumes of 7 cortical regions were delineated on T1-weighted magnetic resonance imaging scans. Participants without cognitive decline did not exhibit an age effect on the gray matter volume. Conversely, participants with cognitive decline exhibited a significant age effect in all the 7 areas. These results suggest that cortical gray matter atrophy may have been overestimated in studies on healthy aging because most studies were unable to exclude participants with a substantial atypical cognitive decline or preclinical dementia. Our results underscore the importance of establishing stringent inclusion criteria for future studies on normal aging.

Keywords: healthy aging, gray matter atrophy, cognitive decline, cerebral cortex, MRI

Health Psychology
2009, Vol. 28, No. 4, 439–447

© 2009 American Psychological Association
0278-6133/09/$12.00 http://dx.doi.org/10.1037/a0014568

Psychological and Social Risk Factors in Adolescent Smoking Transitions: A Population-Based Longitudinal Study

Jonathan B. Bricker, K. Bharat Rajan, Maureen Zalewski, M. Robyn Andersen,
Madelaine Ramey, and Arthur V. Peterson
Fred Hutchinson Cancer Research Center&University of Washington

Objective: This study longitudinally investigated psychological and social risk factors consistent with the Theory of Triadic Influence (TTI) as predictors of adolescent smoking transitions. *Design:* Among 4218 adolescents, 5 psychological risk factors (i.e., parent-noncompliance, friend-compliance, rebelliousness, low achievement motivation, and thrill seeking) were assessed in 9th grade (age 14), 2 social influence risk factors (i.e., parents' and close friends' smoking) were assessed in Grades 3 (age 8) and 9 (age 14), respectively. *Main Outcome Measures:* Adolescent smoking transitions occurring between the 9th and 12th (ages 14–17) grade interval. *Results:* The probabilities contributed by each of the 5 psychological risk factors to the overall probability of making a specific smoking transition were: 22% to 27% for the transition from never to trying smoking, 10% to 13% for the transition from trying to monthly smoking, and, for 3 of the 5 risk factors, 11% to 16% for the transition from monthly to daily smoking. For predicting trying smoking, the probability contributed by these psychological factors was greater than the probability contributed by each parent's and close friend's smoking. Parent-compliance had a higher contribution to the probability of trying smoking when an adolescent's parent smoked ($p < .05$), whereas friend-compliance had a higher contribution to the probability of trying smoking when an adolescent's friend smoked ($p < .001$). *Conclusion:* These psychological and social factors have an important influence on adolescent smoking transitions. Implications for TTI and smoking prevention interventions are discussed.

Keywords: psychological influences, parents, friends, adolescents, smoking

presented some statistical results and probability levels associated with the findings (as called for in JARS), whereas Burgmans et al. did not (their article did contain results of *t* tests and effect size estimates that could have been included in the abstract).[4] Finally, each abstract concludes with a sentence or two that interpret the findings.

A final point: Both example abstracts are followed by keywords that can also be used to identify the reports for a literature search. In fact, all authors publishing in APA journals are required to supply keywords for their articles. Note that some keywords in the examples are redundant with terms that appear in the title or abstract and others are not. Still other terms appear in the abstract that are not in the title or keywords that could very likely be the object of reference database searches. I would suggest that for Bricker et al. (2009) *theory of triadic influence* and *achievement motivation* and for Burgmans et al. (2009) *dementia*, among others, also be added as keywords.

Introduction

The introduction to your report should include

- a statement of the problem under study and its theoretical or practical importance (especially public health implications);
- a succinct review of relevant scholarship, including
  - its relation to previous work and
  - if the data in this study have been reported on previously, how the current study differs from these earlier studies;
- a statement of the research hypotheses, including
  - the theories or other means used to derive them,
  - which hypotheses are primary or secondary, and
  - other planned analyses; and
- a statement regarding how the hypotheses and research design are related to one another.

The elements of the introduction section that are contained in JARS correspond neatly with the text in the *Publication Manual* (6th ed.; APA, 2010, pp. 27–28, section 2.05, Introduction). The *Publication Manual* asks five questions that you need to answer at the beginning of your report:

- Why is this problem important?
- How does the study relate to previous work in the area? . . .
- What are the primary and secondary hypotheses and objectives of the study, and what, if any, are the links to theory?
- How do the hypotheses and research design relate to one another?
- What are the theoretical and practical implications of the study? (APA, 2010, p. 27)

---

[4]Note as well that I have not updated the abstracts to meet the current requirements of APA Style as set forth in the sixth edition of the *Publication Manual* (APA, 2010). So, for example, Bricker et al.'s (2009) abstract reports two null hypothesis tests as $p < .05$ and $p < .001$. Under the new guidelines, these p levels would be reported precisely, using $p =$ rather than $p <$. At the time of the appearance of Bricker et al.'s article, what they did was perfectly acceptable.

Because most of these are self-explanatory, here I focus on only two elements of JARS: (a) stating whether hypotheses are primary or secondary or analyses are planned but with no associated hypotheses and (b) describing the relationship between the hypotheses and the choice of research design.

Primary and Secondary Hypotheses and Other Planned Analyses

It is important to group hypotheses into those of primary interest and secondary interest. Doing this assists you and your readers in interpreting the results. This is especially critical with regard to the outcomes of statistical tests. For example, suppose you conducted a study concerning the effects of labels on people's evaluations of fragrances or perfumes. For a random half of the subjects, you labeled a fragrance (rated as "mildly pleasing" in previous tests) *roses*, and for the other half, you labeled it *manure*. After smelling the fragrance, you asked subjects to rate it along, say, five dimensions (e.g., one of which might have been pleasant–unpleasant). Your primary hypothesis (contrary to Juliet's prediction that you would uncover a null finding) was that the scent labeled *roses* would be rated as more pleasant than the same one labeled *manure*.

In addition, you asked subjects questions about whether they would purchase the perfume, recommend it to a friend, and so on. For these measures, you are less confident you will find an effect of the label because you think the effect itself is not large and other considerations may obscure its impact. For example, intention to buy might be influenced by how much money subjects have as well as their liking of the fragrance. Or subjects might already have a favorite fragrance. Therefore, intention to buy might be of interest to you but only as a secondary consideration; this hypothesis is secondary to your primary interest.

In your study, you also did some exploratory analyses by breaking your data down into subgroups and looking for interactions, for example, by examining whether the labeling effect is greater for male or female subjects. You have no real predictions about what the outcome of the test might be, but you are interested in possible effects, perhaps to guide future research. If you found that female subjects were more affected by the label than male subjects, why might this be so? You could speculate on this and call for the findings to be replicated to test your new hypothesis.

By dividing your hypotheses a priori into primary and secondary concerns and designating others as exploratory, you accomplish two things. First, suppose you had no a priori groupings of hypotheses. You ran a total of 20 t tests (on 20 dependent variables) pitting the null hypothesis against some alternative. You found that three tests proved significant ($p < .05$). Given that we would expect one significant result even if all of your numbers were generated by chance, this is not a terribly impressive result.[5] (Juliet would be vindicated.) However, suppose all three significant findings were obtained on your three primary measures and all in the predicted direction. Now a more convincing argument for your hypothesis can be made.

---

[5]You may be familiar with the notion of experiment-wise error rates. This refers to the fact that because you have conducted more than one statistical comparison, the probability that you will get at least one false rejection of the null hypothesis is greater than the probability associated with each individual comparison. The more tests you do, the more likely an experiment-wise error will occur.

Also, because the other 17 statistical tests have been labeled secondary or exploratory, readers know to interpret these results in a different context. If the intent to purchase measure does not prove significant, readers know that a priori you viewed this test as less diagnostic of your main hypothesis. Conversely, if you find male and female subjects did differ in the effect of the label, you will have to provide a post hoc explanation for why one sex was more affected than the other. This after-the-fact explanation will need further testing before it gains the credibility that your study bestowed on your primary hypotheses. In this way, an a priori grouping of hypotheses helps both you and your audience interpret your results.[6]

Relationship Between Your Hypotheses and Research Design

It is also important in the introduction section to briefly explain your research design and why the design is well suited to answer your research question. So, for example, if your research question addresses a causal relationship (e.g., does the label of a fragrance cause people to react to it differently?), an experimental or quasi-experimental research design is appropriate for answering it. If the question relates to a simple association (are labels for fragrances that are rated more positively associated with more positive reactions to the fragrance itself?), then a simple correlational analysis may provide the answer. If you are interested in how people differ, then a between-subjects design is called for. If your interest is in how people change over time, then a within-subjects design is most appropriate.

JARS recommends that you provide your audience with an analysis of the fit between your research question and research design in the introduction to your article. Why did you pick this design to answer this question? How well can this design answer the question? Answers to these questions will be critical to readers' evaluation of your article. If you ask a causal question but your design does not support a causal interpretation, you have made a mistake. By setting this out explicitly in the introduction, you will be less likely to make an inferential error, and your readers will be less likely to misinterpret your results.

On occasion, your intentions (the design you hoped to carry out) will be thwarted by the realities you face in conducting the study. For example, a lot of subjects might withdraw from the condition that asks them to sniff manure whereas few withdraw from the roses condition, suggesting that the subjects in the two conditions were different before the experiment began. In the end, your hoped-for inferences and design will not match up. In such cases, you need to describe these problems in the Method section (which I turn to in Chapters 3 and 4) and address their implications in the Discussion section (which I discuss in Chapter 7).

---

[6]Another way to address the issue of experiment-wise error would be to combine your related measures, perhaps through factor analysis, so that you do fewer tests. The optimal strategy to address experiment-wise error may be to do both: Combine related measures, and group the combined measures on the basis of their primary or secondary status.

Detailing What You Did: The Method Section

The Method section of your article is the place where you describe how you carried out your study. The information shared here should include who participated, what procedures you followed, what instruments and measures you used, and how you planned to treat and analyze your data.

Cast broadly, these are the most important questions to answer as you write your Method section:

- What information will readers need to evaluate the validity of your study's conclusions and to interpret its findings?
- What information would readers need to know if they wished to replicate your research?

Both of these questions need to be answered in full for your article and your research to be of maximum use to others.

Answering the first question completely will almost certainly cause you some anxiety. Because the perfect study has yet to be conducted, you will find yourself in the uncomfortable situation of having to reveal the flaws in your work. Should you report the number of participants who chose not to take part in the study after it was explained to them? Should you describe the measure you collected that proved unreliable or was misunderstood by many participants and therefore went unanalyzed? The answer is, yes, report the flaws.

Answering the second question requires you to think about those things you did that were critical to getting your results. Replication is central to science. It is always in your interest to provide enough details, the good and the bad, so that someone else can verify what you found by redoing your study.

http://dx.doi.org/10.1037/0000103-003

Reporting Quantitative Research in Psychology: How to Meet APA Style Journal Article Reporting Standards, Second Edition, by H. Cooper

When it comes to writing about the methods of your study, the Journal Article Reporting Standards (JARS; Appelbaum et al., 2018) can be thought of as an attempt to systematize aspects of research methodology known to have a significant influence on how a study is interpreted and what is needed to replicate it. The JARS items take some of the guesswork out of reporting the methods of your research. They also are meant to protect you against accusations that you purposely did not report things. Again, however, for any particular study in any particular subfield of psychology, there will be unique features that render some of the JARS items irrelevant, whereas other important items may need to be included in your report.

Because of this, I draw on 16 articles across a wide range of topics to present examples of the different items on JARS. I skip around from article to article, so I will remind you of the important characteristics of each study as it is reintroduced. If you get lost, the Appendix at the end of the book provides the abstract for each of the example articles in alphabetical order by first author. You can refer to these to keep on track. Included as examples are studies in Chapter 5 through 8 that are introduced because they demonstrate particular research designs and data analysis techniques.

Characteristics of Participants and Sampling Procedures

The description of participant characteristics in your report should include

- the inclusion and exclusion criteria you applied when picking participants, including any restrictions based on demographic characteristics;
- the major demographic characteristics (e.g., age, sex, ethnicity, socioeconomic status) as well as important topic-specific characteristics (e.g., achievement level in studies of educational interventions) of the included sample; and
- in the case of animal research,
  - the genus, species, and strain number or other specific means for identifying animals, such as the name and location of the supplier and the stock designation;
  - the number of animals and the animals' sex, age, weight, physiological condition, genetic modification status, genotype, health–immune status and, if known, drug- or test-naïve; and
  - previous use in testing or previous procedures to which the animal may have been subjected.

The description of the sampling procedures in your report should include

- the sampling method if a systematic sampling plan was implemented;
- the percentage of the sample approached that participated;
- whether self-selection into the study (by either individuals or units) or selection by administrators (e.g., school officials, clinic directors) occurred;
- the settings and locations where data were collected as well as dates of data collection;
- agreements and payments made to participants; and
- institutional review board agreements, ethical standards met, and safety monitoring.

Most Method sections begin with a description of who took part in the study and how they were recruited. Some people will always be more likely than others to participate in a study, often simply because some people are convenient to recruit. For example, your hypothetical fragrance labeling study, like many studies in psychology, may have been conducted with undergraduates drawn from the subject pool of your psychology department who may have participated as a course requirement or who have at least a curiosity about psychology. Studies drawing participants from communities that are near an institution of higher learning are also restricted in some ways, if only geographically. Even samples meant to be nationally representative can include restrictions based on, for example, language or accessibility.

It is important to identify and report the ways in which your recruitment procedure might have restricted the types of people in your study. Restrictions on who participated may influence the interpretation of your data. Readers will ask, "Whom do the results of this study apply to?" and you will address this question explicitly in your Discussion section. More specifically, you and your readers will ask the following questions:

- What is the target population to which the issue under study pertains?
- Are the people in the study drawn from this population? If the answer to this question is no, then your study may not be relevant to the pertinent issue. If the answer is yes, then a third question would be
- Are the people in the study in some way a restricted subsample of the target population? If they are,
- Do the restrictions suggest that the results pertain to some, but not all, members of the target population?

This last question rules the day. Drawing a random sample from your target population (a sample in which each population element had an equal chance of being picked) is ideal. However, researchers know this is rarely feasible. Given this, what becomes most important is that either (a) the ways your sample differs from the target population are irrelevant to drawing inferences about the population of interest or (b) you are careful (in your Discussion section) to point out how the restrictions on your sample might limit your ability to draw inferences about certain subpopulations within the target population.

To continue with the example of the fragrance labeling study, what was the population of interest? Presumably it was all human adults, unless, perhaps, it was a marketing study aimed at women in the United States. Are undergraduates drawn from this population? Yes. Are undergraduates a restricted subsample of all human adults or all U.S. women? Yes, but does it matter? To answer this extrastatistical question about your data and inferences, readers (and you) need to know as precisely as possible what the characteristics of your sample were and how participants were recruited.

Let's look at some examples of how participant characteristics and sampling procedures are described in published research articles. Goldinger, He, and Papesh (2009) reported a study in their article "Deficits in Cross-Race Face Learning: Insights From Eye Movements and Pupillometry," which was published in the *Journal of Experimental Psychology: Learning, Memory, and Cognition.* They examined the *own-race bias*, a phenomenon in which people are better at recognizing and discriminating faces from their own race than those from other races. They conducted two experiments, one with Caucasian subjects and one with Asian subjects. Here is how Goldinger et al. (2009) described the subjects in their first study:

> *Participants.* The initial sample included 46 Arizona State University students, all volunteers who received course credit. All participants reported either normal or corrected vision. From the original sample, data were excluded from six students. Two were Asian, three had excessive periods of eye-tracking failure, and one failed to complete the recognition test. The final sample included 40 students, with 20 per study-time condition. All were Caucasian and reported no special familiarity with Asian faces. (p. 1107)

Even though this description is brief, Goldinger et al. (2009) did a good job of addressing the issues regarding subject characteristics and sampling procedures called for by JARS. They made it clear that the subjects were in Arizona (location), that they were drawn from a college subject pool (setting), and that they received course credit for participating (agreements and payments). In this first of two studies, an eligibility criterion was that subjects had to be Caucasian (in the second study, they had to be Asian) and had no special familiarity with Asian faces (what this might be is not defined). Subjects had to have normal or corrected vision.

As a critical reader or potential replicator of this study, do you have the information you need? It is hard to see much missing. For example, you are not told the sex composition of the sample. But does this matter? Probably not; at this time, theories about the own-race bias suggest no reason to believe that the phenomenon operates differently for men and women.[1]

Note as well that Goldinger et al. (2009) reported that four subjects were eliminated for procedural reasons, eye-tracking failures, and incomplete data. This is a small portion of the otherwise eligible initial sample, probably not large enough to concern you. What if eight or 18 subjects had to be dropped from the experiment? Then you might consider whether the exclusion criteria were related to own-race bias. To push a point, only college students were subjects. If you want to draw inferences about all humans, could it be that college students are less (or more) susceptible to the own-race bias than younger or older humans with more or less education? These are issues that might interest you. From the JARS point of view, however, the authors have given you what you need to consider the potential impact of these subject characteristics.

Another example is a more complex description of a sampling procedure and the resulting participants' characteristics. It is from Fagan, Palkovitz, Roy, and Farrie's (2009) article "Pathways to Paternal Engagement: Longitudinal Effects of Risk and Resilience on Nonresident Fathers," published in *Developmental Psychology*. The researchers wanted to know whether risk factors (e.g., fathers' drug problems, incarceration, or unemployment) were associated with resilience factors (e.g., fathers' positive attitudes, job training, or religious participation) and paternal engagement with

---

[1]At some later date, if the sex of the perceiver does come to be seen as a potential moderator of own-race bias, future replicators may wish they had this information (and meta-analysts would be frustrated over it not being given), but Goldinger et al. (2009) cannot be faulted for this lack of prescience. That said, to the extent that you can foresee and describe the characteristics of participants in your studies that might prove critical in the future to the understanding of a result, the long-term value of your study will be greater.

offspring. Here is how Fagan et al. described their sampling procedure and participant characteristics:

> The FFCW [Fragile Family and Child Wellbeing Study] follows a cohort of nearly 5,000 children born in the United States between 1998 and 2000 (McLanahan & Garfinkel, 2000). The study oversamples births to unmarried couples, and when weighted, the data are representative of nonmarital births in large U.S. cities at the turn of the century. . . . The sample is made up of 3,712 unwed couples and 1,186 married couples.
>
> The present study made use of the birth (baseline), 1-year follow-up (Year 1), and 3-year follow-up (Year 3) fathers' and mothers' data. Our sample was selected in several steps. First, we selected fathers who participated at baseline and who were not married and were not residing with the mother most or all of the time. . . . We excluded married and cohabiting couples at baseline to ensure that the study focused on the most fragile families at the time of the child's birth. Next, we selected fathers who also participated at Year 1. Of the 815 eligible fathers who participated at baseline and Year 1, 130 were missing substantial data, so we removed them from the sample. These steps resulted in a sample of 685 fathers. We then excluded fathers who were not interviewed at Year 3, yielding a sample of 569 fathers. About 4% of the 569 fathers had substantial missing Year 3 data that could not be easily imputed. We omitted these fathers from the study, yielding a final sample of 549 fathers with complete data.
>
> *Participants*
>
> The average age of the fathers in the sample was about 26 years at the baseline interview. . . . The majority of fathers were African American (72.3%), followed by Hispanic (16.2%) and White (9.5%). Nearly 40% of the fathers completed less than high school or less than a general equivalency diploma. Shifts in father–mother relational quality occurred across time. One year after the child's birth, most fathers were in romantic relationships (51.9%) with the mother, 6.4% were married, 28.4% were friends, 13.2% were acquaintances, and one father was separated from the mother. By the 3rd-year follow-up, 9% of fathers were married, 36% were in romantic relationships with the mother, 35% were friends, and 15.5% described the mother of the baby as an acquaintance. Substantial proportions of fathers resided with their child at Year 1 (37.7%) and Year 3 (41.2%). (pp. 1392–1393)

Fagan et al. (2009) made the case that the sample used in their study was initially drawn from a wide geographic space and with the intent of being representative of non-marital births in the United States. They also carefully filled in readers about a series of exclusion criteria they applied to the initial sample. Some of the exclusion criteria relate to identifying the subpopulation of interest to them, and some, regrettably, relate to their inability to obtain complete data from participants in the broader study, families that would have been included had data been complete.

Let me highlight two aspects of the description. First, Fagan et al. (2009) made it clear that they were using a data set that had been used to study other questions related to fragile families and child well-being. They told readers where to obtain more information about the larger sample (McLanahan & Garfinkel, 2000). Thus, as detailed as Fagan et al.'s description is, it still does not answer all of the JARS questions. Not to worry. McLanahan and Garfinkel (2000), in their working paper, did this for you.[2] In fact, nearly all of the working paper is a detailed description of the instruments, sampling procedures, and characteristics of the sample. It would have been a poor use of journal space for Fagan et al. to reproduce all of this material when the original report is easily available on the Internet. Instead, they focused on how they resampled from the initial sample and the resulting characteristics of their subsample.

Second, note that the description of the final sample used in the study is very detailed. The authors even provide a table (reproduced here as Table 3.1) with information more specific than that included in the text. This will make it much easier for future researchers who attempt to replicate the findings to compare their sample with that used by Fagan et al. (2009). The description is an excellent example of how to report sampling procedures and participant characteristics when samples are drawn to be broadly representative. It meets the JARS standards. As a critical reader, between this document and the earlier working paper, you have all you need to determine who the target population was, how the sample in the study might differ from the target population, and whether you think the differences matter. As a potential replicator, you would not have to ask for more information.

Neither Goldinger et al. (2009) nor Fagan et al. (2009) explicitly stated that they received permission from an institutional review board to run their study or that they followed ethical standards in doing so. Requiring such a statement is a relatively new practice and one that should be followed in the future. In your study of labeling effects, you might write, "The Capulet University institutional review board gave approval for the research." Sometimes you will see a statement of this type in the author note rather than the Method section.

Finally, it is important to point out that although the characteristics of settings and participants are very different, researchers who work with animals are under the same obligations to provide detailed descriptions of participants. Here, for example, is a description of the animals used in a study by Killeen, Sanabria, and Dolgov (2009) reported in an article titled "The Dynamics of Conditioning and Extinction" that was published in the *Journal of Experimental Psychology: Animal Behavior Processes*:

Subjects

Six experienced adult homing pigeons (*Columba livia*) were housed in a room with a 12-hr light–dark cycle, with lights on at 6:00 a.m. They had free access to water and grit in their home cages. Running weights were maintained just above their 80% ad libitum weight [i.e., feed was made available at the desire of the animal]; a pigeon was excluded from a session if its weight exceeded its running weight by more than 7%. When required, supplementary feeding of Ace-Hi pigeon pellets (Star Milling Co., Perris, CA) was given at the end of each day, no fewer than 12 hr before experimental sessions were conducted. Supplementary feeding amounts were based equally on current deviation and on a moving average of supplements over the past 15 sessions. (p. 449)

---

[2]McLanahan and Garfinkel (2000) stated that "the sample is representative of nonmarital births in each [sampled] city and is nationally representative of nonmarital births to parents residing in cities with populations over 200,000" (pp. 14, 16).

▨ Table 3.1. Example of Table Reporting Demographic Characteristics of a Sample

Table X

Demographic Characteristics of Sample

Variable	Baseline	Year 1	Year 3
Father's age, *M* (*SD*)	25.65 (7.36)		
Father's race/ethnicity, *n* (%)			
White	52 (9.5)		
African American	397 (72.3)		
Hispanic	89 (16.2)		
Other	11 (2)		
Father's education, *n* (%)			
Less than high school diploma	213 (38.8)		
High school diploma	146 (26.6)		
General equivalency diploma	55 (10)		
Some college	95 (17.3)		
Technical training	19 (3.5)		
College graduate	13 (2.4)		
Graduate school	8 (1.5)		
Father–mother relationship, *n* (%)			
Romantic	436 (79.4)	285 (51.9)	198 (36.1)
Friends	71 (12.9)	156 (28.4)	192 (35)
Acquaintances	42 (7.7)	72 (13.2)	85 (15.5)
Married		35 (6.4)	51 (9.3)
Separated		1 (0.2)	23 (4.2)
Father resides with child, *n* (%)		207 (37.7)	226 (41.2)
Child's gender, *n* (%)			
Male	276 (50.3)		
Female	273 (49.7)		
Father has other biological children, *n* (%)	280 (51)		

Note. From "Pathways to Paternal Engagement: Longitudinal Effects of Risk and Resilience on Nonresident Fathers," by J. Fagan, R. Palkovitz, K. Roy, and D. Farrie, 2009, *Developmental Psychology, 45*, p. 1393. Copyright 2009 by the American Psychological Association.

Clearly, not only the type of pigeon but also the pigeons' weights were important considerations in this study. In some areas of animal research, researchers are expected to report the genus, species, and strain number or other characteristics needed to identify animals, such as the name and location of the supplier and the stock designation. Sometimes, researchers are expected to report the animals' sex, age, and other physiological conditions. The reasoning that you must apply in deciding what to report about animals in a study is no different than the reasoning applied when deciding what to report for people. As the *Publication Manual* states, "Appropriate identification of research participants is critical to the science and practice of psychology, particularly for generalizing the findings, making comparisons across replications, and using the evidence in research syntheses and secondary data analyses" (APA, 2010, p. 29).

Sample Size, Power, and Precision

When describing the size, power, and precision of your sample, your report should include

- the intended sample size;
- the achieved sample size, if different from the intended sample size;
- how the intended sample size was determined, including
  - whether a power analysis was performed or another method was used to determine the precision of parameter estimates and
  - an explanation of any interim analyses and stopping rules you used.

All of the descriptions of sampling procedures and participant characteristics I provide here present the total number of participants who took part in the study and also give the number of participants included in the various subgroups. JARS asks for more than that. It recommends that you also report (a) the number of participants you intended to have in the study if it was different from the number you actually included, (b) how you arrived at this number, (c) whether you conducted a power analysis, and (d) whether you conducted any interim analyses or used some other stopping rule to help you decide when you could cease collecting data from participants. I briefly discuss each of these, in reverse order for ease of exposition.

Stopping Rules

Stopping rules refers to predetermined criteria for deciding what statistical results you would find adequate to stop collecting data from additional participants. Typically, this relates to the acceptable Type I error rate you have selected or, put differently, the chance that you falsely rejected a true null hypothesis. For example, you might decide that you will collect data from subjects in your labeling study until your statistical test of the difference between the two groups (the roses and manure groups) rejects the null hypothesis of no difference at the $p < .05$ level of significance. You intend to check your significance level frequently after collecting data from new subjects and to stop data collection when the designated p level is reached.

The use of stopping rules is rare in most areas of psychology; when they are used, there is some possibility that the researchers will capitalize on chance. That is, because of a run of good luck in gathering participant data, the difference between groups on the primary dependent variables in the observed sample might be larger than the true difference in the population. If more participants took part in the study, the observed difference could return to a smaller estimated value but one that is closer to the population difference.[3]

Stopping rules are used most often in medical research and some psychology research related to health and medicine (but not in labeling studies). Their use is most likely to occur when researchers are evaluating a critical treatment—for example, the effectiveness of a cancer drug. In such a case, there are ethical concerns raised by not stopping the research when lives may be lost by withholding the treatment while further evidence is collected.[4]

Interim Analysis

An interim analysis looks a lot like a stopping rule, but here the decisions are more post hoc. You might decide that you will collect data from 15 participants in each of your labeling conditions and then look at the data to determine whether your results have reached statistical significance. If they have, your study might be over. If not, you might calculate the effect size in the collected data and use this to conduct a power analysis. The result of this power analysis is then used to decide how many more subjects to test. A brief treatment of ethical and statistical issues related to stopping rules and interim analyses in medicine was provided by Pocock (1993).

Effect Size

It is important to define two terms I just introduced: *effect size* and *power analysis*. Cohen (1988) defined *effect size* as "the degree to which the phenomenon is present in the population, or the degree to which the null hypothesis is false" (pp. 9–10). Although numerous metrics for expressing effect sizes are available, three metrics are used most often in the literature: standardized mean difference, *r* index, and odds ratio.

The first is called the *standardized mean difference*, or *d* index. This is the metric you would use in your labeling study. The *d* index is a scale-free measure of the separation between two group means. Continuing the fragrance labeling study example, calculating the *d* index involves dividing the difference between the roses and manure group means by their average standard deviation.[5] So, if $d = 0.50$, it means half of a standard deviation separates the two group means.

---

[3]As an example, a study of treatments for leukemia initially showed unusually large effects, but the evaluation was continued anyway. With more data, the effects disappeared. This led Wheatley and Clayton (2003) to suggest,

> Lessons to be learned from this example are that: fixed stopping rules based on some predetermined *p*-value should not be used and the decision to close a randomization or not should take account of other factors such as the medical plausibility of the magnitude of the treatment effect; chance effects do occur and happen more frequently than many clinicians realize. (p. 66)

It is also the case that stopping rules can be used to halt experiments in which the treatment appears to be ineffective (Lachin, 2005).
[4]Stopping rules are also used in other statistical contexts—for example, in stepwise regression (for deciding how many variables to add to or remove from a model) and factor analysis (for deciding how many factors to retain).
[5]There are finer nuances to the calculation of *d* indexes that I do not go into here (see Cummings, 2012).

Another effect-size metric is the *r* index, or the Pearson product–moment correlation coefficient. (You may be familiar with this effect size.) Typically, it is used to measure the linear relation between two continuous variables. You would use this measure if you studied, for example, the relationship between peoples' affective ratings of the names of perfumes currently on the market and their reactions to the fragrance itself (say, on a scale from 1 = *very unpleasant* to 10 = *very pleasant*).

The third effect-size metric is the odds ratio. It is used when both variables are dichotomous, and findings are presented as frequencies or proportions. You might use an odds ratio (or a number of related metrics) to express the strength of the relationship between your two labels and whether participants said they would buy the fragrance. To calculate an odds ratio, you would determine the odds of purchasing in each condition, say 6:1 in the manure condition and 3:1 in the roses condition. The odds ratio in this situation is 2, meaning that the odds of purchasing the fragrance are twice as great when it is called "Roses" than when it is called "Manure."

How do you know what effect size to expect in your study? This is where the interim analysis comes in: Use it to estimate your expected effect size. Or, you can look at the effect sizes that were found in previous studies on the same topic when similar methods were used (meta-analyses are especially good for this purpose; they always include effect-size estimates). Another option would be to decide what size effect would be theoretically or practically meaningful—for example, how large a sales difference would matter in a perfume company's decision about what to call a perfume.

Power Analysis

A *power analysis* most often is used to determine how many participants should be included in a study if it is to have a good chance to reject the null hypothesis. When you conduct a power analysis, you decide a priori (a) what you expect the effect size to be (or what effect size will be meaningful),[6] (b) what *p* level you will use to reject the null hypothesis, and (c) the likelihood with which you want to be able to reject the null hypothesis if there truly is a relationship in the population. This last number is referred to as the *power* of your study. If power equals .80, it means you have an 80% chance of rejecting the null hypothesis given your chosen statistical significance level, sample size, and expected effect size.[7] Say you expect an effect size of $d = 0.50$, and you want an 80% chance of rejecting the null hypothesis at $p < .05$ (two-tailed). With these three numbers, you can then calculate power, or more likely, you will consult a power table (see Cohen, 1988; power tables can also be found on the Internet). You will discover that you need to include 64 participants per condition to have 80% power.

An example of how a power analysis should be reported is taken from Amir et al.'s (2009) article titled "Attention Training in Individuals With Generalized Social Phobia: A Randomized Controlled Trial" that was published in the *Journal of Consulting and Clinical Psychology*. The researchers reported an experimental study on generalized

---

[6]Again, this can be determined by what was found in past research or by theoretical or practical importance. Still, it is important to keep in mind that in addition to setting your tolerance for making false positive conclusions and for missing true positive conclusions, the power of your study will depend on your expectations about (estimated impact of) the very thing you are trying to determine.

[7]Sometimes power analyses are conducted after a study has been run and has failed to reject the null hypothesis; the researchers may be hoping to make the case that the study was underpowered for revealing a significant result (i.e., the sample was too small or the effect was too subtle).

anxiety disorder (GAD) that examined the effectiveness of an attention modification training procedure in which individuals were trained to divert their attention from a threatening social stimulus:

> On the basis of prior research examining the effect of a similar eight-session attention bias modification procedure on symptoms of anxiety in a sample of individuals diagnosed with GAD (Amir et al., 2009), we estimated an average effect size of [$d =$] 1.0 on our primary dependent measures. With alpha set at .05 and power (1 − beta) set at .80, a sample size of at least 17 participants per group was needed to detect an effect of this magnitude between the AMP [attention modification program] and ACC [attention control condition] groups on the primary outcome measures of social anxiety symptoms. (Amir et al., p. 966)

Amir et al. included 22 participants in one condition and 26 in the other.

Intended Sample Size

It is rare to find explicit statements of the sample size that researchers intended to include in their studies. It is more often the case that you can discern this from other information. Amir et al. (2009) made it clear that a minimum sample size was 17 per condition, and they surpassed this figure. In other instances, the researchers provide the total number of people in the population or subpopulation of interest, and this can be taken as an indication of the intended sample size. For example, O'Neill, Vandenberg, DeJoy, and Wilson (2009) reported a study titled "Exploring Relationships Among Anger, Perceived Organizational Support, and Workplace Outcomes" in the *Journal of Occupational Health Psychology*. They examined the relationships among perceived organizational support, employee anger, and turnover, absences, and accidents on the job:

> Respondents were 1,136 employees from 21 stores of a national retail organization headquartered in the southeastern United States. There were a total of 4,274 employees across the 21 locations; 1,495 people (35%) completed the survey and, of those, 76% provided usable responses for purposes of this study. . . . In summary, 27% of all employees in the 21 locations provided usable data. The average number of respondents per store was 71, with a range of 36 to 138. (O'Neill et al., 2009, p. 323)

Clearly, the intended sample was all of the employees ($N = 4{,}274$) in the 21 locations.

If you are conducting a study that involves the comparison of people in different conditions, the best way to ensure that you have provided complete information about your sample size is to use a variation of the flowchart in Figure 5.1. This chart guides you through each of the steps involved in the sampling process and helps you document when and why participants were lost from your study. Figure 5.1 can help you and your readers determine both the legitimate generalizations (about people) that can be made from your study and whether your study had sufficient power to reject the null hypothesis or, in effect size terms, whether your study could estimate the effect sizes with sufficient precision. I provide an example of the use of Figure 5.1 in Chapter 5, when I discuss how you report the results of your study.

Measures, Methods of Data Collection, Measurement Quality, and Instrumentation

The description in your report of the measures you used should include

- definitions of all primary and secondary measures and measures used as covariates, including measures collected but not included in this report, and
- the methods you used to collect data.

In addition, your report should present evidence about the quality of your measures, including

- methods used to enhance the quality of measurements, including
  - the training and reliability of data collectors and
  - the use of multiple observations, and
- information on the validity of any instruments you created for your individual study—for example, their psychometric and biometric properties.

JARS recommends that your Method section include a subsection that provides definitions of all measures you collected on participants. Definitions of measures should be provided regardless of whether they were outcome variables of primary or secondary interest to you or whether you used them as covariates in your analyses of outcome variables. Also, describe measures that you collected but did not use in the reported analyses. These unanalyzed measures can be mentioned briefly, sometimes in a footnote. Or, if they are described in another document that is publicly available, such as an already-published journal article based on the same data collection, a dissertation, or a technical report, you can simply include a reference for this work.

This subsection should also describe the methods used to collect the measures. Did you use written questionnaires, interviews, or behavior assessments or observations? I discussed in Chapter 2 of this volume (see Primary and Secondary Hypotheses and Other Planned Analyses section) the distinction between primary and secondary measures, so I do not repeat that information here. *Covariates* are variables that may be predictive of the outcome variable in your study. You enter them into your data analysis either (a) to reduce the error in the outcome measure to make your statistical tests more sensitive to the effects of other variables or (b) to adjust for initial differences between experimental groups (on the covariate and therefore possibly on the outcome measure) because participants were not randomly assigned to conditions (or randomization failed).

An example of a measurement description that meets the JARS recommendations comes from a study by Tsaousides et al. (2009) in the article "The Relationship Between Employment-Related Self-Efficacy and Quality of Life Following Traumatic Brain Injury," published in *Rehabilitation Psychology*:

Predictor Variables

Employment-related self-efficacy. The Perceived Employability subscale (PEM) of the Bigelow Quality of Life Questionnaire (BQQ; Bigelow, McFarland, Gareau, & Young, 1991) was used to measure employment-related self-efficacy. The PEM consists of eight items that assess an individual's confidence to find and maintain employment (e.g., how comfortable do you feel going out to look for a job?). Items are rated on a 4-point Likert scale and summed, with higher scores indicating higher efficacy. Only five of the eight items from the PEM subscale were included . . . with adequate internal consistency (Cronbach's α = .72). (p. 301)

This description reveals the construct of interest (employment-related self-efficacy), how it was measured (with a questionnaire), and that the measure had five questions each with four possible responses.

Masking

> The description in your report of the measurements you used should give information about the awareness of data collectors regarding (a) the experimental condition to which the subject was assigned or (b) the primary hypotheses of the study.

Masking refers to steps to ensure that subjects, those administering the interventions or experimental manipulations, and those assessing the outcomes are unaware of which condition each subject is in. In the context of measurement, it is the awareness of the person either collecting the data directly from the subject or transferring the data from, say, written questions to a spreadsheet that is at issue. If the data collectors know the primary hypotheses of the study, they may alter the data collection in subtle (and sometimes unconscious) ways that influence subjects' responses or the transcribed data.

For example, a data collector in your perfume experiment who is aware of whether the fragrance a subject has sniffed was labeled *roses* or *manure* may smile more or act friendlier when the subjects who are responding are ostensibly smelling roses. You would try to prevent this bias by not letting data collectors see the labels on the bottles. Anything you did to keep data collectors or transcribers unaware of the subjects' condition should be presented in the section on psychometrics. I return to discussion of masking in other contexts in Chapter 4.

Psychometrics

> The description in your report of the psychometric characteristics of the measures you used should include
>
> - estimates of the reliability of the scores analyzed, including
>   - interrater reliability for subjectively scored measures and ratings,
>   - test–retest coefficients in longitudinal studies, and
>   - internal consistency coefficients for composite scales
> - estimates of convergent and discriminant validity, when relevant.
>
> If the reported reliability and validity information was not collected on your sample but was taken from another source, report the basic demographic characteristics of the other sample.

The example description from Tsaousides et al. (2009) also gives the internal consistency of the measure and declares that this was adequate. Tsaousides et al. provided Cronbach's alpha, which uses the correlations between items to estimate internal consistency. Many other measures of internal consistency also exist (T. J. B. Kline, 2005). Had the authors not calculated Cronbach's alpha from their own data but instead provided alpha coefficients from another source—say, the original article presenting the Bigelow Quality of Life Questionnaire—JARS would recommend that the authors also provide demographic information on the sample used in the original study. With this information, readers can compare the characteristics of the original and new samples and decide, on the basis of their similarities and difference, whether the original alpha estimate pertains to the new sample.

Fagan et al. (2009) provided a measure of the correlation between two of their measures of how often fathers participated in activities with their child:

> The father and mother reports of paternal engagement with the child were moderately correlated with each other at Years 1 and 3 (*r*s = .56 and .58, respectively). (p. 1393)

This is a measure of the convergent validity of the two measures because they are two different ways (asking mothers or fathers) of measuring the same construct (fathers' parental engagement). As such, a high correlation between the two enhances our confidence that each is measuring the construct of interest.

A study that provided an estimate of test–retest reliability and concurrent validity was conducted by Vadasy and Sanders (2008). The study was titled "Repeated Reading Intervention: Outcomes and Interactions With Readers' Skills and Classroom Instruction," and it appeared in the *Journal of Educational Psychology*. This study examined the effects of a reading intervention on second and third graders' reading fluency. Here is some of what the authors wrote about their measures:

> Students were presented with a card that had five randomly sorted letters (a, d, o, p, s) repeated 10 times each and were asked to say the names of the letters as quickly as they could. The raw score was the total number of seconds the student used to name all of the letters. Test–retest reliability reported in the test manual is .87 for elementary grades. We also measured students on the Number Naming subtest to obtain concurrent validity: The correlation between Letter Naming and Number Naming (in number of seconds) was .79. (p. 277)

Note that for the test–retest information, the authors did not give information on the original sample, other than to say that students were drawn from similar grades. The estimate of concurrent validity is based on a comparison within their sample.

Tsaousides et al. (2009) also provided an example of an item on their questionnaire. This is good practice, especially when the content of questions is not clear or when the measure involves multiple items that are summed to derive a participant's score. It is best practice to provide a reference to a document that spells out the entire measure and its measurement characteristics or a link (along with your example) to an online supplemental archive, where you provide the reader with the complete measurement instrument.

The following is a good description of a measurement scale based on observer ratings that, rather than measuring behavior, measures the quality of preschool classrooms, taken from Moller, Forbes-Jones, and Hightower's (2008) article, "Classroom Age Composition and Developmental Change in 70 Urban Preschool Classrooms," published in the *Journal of Educational Psychology*:

> **Early Childhood Environment Rating Scale—Revised (ECERS–R).** The ECERS–R is among the most widely used observational tools allowing for objective assessment of preschool classroom quality (Henry et al., 2004; Howes & Smith, 1995; Scarr, Eisenberg, & Deater-Deckard, 1994). The seven areas of classroom quality that the ECERS–R measures are space and furnishing, personal care routines, language and reasoning, activities, interaction, program structure, and parents and staff. Each area contains 5–10 items that represent various elements of that area. For the present investigation, we averaged scores across all seven areas to create an overall, composite measure of classroom quality. . . .
>
> ECERS–R observations of classroom quality were conducted by 24 observers midway through the academic year (in the months of February, March, and April). For classroom observers in their 1st year of training, ECERS–R observers attended a 15-hr training program and reached an interrater reliability of 85% agreement with a master observer who was trained by the ECERS–R authors. For observers in their 2nd year, an additional 4–5 hr of training were required. All observers maintained an interrater reliability of 80% agreement, with 20% of their observations being checked. (pp. 744–745)

Moller et al. (2008) gave several references in which readers can find additional information on the measure. Because this measure involves observations, the authors were careful to describe how raters were trained and how reliable their ratings were. Moller et al. provided an agreement percentage as a measure of interrater reliability. Other measures of rater equivalence could also have been reported (T. J. B. Kline, 2005).

Finally, *biometric properties* refers to the characteristics of individuals' physical or physiological makeup. Some biometric properties, such as age, are easy to collect with great reliability. Others require descriptions with much detail. For example, an electrocardiogram (EKG) obtained by strategically placing electrodes on the skin of participants is a measure of the heart's electrical activity. In Taylor and James's (2009) article "Evidence for a Putative Biomarker for Substance Dependence," published in *Psychology of Addictive Behaviors*, the authors used an EKG as one measure in a study examining differences in responses to predictable and unpredictable bursts of white noise by people with and without substance dependence. Here is their description of how they collected their EKG data:

> For all participants, the electrocardiograph (EKG) was recorded from solid-gelled Ag-AgCl disposable electrodes through an AC amp from Contact Precision Instruments. Low-pass and high-pass filters were set to 30 and 0.3 Hz, respectively. All data were digitized online at 100 Hz (128 Hz in the earlier study). All physiological data were acquired with software from Contact Precision Instruments running on an IBM-compatible computer. (p. 493)

Each biometric marker has a unique set of parameters that need to be reported. As with psychological measures, JARS recommends that enough information be provided to allow others to judge the adequacy of the measures and to replicate results.

Conditions and Design

The description in your report of the research design should include

- whether conditions were manipulated or naturally observed and
- the type of research design (see appendices in Chapters 4, 6, and 8).

If your design is not covered in JARS, it would have different reporting needs associated with it. In this case,

- report the common name associated with the design, and
- look for standards developed by others (e.g., organizations, journals) that might guide your reporting.

The Method section must also contain information on your research design and the procedures you used to implement it. Elsewhere, I have discussed the basic issues involved in the choice of a research design (Cooper, 2006). Briefly, three principal questions need to be asked to determine the appropriateness of a design for answering a research question:

1. Should the results of the research be expressed in numbers or narrative?
2. Is the problem you are studying a description of an event, an association between events, or a causal explanation of an event?
3. Does the problem or hypothesis address (a) how a process unfolds within an individual person or other type of unit over time or (b) what is associated with or explains variation between participants or groups of participants?

The JARS material presented in this book covers only designs that seek explanations that are arrived at through analyses of qualities expressed in numbers. If you answered "narrative" to the first question, you should refer to Levitt (in press) and Levitt et al. (2018) for reporting guidelines.

Chapter 4 provides reporting standards for designs that express results in numbers. It addresses design variations that

- experimentally or purposively manipulate conditions to examine the effects of the manipulations on selected outcome or dependent variables and
  - within this type of design, assign participants to conditions either randomly or not at random—for example, through self- or administrative selection (your hypothetical study involving the effects of labeling perfume *roses* vs. *manure* would be an experiment with random assignment) and
- do not contain an experimental manipulation but instead involve observations of naturally occurring events.

In Chapter 6, you will find design features of studies that

- collect data on multiple occasions,
- attempt to replicate a study that was previously conducted,
- use only one person or unit in the study, and
- involve clinical trials.

In Chapter 8, reporting standards for research syntheses and meta-analyses are described. Again, you can use Figure 1.1 to assist in picking the tables most applicable to your study.

The variety of designs illustrated in the examples I have given thus far demonstrate that the JARS items covering participants' characteristics, sampling procedures, and measurement characteristics relate to all studies, regardless of the researchers' answers to the research design questions, as does the material in Chapter 2 (on setting the stage), Chapter 5 (on describing your data and statistical analyses), and Chapter 7 (on interpreting your results). Regardless, an extremely important JARS recommendation is that your report include a description of the research design, one that will allow readers to decide whether the design you have chosen and the way it was implemented allow you to draw the inferences you desire.

Data Diagnostics

The description in your report of your planned data diagnostics should include your

- criteria for exclusion of subjects after the data have been collected, if any;
- criteria for deciding when to infer missing data and methods used for imputation of missing data;
- definition and processing of statistical outliers;
- analyses of data distributions; and
- data transformations you will use, if any.

Your report should also describe the analytic strategy for any inferential statistics you will calculate and how you plan to protect against experiment-wise error for

- primary hypotheses,
- secondary hypotheses, and
- exploratory hypotheses.

You may be wondering why details of your planned data diagnostics and analysis strategy need to be presented in the Method section rather than the Results section. The answer lies in the word *planned*. In the Method section, you should briefly detail what your strategy was for examining your data and subjecting it to analyses *before* you actually collected the data and began to look at them. JARS asks you to provide this information because it is often the case that plans change once the data collection process begins or is complete, and this change in plans can change the inferences you can make from your data.

It is OK to change your plans when unforeseen circumstances arise. However, it is not OK to change your approach to the data after you have seen the results and maybe don't like what you see. For example, suppose you collected your data on the pleasantness of fragrances and discovered that there was no difference between the ratings of the scents labeled *roses* and *manure*. However, after the fact you discover that the scent generally had very low ratings—that is, the scores are skewed to the right. Then, you decide to log transform your data, and voilà, a difference between the two labeling groups appears.

The status of this conclusion is different from the conclusion you could arrive at if you had planned to use an odious odor and to transform the data before conducting the analysis. Why? Because it is the second test you have conducted, and a post hoc one at that. Therefore, there is a greater likelihood that your new result has capitalized on chance. It may be harder to replicate your finding. If you do this post hoc analysis, you need to say first what you intended to do, what you found when you did it, what you did next, and what you found. You can't ignore your original planned analysis and what it revealed. I return to this topic in Chapter 5 when I describe several diagnostic and analytic procedures individually.

Reporting on data diagnostics and analysis intentions in a Method section is still rather rare, but hopefully will be less so now that JARS and other reporting standards have drawn attention to the need for reporting it. The objective of adding this new section to the end of the Method section is to encourage researchers to fully report their data handling strategies. Sometimes, when researchers report lots of data diagnostics that lead to removed data, data transformations, and exotic data analyses, unless these are justified a priori, readers will smell something fishy.

Describing Your Research Design: Studies With and Without Experimental Manipulations

As I mentioned in Chapter 1, Table A1.1 should be filled out whenever the research project involves the collection of new data. This table will get you through the common material that should be contained in all research reports, regardless of the research design and statistical analyses used. But different research designs require that different aspects of the design be reported. This chapter describes these standards for studies with research designs that involve a manipulation of experimental conditions.

Table A4.1 describes reporting standards for all research designs involving purposive or experimental manipulations. Table A4.2a provides separate items for reporting a study that used random assignment of subjects to conditions and Table A4.2b for reporting a study that used a purposive manipulation but in which subjects were assigned to conditions using a procedure other than random assignment. You would choose to use either Table A4.2a or Table A4.2b but not both. Table A6.4 presents some additional reporting standards for reporting clinical trials. It also highlights a few extra reporting standards for the abstract and the introduction. These are primarily included to emphasize their particular importance in the case of clinical trials.

Studies With Experimental Manipulations or Interventions

The Journal Article Reporting Standards for quantitative studies (JARS; Appelbaum et al., 2018) recommends that research reports contain detailed descriptions of all of the different conditions that subjects were exposed to in studies with experimental manipulations

http://dx.doi.org/10.1037/0000103-004
Reporting Quantitative Research in Psychology: How to Meet APA Style Journal Article Reporting Standards, Second Edition, by H. Cooper

(Table A4.1). To illustrate the different items in JARS, I use primarily an article by Adank, Evans, Stuart-Smith, and Scott (2009) titled "Comprehension of Familiar and Unfamiliar Native Accents Under Adverse Listening Conditions," published in the *Journal of Experimental Psychology: Human Perception and Performance*. The researchers created two groups of listeners. One group of listeners was drawn from the residents of London, England. They heard taped sentences spoken in standard English (SE) or Glaswegian English (GE) and were assumed to be familiar with the former but unfamiliar with the latter. The second group of listeners was drawn from Glasgow, Scotland, and listened to the same tapes but were assumed to be familiar with both accents (because of media exposure). Also, noise at three volumes was added to the tapes to create four conditions of noise (one being a no-noise condition). Therefore, there were eight experimental conditions. In their overview of their design, Adank et al. also informed readers that

> Ninety-six true/false sentences were presented to the participants, that is, 12 sentences per experimental condition. The sentences were counterbalanced across conditions, so that all 96 sentences were presented in all conditions across all subjects within a listener group. All listeners heard sentences in all four conditions. This was repeated for the SE and GE listener groups, thus ensuring that all sentences were presented in all conditions for both groups. Furthermore, not more than two sentences of one speaker were presented in succession, as Clarke and Garrett (2004) found that familiarization occurs after as few as two sentences from a speaker. (p. 521)

Thus, Adank et al. used a two-factor (2 × 4) within-subjects experimental design with an additional individual difference—whether the subject spoke SE or GE—serving as a between-subjects factor. The study focused on perceptual processes and was conducted in a laboratory.

Experimental Manipulation

If your study involved an experimental manipulation, your report should describe

- the details of the experimental manipulations intended for each study condition, including the comparison conditions, and
- how and when manipulations were actually administered, including
  - the content of the specific experimental manipulations (a summary or paraphrasing of instructions is OK unless they are unusual, in which case they may be presented verbatim) and
  - the method of experimental manipulation delivery, including a description of apparatus and materials used, such as specialized equipment by model and supplier, and their function in the experiment.

The methods and materials used by Adank et al. (2009) to deliver the spoken sentences in their study involved, first, the creation of the spoken sentences stimulus materials. They gave an impressive amount of detail about how the manipulation was delivered. First, Adank et al. described how the tapes were made to ensure that only the speakers' accents varied across the spoken sentences:

> For every speaker, recordings were made of the 100 sentences of Version A of the SCOLP [Speed and Capacity of Language Processing] test (Baddeley et al., 1992). The sentence was presented on the screen of a notebook computer, and speakers were instructed to quietly read the sentence and subsequently to pronounce the sentence as a declarative statement. All sentences were recorded once. However, if the speaker made a mistake, the interviewer went back two sentences, and the speaker was instructed to repeat both. . . .
>
> The GE speakers were recorded in a sound-treated room, using an AKG SE300B microphone (AKG Acoustics, Vienna, Austria), which was attached to an AKG N6-6E preamplifier, on a Tascam DA-P1 DAT recorder (Tascam Div., TEAC Corp., Tokyo, Japan). Each stimulus was transferred directly to hard disk using a Kay Elemetrics DSP sonagraph (Kay Elemetrics, Lincoln Park, NJ). . . . The recordings of the SE speakers were made in an anechoic room, using a Brüel and Kjær 2231 sound level meter (Brüel and Kjær Sound & Vibration Measurement, Nærum, Denmark) as a microphone/amplifier. This microphone was fitted with a 4165 microphone cartridge and its A/C output was fed to the line input of a Sony 60ES DAT recorder (Sony Corp., Tokyo) and the digital output from the DAT recorder fed to the digital input of a Delta 66 sound card (M-Audio UK, Watford, UK) in the Dell Optiplex GX280 personal computer (Dell Corp., Fort Lauderdale, FL). . . . The difference in recording conditions between the two speaker groups was not noticeable in the recordings, and it is thus unlikely that intelligibility of the two accents was affected.
>
> Next, all sentences were saved into their own file with beginning and end trimmed at zero crossings (trimming on or as closely as possible to the onset and offset of initial and final speech sounds) and resampled at 22,050 Hz. Subsequently, the speech rate differences across all eight speakers were equalized, so that every sentence had the same length across all eight speakers. This was necessary to ensure straightforward interpretation of the dependent variable (i.e., to be able to express the results in milliseconds). First, for each of the 96 sentences, the average duration across all speakers was calculated. Second, we used the Pitch Synchronous Overlap Add Method, or PSOLA (Moulines & Charpentier, 1990), as implemented in the Praat software package (Boersma & Weenink, 2003), to digitally shorten or lengthen the sentence for each speaker separately. The effect of the shortening or lengthening was in some cases just audible, but it was expected that any effects due to this manipulation were small to negligible, as the manipulations were relatively small and were carried out across all sentences for all speakers in the experiment. (p. 522)

This level of detail is called for in the *Publication Manual of the American Psychological Association* (APA, 2010):

> If a mechanical apparatus was used to present stimulus materials or collect data, include in the description of procedures the apparatus model number and manufacturer (when important, as in neuroimaging studies), its key settings or parameters (e.g., pulse settings), and its resolution (e.g., regarding stimulus delivery, recording precision). (p. 31)

The level of detail also suggests that this area of research is probably working with very subtle and sensitive effects (note the attention to the speed of speech). This requires of the experimenters a great deal of control over what and how stimulus materials are presented to produce it. Note that Adank et al. also mentioned the locations (London and Glasgow) at which the recordings for the experiment took place.

Adank et al. (2009) then went on to describe how they accomplished the noise manipulation:

> Finally, speech-shaped noise was added. . . . This speech-shaped noise was based on an approximation to the long-term average speech spectrum for combined male and female voices. . . . The root mean square levels per one third of the octave band were converted into spectrum level and plotted on an octave scale. A three-line approximation was used to capture the major part of the shape from 60 Hz to 9 kHz. This consisted of a low-frequency portion rolling off below 120 Hz at 17.5 dB/octave and a high frequency portion rolling off at 7.2 dB/octave above 420 Hz, with a constant spectrum portion in between. Per sentence, the noise sound file was cut at a random position from a longer (6-s) segment of speech-shaped noise, so that the noise varied randomly across sentences. The speech-shaped noise had the same duration as the sentence and started and ended with the onset and offset of the sentence. The root mean squares of the sentence and the noise were determined and scaled as to fit the SNR [signal-to-noise] level and finally were combined through addition. Finally, using Praat, we peak normalized and scaled the intensity of the sound file to 70 dB sound pressure level (SPL). (p. 522)

Deliverers

If your study involved an experimental manipulation, describe

- the deliverers, including
  - who delivered the manipulations,
  - their level of professional training, and
  - their level of training in the specific experimental manipulations;
- the number of deliverers; and
- the mean, standard deviation, and range of number of individuals or units treated by each deliverer.

For Adank et al. (2009), the deliverers of the manipulation might be considered the people whose voices were recorded:

> Recordings were made of four SE speakers and four GE speakers. All speakers were male, middle class, and between 20 and 46 years old. Only male speakers were selected because including both genders would have introduced unwanted variation related to the gender differences in larynx size and vocal tract length. . . . The GE speakers were recorded in Glasgow, and the SE speakers were recorded in London. (p. 552)

Taking extra precaution, these researchers also described the persons helping the speakers create the tapes:

> Because our investigative team speaks in Southern English accents, we arranged for the GE recordings to be conducted by a native GE interviewer to avoid the possibility of speech accommodation toward Southern English (Trudgill, 1986). . . . The SE recordings were conducted by a native SE interviewer. (p. 522)

The level of detail these authors provide for how their experimental conditions were delivered also is impressive. What might seem like trivial detail to an outsider can be critical to enabling someone immersed in this field to draw strong causal inferences from a study. How will you know what these details are? By reading the detailed reports of those who have done work in your area before you.

Setting, Exposure, and Time Span

If your study involved an experimental manipulation, describe

- the setting where the experimental manipulations occurred and
- the exposure quantity and duration, including
    - how many sessions, episodes, or events were intended to be delivered;
    - how long they were intended to last; and
    - the time span, or how long it took to deliver the manipulation to each unit.

Adank et al.'s (2009) description of the experimental procedures focused on the physical characteristics of the experimental room, the mode of the manipulation delivery, and what subjects had to do to respond:

> *Procedure.* The SE listeners were tested in London, and the GE listeners were tested in Glasgow. All listeners were tested individually in a quiet room while facing the screen of a notebook computer. They received written instructions. The listeners responded using the notebook's keyboard. Half of the participants were instructed to press the *q* key with their left index finger for true responses and to press the *p* key with their right index finger for false responses. The response keys were reversed (i.e., *p* for true and *q* for false) for the other half of the participants. Listeners were not screened for handedness. The stimuli were presented over headphones (Philips SBC HN110; Philips Electronics, Eindhoven, the Netherlands) at a sound level that was kept constant for all participants. Stimulus presentation and the collection of the responses were performed with Cogent 2000 software (Cogent 2000 Team, Wellcome Trust, London, UK), running under Matlab (Mathworks, Cambridge, UK). The response times were measured relative to the end of the audio file, following the computerized SCOLP task in May et al. (2001).
>
> Each trial proceeded as follows. First, the stimulus sentence was presented. Second, the program waited for 3.5 s before playing the next stimulus, allowing the participant to make a response. If the participant did not respond within

3.5 s, the trial was recorded as *no response*. The participants were asked to respond as quickly as they could and told that they did not have to wait until the sentence had finished (allowing for negative response times, as response time was calculated from the offset of the sound file).

Ten familiarization trials were presented prior to the start of the experiment. The familiarization sentences had been produced by a male SE speaker. This speaker was not included in the actual experiment, and neither were the 10 familiarization sentences. The experiment's duration was 15 min, without breaks. (pp. 522–523)

Activities to Increase Compliance

If your study involved an experimental manipulation, describe in detail the activities you engaged in to increase compliance or adherence (e.g., incentives).

Adank et al. (2009) did little to increase compliance, but in this type of study it is likely that little was needed. They told readers that the subjects in their study were recruited from London and Glasgow and that "all were paid for their participation" (p. 522). We can consider the payments as a method to increase compliance.

Use of Language Other Than English

If your study involved an experimental manipulation, describe the use of a language other than English and the translation method.

In Adank et al.'s (2009) study, the use of a language other than SE was one of the experimental manipulations. JARS recommends (see Table A4.1) that the research report indicate whether the language used to conduct the study was other than English. According to the *Publication Manual*,

When an instrument is translated into a language other than the language in which it was developed, describe the specific method of translation (e.g., back-translation, in which a text is translated into another language and then back into the first to ensure that it is equivalent enough that results can be compared). (APA, 2010, p. 32)

Replication

If your study involved an experimental manipulation, include sufficient detail to allow for replication, including

■ reference to or a copy of the manual of procedures (i.e., whether the manual of procedures is available and, if so, how others may obtain it).

The design descriptions presented above provide excellent examples of the details that should be presented so that others might be able to repeat the studies with excellent fidelity. Adank et al.'s (2009) report went to great lengths to describe the manipulations, equipment, deliverers, and setting of their study.

Unit of Delivery and Analysis

> If your study involved an experimental manipulation, describe the unit of delivery—that is, how participants were grouped during delivery—including
>
> ■ a description of the smallest unit that was analyzed (in the case of experiments, that was randomly assigned to conditions) to assess manipulation effects (e.g., individuals, work groups, classes) and
> ■ if the unit of analysis differed from the unit of delivery, a description of the analytical method used to account for this (e.g., adjusting the standard error estimates by the design effect, using multilevel analysis).

JARS calls for a description of how subjects were grouped during delivery of the experimental manipulation. Was the manipulation administered individual by individual, to small or large groups, or to intact, naturally occurring groups? It also recommends that you describe the smallest unit you used in your data analysis.

The reason for recommending that this information be reported goes beyond the reader's need to know the method of manipulation delivery and analysis. In most instances, the unit of delivery and the unit of analysis need to be the same for the assumptions of statistical tests to be met. Specifically, at issue is the assumption that each data point in the analysis is independent of the other data points. When subjects are tested in groups, it is possible that the individuals in each group affect one another in ways that would influence their scores on the dependent variable.

Suppose you conducted your fragrance labeling study by having 10 groups of five subjects each smell the fragrance when it was labeled *roses* and another 10 groups of five subjects each smell it when it was labeled *manure*. Before you had subjects rate the fragrances, you allowed them to engage in a group discussion. The discussions might have gone very differently in the different groups. The first person to speak up in one of the manure groups might have framed the discussion for the entire group by stating, "I would never buy a fragrance called *manure*!" whereas in another group, the first speaker might have said, "*Manure*! What a bold marketing strategy!" Such comments could lower and raise, respectively, all group members' ratings. Therefore, the ratings within groups are no longer independent. By knowing the subjects' groups, you know something about whether their ratings will be lower or higher than those of other subjects not in their group, even within the manure and roses conditions.

This example, of course, is unlikely to happen (I hope); clearly, subjects should complete this type of labeling study individually, unless the research question deals with the influence of groups on labeling (in which case the framing comments likely would also be experimentally manipulated). However, there are many instances in which treatments are applied to groups formed purposively (e.g., group therapy) or naturalistically (e.g., classrooms). Still, in many of these instances, there will be a temptation to conduct the data analysis with the individual participant as the unit of analysis because either (a) the analysis is simpler or (b) using the participant as the unit of analysis increases the power of the test by increasing the available degrees of freedom. In your labeling experiment run in groups, there are 100 subjects but only 20 groups.

Some data analysis techniques take into account the potential dependence of scores within groups (Luke, 2004). If you used such an analytic method, describe it. Describing these techniques is beyond the scope of this discussion; for now, it is important only that you understand the rationale behind why JARS asks for this information.

A study that addressed the issue of units of delivery and analysis was conducted by Vadasy and Sanders (2008), who examined the effects of a reading intervention on second and third graders' reading fluency. The intervention was delivered in groups of two students. Here is how Vadasy and Sanders described their method of composing the units of delivery:

> Group assignment was a two-stage process. First, eligible students were randomly assigned to dyads (pairs of students) within grade and school using a random number generator. Although it would have been preferable to randomly assign students to dyads within classrooms in order to minimize extreme mismatches between students within a dyad, there were too few eligible students within classrooms to make this practical. Nevertheless, there were sufficient numbers of eligible students for random assignment of dyads within grades (within schools). For schools with uneven numbers of students within grades, we used random selection to identify singletons that were subsequently excluded from participation. Dyads were then randomly assigned to one of two conditions: treatment (supplemental fluency tutoring instruction) or control (no tutoring; classroom instruction only). (p. 274)

These researchers went on to describe their unit of analysis and the rationale for their choice of data analysis strategy by simply stating,

> Due to nesting structures present in our research design, a multilevel (hierarchical) modeling approach was adopted for analyzing group differences on pretests and gains. (Vadasy & Sanders, 2008, p. 280)

Studies Using Random Assignment

If your study used random assignment to place subjects into conditions, your report should describe

- the unit of randomization and
- the procedure used to generate the random assignment sequence, including details of any restriction (e.g., blocking, stratification).

Knowing whether subjects have been assigned to conditions in a study at random or through some self-choice or administrative procedure is critical to readers' ability to understand the study's potential for revealing causal relationships. Random assignment makes it unlikely that there will be any differences between the experimental groups before the manipulation occurs (Christensen, 2012; see Table A4.2a). If subjects are placed into experimental groups using random assignment, then you can assume the groups do not differ on characteristics that might be related to the dependent variable.[1]

In the case of self- or administrative selection into groups, it is quite plausible that the groups will differ on many dimensions before the manipulation is introduced, and some of these dimensions are likely related to the dependent variable. This potential compromises the ability of studies using self- or administrative assignment techniques to lead to strong causal inferences about the manipulation. For example, if subjects in the labeling study were first asked whether they would like to smell a fragrance called "Roses" or one called "Manure" and then they were assigned to their preference, there is simply no way to determine whether their subsequent ratings of the fragrances were caused by a labeling effect or by individual differences subjects brought with them to the study (perhaps more subjects in the manure condition grew up on a farm?). For this reason, studies using random assignment are called *experiments* or *randomized field trials*, whereas those using nonrandom assignment are called *quasi-experiments*.

Types of random assignment. It is essential that your report tells readers what procedure you used to assign subjects to conditions. When random assignment is used in a laboratory context, it is often OK to say only that random assignment happened. However, you can add how the random assignment sequence was generated—for example, by using a random numbers table, an urn randomization method, or statistical software.

Your study may also have involved a more sophisticated random assignment technique. For example, when the number of subjects in an experiment is small, it is often good practice to first create groups that include a number of subjects equal to the number of conditions in the study and then to randomly assign one member of the group to each condition. This technique, called *blocking*, ensures that you end up with equal numbers of subjects in each condition.

Sometimes *stratified random assignment* is used to ensure that groups are equal across important strata of subjects—for example, using the blocking strategy to assign each pair of women and each pair of men to the two labeling conditions. In this way, you can ensure that the roses and manure conditions have equal numbers of subjects of each sex. This is important if you think fragrance ratings will differ between sexes. If your study uses such a technique, say so in your report.

Random assignment implementation and method of concealment.

If your study used random assignment, state whether and how the sequence was concealed until experimental manipulations were assigned. Also state

- who generated the assignment sequence,
- who enrolled participants, and
- who assigned participants to groups.

---

[1]Of course, the use of random assignment does not rule out differences between groups arising after assignment has occurred. For example, more participants assigned to smell a fragrance called *manure* may choose not to complete the study than would those assigned to smell a fragrance called *roses*. The decision to quit the study could be related to their predisposition to like the things they smell. This is called *differential attrition* and is discussed more fully in Chapter 6. Also, sometimes random assignment fails simply because it is a chance process; by bad luck alone, groups are created that differ on the dependent variable.

The next JARS recommendation concerns the issue of concealment of the allocation process. It raises the issue of whether the person enrolling people in a study knew which condition was coming up next. In most psychology laboratory experiments, this is of little importance; the enrollment is done by computer.

Studies Using Nonrandom Assignment: Quasi-Experiments

If your study used a method other than random assignment to place subjects into conditions, describe

- the unit of assignment (i.e., the unit being assigned to study conditions; e.g., individual, group, community);
- the method used to assign units to study conditions, including details of any restriction (e.g., blocking, stratification, minimization); and
- the procedures employed to help minimize selection bias (e.g., matching, propensity score matching).

When a nonrandom process is used to assign subjects to conditions, some other technique typically is used to make the groups as equivalent as possible (Table A4.2b; see Shadish, Cook, & Campbell, 2002, for how this is done). Frequently used techniques include (a) matching people across the groups on important dimensions and removing the data of subjects who do not have a good match and (b) post hoc statistical control of variables believed related to the outcome measure using an analysis of covariance or multiple regression.

Evers, Brouwers, and Tomic (2006) provided an example of reporting a quasi-experiment in their article "A Quasi-Experimental Study on Management Coaching Effectiveness," published in *Consulting Psychology Journal: Practice and Research*. In this study, the experimental group was composed of managers who had signed up (self-selected) to be coached. Evers et al. were then faced with constructing a no-coaching comparison group. Here is how they described the process:

The Experimental Group

We asked staff managers of various departments which managers were about to be coached. . . . We got the names of 41 managers who were about to register for coaching; 30 managers agreed to participate in our quasi-experiment, 19 men (63.3%) and 11 women (36.7%). Their ages ranged between 27 and 53 years ($M = 38.8$; $SD = 8.20$). The mean number of years as a manager was 5.34 years ($SD = 5.66$), and the mean number of years in the present position was 1.76 years ($SD = 2.52$).

The Control Group

We asked 77 managers of the Department of Housing and Urban Development to fill out our questionnaires: Of this group, 22 did not respond, whereas 48 of them answered the questionnaires both at the beginning and at the end of our quasi-experiment. We matched the groups with the help of salary scales, for these scales of the federal government are indicative of the weight of a position. We also matched the groups as much as possible according to sex and age, which ultimately resulted in a control group of 30 managers, of which 20 (66.7%) were men and 10 (33.3%) were women. Their ages ranged from 26 to 56 years, with a mean of 43.6 years ($SD = 8.31$), which means that the mean age of the control group is 4.8 years older. The mean number of years as a manager was 8.64 years ($SD = 7.55$), which means that they worked 3.3 years longer in this position than members of the experimental group did. The members of the control group had been working in the present position for a mean of 2.76 years ($SD = 2.39$), which is 1 year more than the members of the experimental group.

The experimental and the control group . . . were equal on sex, $\chi^2(1) = 0.14$, $p = .71$; the number of years as a manager, $t(58) = 1.91$, $p = .06$; and the total number of years in the present position, $t(58) = 1.58$, $p = .12$; but not on age, $t(58) = 2.25$, $p = .03$. (pp. 176–177)

First, as recommended in JARS, it is clear from Evers et al.'s (2006) description that the individual manager was the unit of assignment. The first sentence tells readers that subjects had not been randomly assigned to the coaching condition; the method of assignment was self-choice or administrative selection. We do not know (and I suspect the researchers did not either) whether subjects requested coaching or were nominated for it (or both), but the managers in the coaching group were clearly people who might have been different from all managers in numerous ways: They might have needed coaching because of poor job performance, or they might have been good managers who were highly motivated to become even better. The group of not-coached managers who were invited to take part was chosen because they were similar in salary.

The researchers stated that 77 managers were asked to be in the control group, of which 48 provided the necessary data. These numbers relate more to our assessment of the representativeness of control group managers than to issues related to condition assignment. Then, within the responding invitees, further matching was done on the basis of the managers' sex and age. This resulted in a control group of 30, comprising the best matches for the managers in the coached group.

Finally, Evers et al. (2006) informed readers that their matching procedure produced groups that were equivalent in sex and experience but not in age. The researchers found that coached managers had some higher outcome expectancies and self-efficacy beliefs. Because the coached and not-coached groups also differed in age, is it possible that managers scored higher on these two variables simply because these two self-beliefs grow more positive as a function of growing older?

Methods to Report for Studies Using Random and Nonrandom Assignment Masking

Regardless of whether random assignment or another method was used to place subjects into experimental conditions, your Method section should

- report whether participants, those administering experimental manipulations, and those assessing the outcomes were unaware of condition assignments, and
- provide a statement regarding how masking was accomplished and how the success of masking was evaluated.

If you did not use masking, this should be stated as well.

As I mentioned in the Chapter 3, *masking* refers to steps to ensure that subjects, those administering the interventions or experimental manipulations, and those assessing the outcomes are unaware of which condition each subject is in. Masking is most likely to take place in circumstances in which knowledge of the condition could itself influence the behavior of the subject or the person interacting with him or her. In the fragrance labeling experiment, for example, subjects should not know that there is also another condition in which people are reacting to a fragrance called something else. Otherwise, they might react to their assignment ("Why did I have to smell *manure*?") rather than the fragrance itself.

The person interacting with the subject also should not know what the label is for this subject; this knowledge might influence how the person behaves, either wittingly or unwittingly (e.g., smiling more at subjects in the roses condition). Also, if you had someone rate, say, the facial expression of subjects after sniffing the fragrance, you would want them to be unaware of the subjects' condition to guard against a possible bias in their ratings.

Masking used to be referred to as *blinding*, and it still is not unusual to see reference to *single-blind* and *double-blind* experiments. The first refers to a study in which subjects do not know which condition they are in, and the second refers to a study in which neither the subject nor the experimenter knows the condition.[2] For example, Amir et al.'s (2009) article "Attention Training in Individuals With Generalized Social Phobia: A Randomized Controlled Trial" was discussed earlier for its power analysis. In this study, all parties who could introduce bias were kept unaware of condition assignment. Clinicians rated some outcome measures and did not know whether the subjects received the experimental treatment or placebo:

Measures

We used a battery of clinician- and self-rated measures at pre- and postassessment. Clinician ratings were made by raters blind to treatment condition. (Amir et al., 2009, p. 964)

Also, subjects and experimenters were kept unaware of the subjects' condition:

Procedure

Prior to each experimental session, participants entered the number in their file into the computer. . . . Participants did not know which condition the numbers represented, and the research assistants working with the participants could not see the number in the envelope. Thus, participants, experimenters, and interviewers remained blind to a participant's condition until all posttreatment assessments had been conducted. (Amir et al., 2009, p. 965)

---

[2]The term *blinding* was abandoned by APA in the mid-1980s because it used a description of a disability in a metaphoric sense. Even though the term has not been used in APA guidelines for more than 2 decades, it still appears in some APA journals. Personally, I don't like *masking* either and use *were kept unaware* as an alternative.

Further, the researchers assessed whether their procedure to keep subjects unaware of their condition was successful:

> To assess whether participants remained blind to their respective experimental condition, we asked participants at postassessment whether they thought they had received the active versus placebo intervention. Of the participants who provided responses, 21% (4/19) of participants in the AMP [attention modification program] and 28% (5/18) of ACC [attention control condition] participants thought they had received the active treatment, $\chi^2(1, N = 37) = 0.23$, $p = .63$. These findings bolster confidence that participants did not systematically predict their respective experimental condition. (Amir et al., 2009, p. 965)

Amir et al. (2009) also pointed out in their discussion two limitations of the masking procedures they used:

> Follow-up data should be interpreted with caution because assessors and participants were no longer blind to participant condition. . . . (p. 969)
>
> We did not collect data regarding interviewers' or experimental assistants' guesses regarding participants' group assignment and therefore cannot definitively establish that interviewers and assistants remained blind to participant condition in all cases. (p. 971)

From these descriptions, it is easy for the reader to assess whether knowledge of the treatment condition might have affected the study's outcomes (unlikely, I suspect) and for replicators to know what they need to do to reproduce or improve on what Amir et al. did.

Statistical Analyses

Regardless of whether random assignment or another method was used to place subjects into experimental conditions, your Method section should describe the statistical methods used

- to compare groups on primary outcomes;
- for additional analyses, such as subgroup comparisons and adjusted analysis (e.g., methods for modeling pretest differences and adjusting for them when random assignment was not used); and
- for mediation or moderation analyses, if conducted.

Research reports should conclude the Method section with a subsection titled "Statistical Analysis" or "Analysis Strategy" or some variation thereof. Sometimes this is presented as a subsection of the Method section. Other times, the description of each analysis strategy appears in the Results section just before the results of that analysis are described. Regardless of where it appears, you should lay out the broad strategy you used to analyze your data and give the rationale for your choices.

As an example of how the analysis strategy might be described in a study using nonexperimental data, here is how Tsaousides et al. (2009) described their two-step analytic approach in their study of efficacy belief and brain injury:

Data Analysis

First, correlations were conducted to explore the relationship among demographic, injury related, employment, predictor (PEM [Perceived Employability subscale] and IND [Independence subscale of the Bigelow Quality of Life Questionnaire]), and outcome variables (PQoL [perceived quality of life] and UIN [unmet important needs]). Subsequently, two hierarchical regression analyses were conducted, to determine the relevant contribution of each predictor to each outcome variable. In addition to the predictor variables, all demographic variables that correlated moderately ($r \le .20$) with either outcome variable and all injury-related variables were included in the regression analysis. . . . Employment status was included in both regression analyses as well, to compare the predictive value of employment to the self-efficacy variables. (p. 302)

Amir et al. (2009) provided an example of how to report the analytic strategy for an experiment using analysis of variance (ANOVA). The researchers' subsection on their statistical analysis of the study on attention training covered about a column of text. Here is a portion of what they wrote about their primary measures:

To examine the effect of the attention training procedure on the dependent variables, we submitted participants' scores on self-report and interviewer measures to a series of 2 (group: AMP, ACC) × 2 (time: preassessment, postassessment) ANOVAs with repeated measurement on the second factor. Multivariate ANOVAs were used for conceptually related measures . . . and a univariate ANOVA was used for disability ratings. . . . Significant multivariate effects were followed up with corresponding univariate tests. We followed up significant interactions with within-group simple effects analyses (*t* tests) as well as analyses of covariance on posttreatment scores covarying pretreatment scores to determine whether the AMP resulted in a significant change on the relevant dependent measures from pre- to postassessment. . . . A series of 2 (group) × 2 (time) × 2 (site: UGA [University of Georgia], SDSU [San Diego State University]) analyses established that there was no significant effect of site on the primary dependent measures (all $ps > .20$). The magnitude of symptom change was established by calculating (a) within-group effect sizes = (preassessment mean minus postassessment mean)/preassessment standard deviation, and (b) between-group controlled effect sizes (postassessment ACC covariance adjusted mean minus postassessment AMP covariance adjusted mean)/pooled standard deviation. (Amir et al., 2009, pp. 966–967)

The researchers began by telling readers the variables of primary interest. Then they described how the initial data analysis mirrored the research design; there were two experimental groups with each participant measured at two times, so they had a 2 × 2 design with the time of measurement as a repeated-measures factor. They protected against an inflated experiment-wise error by grouping conceptually related variables and followed up only significant multivariate effects with univariate tests. Significant interactions (tests of potential mediators that might influence the strength of the effect of the treatment) were followed by simple tests of subgroups. They finished by telling readers how they calculated their effect sizes—in this case, standardized mean differences, or *d* indexes. This description perfectly matches the recommendations of JARS.

Studies With No Experimental Manipulation

Many studies in psychology do not involve conditions that were manipulated by the experimenter or anyone else. The main goals of these studies can be to describe, classify, or estimate as well as to look for the naturally occurring relations between the variables of interest. Such studies are sometimes called *observational, correlational,* or *natural history studies.* In an observational study, the investigators watch participants and measure the variables of interest without attempting to influence participants' behavior in any way. The status of the participant is determined by their naturally occurring characteristics, circumstances, or history and is not at all affected (at least not intentionally) by the researchers. Of course, observations can occur in experimental studies as well.

In a correlational study, the researchers observe the participants, ask them questions, or collect records on them from archives. The data gathered are then correlated with one another (or are subjected to complex data analyses, discussed in Chapter 5) to see how they relate to one another. Again, the key is that the data are collected under the most naturalistic circumstances possible, with no experimental manipulation.

A natural history study is used most often in medicine, but it can apply to studies of psychological phenomena as well, especially studies concerned with mental health issues. As the name implies, natural history studies collect data over time on an issue, often a disease or psychological condition, so that the researchers can create a description of how the condition changes or emerges with the passage of time. It is hoped that the progression of the changes will provide insight into how and when it might be best to treat the condition. Thus, a natural history study can be considered a special type of observational study.

Given the nature of the research question, such studies may have special features to their designs or sampling plans. The studies may be prospective—that is, they follow people over time with the intention of collecting planned data in the future. Or they may be retrospective—that is, the participants' states or conditions in the past are gleaned from present-day self-reports, reports from others, or archival records.

A cohort study is a type of nonexperimental design that can be prospective or retrospective. In a prospective cohort study, participants are enrolled before the potential causal effect has occurred. For example, indigent mothers-to-be may be enlisted to take part in a study that tracks the effects of poverty on their children. In a retrospective cohort study, the study begins after the dependent event occurs, such as after the mothers have given birth and their children have exhibited developmental problems in preschool.

In case-control studies, existing groups that differ on an outcome are compared to one another to see if some past event correlates with the outcome. So students who are having trouble reading at grade level and those who are on grade level might be compared to see if they grew up under different conditions, perhaps in or out of poverty.

These are just a few examples of many nonexperimental designs and how they can be described. Table A4.3 presents the additional JARS standards for reporting these types of studies. These standards were added to JARS because they were part of the STROBE standards (Strengthening the Reporting of Observational Studies in Epidemiology; Vandenbroucke et al., 2014) and they either elaborated on the general JARS or asked for additional information. Table A4.3 is intended to be used along with Table A1.1. Because the STROBE guidelines are generally more detailed than JARS and are specific to nonexperimental designs, the article by Vandenbroucke et al. (2014) containing an example and explanation of each STROBE entry is very useful.[3]

Participant Selection

If your study did not include an experimental manipulation,

- describe methods of selecting participants (e.g., the units to be observed or classified), including
  - methods of selecting participants for each group (e.g., methods of sampling, place of recruitment),
  - number of cases in each group, and
  - matching criteria (e.g., propensity score) if matching was used;
- identify data sources used (e.g., sources of observations, archival records) and, if relevant, include codes or algorithms to select participants or link records; and
- define all variables clearly, including
  - exposure;
  - potential predictors, confounders, and effect modifiers; and
  - method of measuring each variable.

I have already introduced several studies that were not experimental in design. The study I described by Fagan, Palkovitz, Roy, and Farrie (2009) looked at whether risk factors such as fathers' drug problems, incarceration, and unemployment were associated with resilience factors (e.g., fathers' positive attitudes, job training, religious participation) and ultimately with the fathers' paternal engagement with offspring. O'Neill, Vandenberg, DeJoy, and Wilson (2009) reported a study on (a) the relationships involving retail store employees' anger, turnover rate, absences, and accidents on the job and (b) the employees' perception of how fully the organization they worked for supported them. All of the variables were measured, not manipulated.

Moller, Forbes-Jones, and Hightower (2008) studied the relationship between the age composition of a classroom, specifically how much variability there was in children's ages in the same preschool class, and the developmental changes they underwent. This also was a correlational study. These researchers measured the variability in classroom age composition and children's scores on the cognitive, motor, and social

---

[3]The STROBE guidelines can also be found online at https://www.strobe-statement.org/index.php?id=available-checklists. Select the document titled "STROBE checklist for cohort, case-control, and cross-sectional studies (combined)."

subscales of the Child Observation Record. They then related the scores to the classrooms' variability in age composition. Finally, Tsaousides et al. (2009) looked at the relationship between self-efficacy beliefs and measures of perceived quality of life among individuals with self-reported traumatic brain injury attending a community-based training center.

I presented the last three of these studies as examples of good descriptions of how to report measures in Chapter 3 under the Intended Sample Size subsection, and the Measures, Methods of Data Collection, Measurement Quality, and Instrumentation section. I will not describe them again here, but you can return to them and see how they fulfilled the JARS requirements for reporting measures in nonexperimental designs. Good descriptions of measures are always important, but this is especially true when the study contains no manipulation. When a manipulation is present, the description of the purposively created conditions also must be detailed and transparent.

Comparability of Assessment

If your study did not include an experimental manipulation, your Method section should describe the comparability of assessment across groups (e.g., the likelihood of observing or recording an outcome in each group for reasons unrelated to the effect of the intervention).

An added reporting standard for the Method section of nonexperimental studies calls for the researchers to describe whether the measurements were taken under comparable conditions across groups. This is especially important when the study compares intact groups, or groups that existed before the study began. Such groups might differ not only because of differences in the measured variable of interest but also because the measurements were taken at different times, in different circumstances, and by different data collectors. If this was true of your study, JARS suggests that you say so in your report and describe what you did to demonstrate that any difference between your static groups were not caused by these differences in measurement.

None of our article examples involve static groups, so let's complicate one for purposes of demonstration. Suppose a retail organization approached you with a problem. They had a store (in a chain) that was experiencing an unusually high rate of absenteeism and employee turnover (similar to O'Neill et al., 2009). They wanted to know why. They suspected the management team at the store was seen as unsupportive by the staff. So they asked you to survey the workers at the location of concern and at another store in the chain. Because the employees were not randomly assigned to store locations, you would need to take special care to determine that absenteeism (did both stores regard personal and sick days in the same way when calculating absences?), turnover (did both consider a request for transfer as an instance of turnover?), and perceived organizational support (how similar were the questionnaires, administrators, and administration circumstances?) were measured in comparable ways. These efforts need to be described in the report. Otherwise, readers will not be able to assess the importance of any of these potential sources of bias in the measures.

With the description of the Method section behind us, let's look at the JARS standards for reporting the results of studies.

Appendix 4.1: Additional Journal Article Reporting Standards for Basic Quantitative Research Designs

Table A4.1. Reporting Standards for Studies With an Experimental Manipulation (in Addition to Material Presented in Table A1.1)

Paper section and topic	Description

Method
  Experimental
    manipulations
	Provide details of the experimental manipulations intended for each study condition, including comparison conditions, and how and when experimental manipulations were actually administered, including
	• Content of the specific experimental manipulations (if experimental manipulation is part of a clinical trial, address Table A6.4)
	  • Summary or paraphrasing of instructions, unless they are unusual or compose the experimental manipulation, in which case they may be presented verbatim
	• Method of experimental manipulation delivery
	  • Description of apparatus and materials used (e.g., specialized equipment by model and supplier) and their function in the experiment
	• Deliverers: who delivered the experimental manipulations
	  • Level of professional training
	  • Level of training in specific experimental manipulations
	• Number of deliverers and, in the case of experimental manipulations, the M, SD, and range of number of individuals or units treated by each
	• Setting: where the manipulations or experimental manipulations occurred

▓ **Table A4.1.** (*Continued*)

Paper section and topic	Description
	• Exposure quantity and duration: how many sessions, episodes, or events were intended to be delivered and how long they were intended to last • Time span: how long it took to deliver the experimental manipulation to each unit • Activities to increase compliance or adherence (e.g., incentives) • Use of a language other than English and translation method • Sufficient detail to allow for replication, including reference to or a copy of the manual of procedures (If the manual of procedures is available, how others may obtain it).
Units of delivery and analysis	State the unit of delivery (how participants were grouped during delivery). Describe the smallest unit that was analyzed (and in the case of experiments, that was randomly assigned to conditions) to assess experimental manipulation effects (e.g., individuals, work groups, classes). If the unit of analysis differed from the unit of delivery, describe the analytic method used to account for this (e.g., adjusting the standard error estimates by the design effect or using multilevel analysis).
Results Participant flow	Report the total number of groups (if the experimental manipulation was administered at the group level) and the number of participants assigned to each group, including • Number of participants approached for inclusion • Number of participants who began the experiment • Number of participants who did not complete the experiment or crossed over to other conditions, with reasons • Number of participants included in primary analyses. Include a figure describing the flow of participants through each stage of the study (see Figure 5.1).
Treatment fidelity	Provide evidence on whether the experimental manipulation was implemented as intended.

(table continues)

▓ **Table A4.1.** (*Continued*)

Paper section and topic	Description
Baseline data	Describe baseline demographic and clinical characteristics of each group.
Adverse events and side effects	Report all important adverse events or side effects in each experimental condition. If none, state so.
Discussion	Discuss results, taking into account the mechanisms by which the experimental manipulation was intended to work (causal pathways) or alternative mechanisms. Discuss the success of, and barriers to, implementing the experimental manipulation and the fidelity of implementation if an experimental manipulation was involved. Discuss generalizability (external validity and construct validity) of the findings, taking into account • Characteristics of the experimental manipulation • How and what outcomes were measured • Length of follow-up • Incentives • Compliance rates. Describe the theoretical or practical significance of outcomes and the basis for these interpretations.

Note. Adapted from "Journal Article Reporting Standards for Quantitative Research in Psychology: The APA Publications and Communications Board Task Force Report," by M. Appelbaum, H. Cooper, R. B. Kline, E. Mayo-Wilson, A. M. Nezu, and S. M. Rao, 2018, *American Psychologist, 73*, p. 11. Copyright 2018 by the American Psychological Association.

Table A4.2a. Reporting Standards for Studies Using Random Assignment (in Addition to Material Presented in Table A1.1)

Paper section and topic	Description
Method	
Random assignment method	Describe the unit of randomization and the procedure used to generate the random assignment sequence, including details of any restriction (e.g., blocking, stratification).
Random assignment implementation and concealment	State whether and how the sequence was concealed until experimental manipulations were assigned, including who • Generated the assignment sequence • Enrolled participants • Assigned participants to groups.
Masking	Report whether participants, those administering the experimental manipulations, and those assessing the outcomes were aware of condition assignments. Provide a statement regarding how any masking (if it took place) was accomplished and whether and how the success of masking was evaluated.
Statistical methods	Describe statistical methods used to compare groups on primary outcomes. Describe statistical methods used for additional analyses, such as subgroup comparisons and adjusted analysis. Describe statistical methods used for mediation or moderation analyses if conducted.

Note. Adapted from "Journal Article Reporting Standards for Quantitative Research in Psychology: The APA Publications and Communications Board Task Force Report," by M. Appelbaum, H. Cooper, R. B. Kline, E. Mayo-Wilson, A. M. Nezu, and S. M. Rao, 2018, *American Psychologist, 73,* pp. 11–12. Copyright 2018 by the American Psychological Association.

■ **Table A4.2b.** Reporting Standards for Studies Using Nonrandom Assignment (in Addition to Material Presented in Table A1.1)

Paper section and topic	Description
Method	
Assignment method	Report the unit of assignment (i.e., the unit being assigned to study conditions; e.g., individual, group, community). Describe the method used to assign units to study conditions, including details of any restriction (e.g., blocking, stratification, minimization). State procedures used to help minimize selection bias (e.g., matching, propensity score matching).
Masking	Report whether participants, those administering the experimental manipulation, and those assessing the outcomes were aware of condition assignments. Report whether masking took place. Provide a statement regarding how it was accomplished and how the success of masking was evaluated, if it was evaluated.
Statistical methods	Describe statistical methods used to compare study groups on primary outcomes, including complex methods for correlated data. Describe statistical methods used for any additional analyses conducted, such as subgroup analyses and adjusted analysis (e.g., methods for modeling pretest differences and adjusting for them). Describe statistical methods used for mediation or moderation analyses if used.

Note. Adapted from "Journal Article Reporting Standards for Quantitative Research in Psychology: The APA Publications and Communications Board Task Force Report," by M. Appelbaum, H. Cooper, R. B. Kline, E. Mayo-Wilson, A. M. Nezu, and S. M. Rao, 2018, *American Psychologist, 73*, p. 12. Copyright 2018 by the American Psychological Association.

Table A4.3. Reporting Standards for Studies Using No Experimental Manipulation (e.g., Single-Case Designs, Natural-Group Comparisons; in Addition to Material Presented in Table A1.1)

Paper section and topic	Description
Abstract	
Study design	Describe the design of the study.
Data use	State the type of data used.
Method	
Participant selection	Describe the methods of selecting participants (i.e., the units to be observed or classified, etc.), including • Methods of selecting participants for each group (e.g., methods of sampling, place of recruitment) and number of cases in each group • Matching criteria (e.g., propensity score) if matching was used. Identify data sources used (e.g., sources of observations, archival records), and if relevant, include codes or algorithms used to select participants or link records.
Variables	Define all variables clearly, including • Exposure • Potential predictors, confounders, and effect modifiers. State how each variable was measured.
Comparability of assessment	Describe comparability of assessment across groups (e.g., the likelihood of observing or recording an outcome in each group for reasons unrelated to the effect of the intervention).
Analysis	Describe how predictors, confounders, and effect modifiers were included in the analysis.
Discussion	
Limitations	Describe potential limitations of the study. As relevant, describe the possibility of misclassification, unmeasured confounding, and changing eligibility criteria over time.

Note. Adapted from "Journal Article Reporting Standards for Quantitative Research in Psychology: The APA Publications and Communications Board Task Force Report," by M. Appelbaum, H. Cooper, R. B. Kline, E. Mayo-Wilson, A. M. Nezu, and S. M. Rao, 2018, *American Psychologist, 73,* p. 14. Copyright 2018 by the American Psychological Association.

5

Summarizing Your Data and Statistical Analyses: The Results Section

The Results section of your manuscript summarizes your data and the statistical analyses you applied to them. The rules here regarding completeness and transparency are the same as those you applied when reporting your method. According to the *Publication Manual of the American Psychological Association* (6th ed.; APA, 2010), you are obligated to report the data "in sufficient detail to justify your conclusions" (p. 32). The *Publication Manual* goes on to say, "Mention all relevant results, including those that run counter to expectation; be sure to include small effect sizes (or statistically nonsignificant findings) when theory predicts large (or statistically significant) ones. Do not hide uncomfortable results by omission" (p. 32).

The *Publication Manual* indicates that you do not need to include the individual scores or raw data in the report except when the study involved a single-case design or for purposes of illustration (and even then, only with proper protection against identifying the individual who provided the data, of course). However, the *Ethical Principles of Psychologists and Code of Conduct* (APA Ethics Code; APA, 2017) encourages data sharing. Therefore, it is important for you to keep your data in interpretable fashion for at least 5 years after any report has been published. I have reproduced in Exhibit 5.1 the relevant section of the APA Ethics Code.

Also, if your research received support from a funding agency, governmental or otherwise, you may find that the funder obligates you to share your data with others if they ask or to make it publicly available on a certain date. Further, it is becoming more common for researchers to make their raw data available in online supplemental archives that are posted on the Internet, with a link provided in the published report.

http://dx.doi.org/10.1037/0000103-005
Reporting Quantitative Research in Psychology: How to Meet APA Style Journal Article Reporting Standards, Second Edition, by H. Cooper

Excerpt from *Ethical Principles of Psychologists and Code of Conduct* Regarding Data Sharing

8.14 Sharing Research Data for Verification

(a) After research results are published, psychologists do not withhold the data on which their conclusions are based from other competent professionals who seek to verify the substantive claims through reanalysis and who intend to use such data only for that purpose, provided that the confidentiality of the participants can be protected and unless legal rights concerning proprietary data preclude their release. This does not preclude psychologists from requiring that such individuals or groups be responsible for costs associated with the provision of such information.

(b) Psychologists who request data from other psychologists to verify the substantive claims through reanalysis may use shared data only for the declared purpose. Requesting psychologists obtain prior written agreement for all other uses of the data.

Note. From *Ethical Principles of Psychologists and Code of Conduct (2002, amended June 1, 2010 and January 1, 2017)*, by the American Psychological Association, 2017 (http://www.apa.org/ethics/code/index.aspx). Copyright 2017 by the American Psychological Association.

Participant Flow

In your Results section, your description of the flow of participants through your study should include

■ the total number of participants in each group and
■ the flow of participants through each stage of the study.

The first subsection of your Results section may be where you decide to report the changes in the number of participants at each stage of your study. I addressed issues related to participant flow in Chapter 3, where I discussed the description of participant characteristics, because many researchers describe participant flow in the Method section. These researchers feel that describing the results of the sampling process at the same time as their description of the intended population for the study and procedure for sampling this population presents a more coherent picture. Therefore, I do not present that material again. Instead, in Figure 5.1, I review an example of the use of a flowchart to visually depict how your sample of participants changed as your study progressed (Appelbaum et al., 2018). It is an adaptation of a flowchart in the Consolidated Standards of Reporting Trials (CONSORT) reporting guidelines (Altman et al., 2001; Moher, Schulz, & Altman, 2001) that is used by many journals in the medical field.

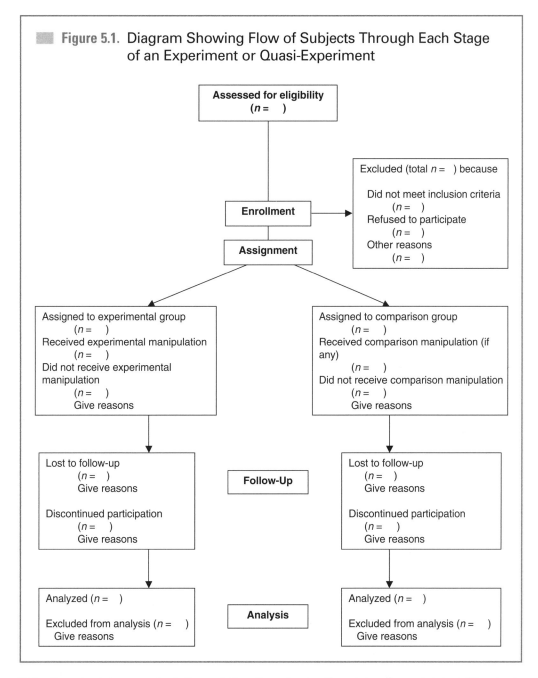

Figure 5.1. Diagram Showing Flow of Subjects Through Each Stage of an Experiment or Quasi-Experiment

This flowchart is an adaptation of the flowchart offered by Consolidated Standards of Reporting Trials (2007). Journals publishing the original CONSORT flowchart have waived copyright protection.

Figure 5.1 details the number and causes of participant loss (often called *attrition*) at each stage of the research, regardless of how participants' assignment to conditions was accomplished. Therefore, it can be regarded as appropriate for use in addition to either Table A4.2a or Table A4.2b.

As an example of how a flowchart might be used, Figure 5.2 reproduces a participant flowchart presented in Norman, Maley, Li, and Skinner's (2008) article, "Using

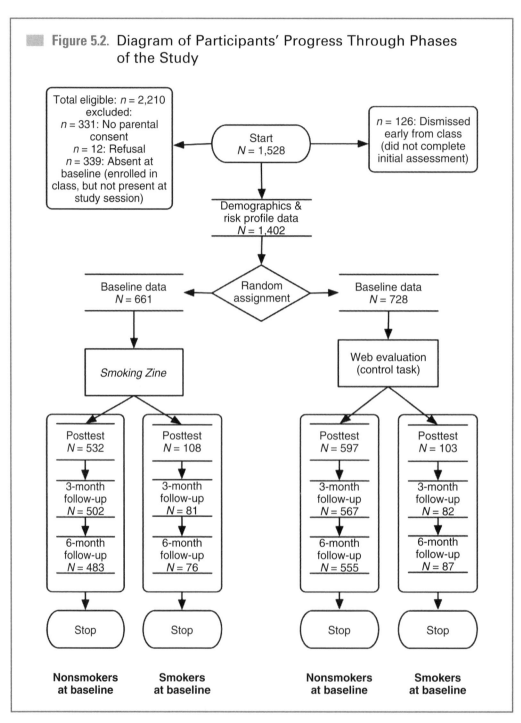

Figure 5.2. Diagram of Participants' Progress Through Phases of the Study

Adapted from "Using the Internet to Assist Smoking Prevention and Cessation in Schools: A Randomized, Controlled Trial," by C. D. Norman, O. Maley, X. Li, and H. A. Skinner, 2008, *Health Psychology, 27,* p. 802. Copyright 2008 by the American Psychological Association.

the Internet to Assist Smoking Prevention and Cessation in Schools: A Randomized, Controlled Trial," published in *Health Psychology*. In the study, subjects were randomly assigned to either a web-based tobacco intervention that involved a website called the Smoking Zine or a control task. Interventions occurred during a single classroom session with a follow-up by e-mail. The intervention website included interactive quizzes and self-assessments with feedback aimed at improving adolescents' resistance to pressure to smoke. In the control group, students did similar web-based activities unrelated to smoking cessation. Note how the flowchart presents lots of information in an easily interpretable manner.

Attrition

Attrition is the loss of participants while a study is in progress (also sometimes referred to as *subject mortality*, but that term has fallen out of use, for obvious reasons). The reason the Journal Article Reporting Standards (JARS; Appelbaum et al., 2018) calls for a detailed description of participant progress through a study relates to the potential impact of attrition on the internal validity of a study, the external validity of a study, or both. Attrition from a study comes in two forms, *overall attrition* and *differential attrition* across conditions.

A large amount of overall attrition often suggests that the study may lack *external validity*—that is, that it does not produce results that generalize to certain subpopulations within the target population. For example, Figure 5.2, from Norman et al.'s (2008) study, shows that of 2,210 eligible students, 331 did not obtain parental consent and 339 were absent on the day of the experiment. Could these exclusions be related to student characteristics that distinguish them from participating students in important ways that relate to the effectiveness of the intervention? Perhaps a lack of parental consent is related to whether the parent is a smoker. If so, the nonparticipating group might have been more likely to contain smokers who were most resistant to intervention, thus restricting the generalizability of findings to the least resistant students. What about the 126 students dismissed early from class? Could they share a characteristic (e.g., are they athletes?) that might relate to the generalizability of findings? These suggestions are far-fetched but illustrate the thinking involved in assessing the effect of attrition on the generalizability of findings.

Differential attrition occurs when more people choose to leave a study from one condition than another. When this happens, even if random assignment was used, you have to wonder whether the groups would still be comparable on all variables other than the experimental manipulation. This is much like the self-selection into conditions that I discussed in Chapter 3. Differential attrition, then, poses a threat to *internal validity*, or the experimenter's ability to draw strong causal inferences about the intervention. In Figure 5.2, you would examine the flow of smokers and nonsmokers through the two conditions from posttest to 6-month follow-up to decide whether differential attrition occurred.

The attrition from conditions in Norman et al.'s (2008) study seems nonproblematic, but, again for illustrative purposes, note that 32 smokers were lost in the Smoking Zine condition, but only 16 were lost in the control condition. Is it possible that smokers for whom the intervention was less effective were unavailable at the 6-month follow-up? Could this have made the intervention look more effective than it might have, had all of the smokers been available?

Here is how Vadasy and Sanders (2008) described the attrition problem in their article describing their reading intervention:

> **Attrition.** After group assignment, the sample comprised 96 students (48 dyads) in the treatment condition and 92 students (46 dyads) in the control condition. By the end of the study, 14 treatment and 12 control students were lost to attrition (14%). To ensure an operational definition of treatment as well as an unbiased attrition pattern across treatment and control groups, we removed any dyad member from study participation if the corresponding member moved from the school. (Although control pairs did not necessarily receive reading instruction together, we assumed that control pairs shared common reading curricula due to the within-grade, within-school pairings.) The sample used for analyses thus comprised 82 treatment students (41 dyads) and 80 control students (40 dyads). As reported in Table 1, there were no significant differences between groups on grade or status variable frequencies (all ps <.05). (pp. 274–275)

Note that the researchers made the case that differential attrition is not a problem by testing for differences between their experimental and control group on some key variables.

Recruitment

> In your Results section, your description of how you recruited participants should include dates defining the periods of recruitment and repeated measures or follow-up.

The dates of participant recruitment are also a detail that researchers often include in the Method section rather than the Results section, sometimes along with the sampling procedures. Again, even though the dates are technically a description of the results of the study, presenting all of this information together may make the information easier for readers to consider (and, frankly, it is more important that the information be in your report somewhere than that it be exactly where it is mentioned in JARS).

For example, Amir et al. (2009), who conducted the study of attention training for people with generalized social phobia discussed in Chapter 3, told readers that

> participants were enrolled in the study serially at two sites, the University of Georgia (UGA; $n = 24$) and San Diego State University (SDSU; $n = 20$), between January 2003 and October 2007. (p. 964)

This study was run over a period of 5 years. Given the nature of the study, this information is likely inconsequential but could be very important if the data are in some way tied to a particular event—for example, reactions to a natural disaster or political event.

Statistics and Data Analysis

In your Results section, your description of the statistics and data analysis procedures you used should include information concerning problems with statistical assumptions and data distributions that could affect the validity of findings.

In the Method section, you may have provided a subsection describing your intended statistical analysis or analysis strategy. Then, in the Results section, you need to describe any problems that arose after you collected your data. These problems might arise because some data points have troubling characteristics or because the data set as a whole does not meet some assumptions of the statistical tests.

What the particular problems might be will vary from data set to data set and statistical test to statistical test. For example, you might find that your data contain a statistical outlier, a value so different from the others it is unlikely to be part of the same population of data. Perhaps there was a recording error, or perhaps a participant wanted to sabotage your study (heaven forbid!). Or perhaps you wanted to conduct a particular analysis requiring that certain assumptions be met by the data. If these assumptions are not met, this might lead you to transform your data or choose another analysis. It is critical to your readers' ability to evaluate and replicate your study that they know (a) what the data analysis problem was and (b) how you solved it, if you did.

Let's look at a couple of examples. Risen and Gilovich (2008) described a problem with a skewed data distribution in an article titled "Why People Are Reluctant to Tempt Fate," published in the *Journal of Personality and Social Psychology*. One measure they used involved *response latencies*, or how long it took participants to choose among a set of possible endings for a story they had just read:

> Because the response latencies were skewed, we used natural log transformations in all response time analyses, but we report the raw means for ease of interpretation. (Risen & Gilovich, p. 296)

In another example, Adank, Evans, Stuart-Smith, and Scott (2009), in their study of comprehension of familiar and unfamiliar accents, conducted an analysis looking for statistical outliers:

> All values larger than the average plus 2.5 standard deviations per noise level as calculated across all participants in both groups were considered to be outliers and excluded from analysis. (p. 524)

Here Adank et al. told us their criterion for identifying a data point as an outlier, but they did not tell us the number of excluded points. Sometimes researchers do not remove outliers but instead reset the participant's value to their next nearest neighbor.

Missing Data

In your Results section, your description of any missing data problems you encountered should include

- the frequency or percentages of missing data;
- the empirical evidence and theoretical arguments for the causes of data that are missing—for example, missing completely at random (MCAR), missing at random (MAR), or missing not at random (MNAR); and
- the methods you used for addressing missing data, if any.

A problem that arises in many studies is missing data. Data typically are missing because (a) participants do not respond to all of the questions on a questionnaire or refuse to respond to certain questions in interviews, (b) equipment fails, or (c) the study included a follow-up phase and participants could not be located. If this happens, you have some (or even most) of the possible data on these participants but not all of the data (this is why missing data is a problem different from attrition).

In these situations, it is important to consider why the data are missing. Little and Rubin (2002) grouped missing data problems into different types. When data are missing completely at random, it means that the reason they are missing has nothing to do with their value or with the value of any other variables in the data analysis. So, in your fragrance labeling study, if you lost data from a participant because the computer you were using crashed just before he or she answered some final questions, you can be fairly certain these data were MCAR.

If data are missing not at random, it means that the reason they are missing is related to the values the variable can take. For example, in your labeling study, you might have wanted to see whether participants' individual differences in suggestibility were related to their ratings of the fragrances (would more suggestible people show more extreme reactions to the *roses* and *manure* labels?). But if people view being susceptible to influence as a negative personal characteristic, then highly suggestible people might be more inclined to leave blank your question "Are you easily influenced by others?"

There are other forms of missing data (e.g., MAR data), but the discussion of these issues quickly becomes complicated.[1] The important point here is that if you encountered a missing data problem in your study, JARS recommends that you describe the problem and what you did to take it into account when you did your analyses.

For example, Norman et al. (2008) described their approach to missing data in their web-based smoking intervention study as follows:

> The influence of missing data was minimized through an assertive tracking approach involving multiple visits to schools after scheduled data collection sessions and working closely with teachers and school administrators who assisted the research team by contacting students in class or sending reminders home. Intensive procedures were used to find students absent at follow-up

---

[1]MAR data are like MNAR data, but they can be adjusted for in your analyses.

through collaboration with participating school officials, which resulted in high follow-up rates: 95% at postintervention, 89% at 3-month follow-up, and 87% at 6-month follow-up. The use of multilevel logistic regression models provided alternative strategies to deal with missing data that are comparable to estimation procedures but rely on less data to effectively assess change over time. (p. 804)

It is also possible to impute missing data or to estimate its most likely value given the value of other data you do have. Here is how Fagan, Palkovitz, Roy, and Farrie (2009) handled missing data in their study of nonresident fathers' engagement with their children, in which they needed data from both mothers and fathers to do the desired analyses:

At Year 1, 19 mothers were not interviewed and 49 had missing data; at Year 3, 29 mothers were not interviewed and 82 had missing data. For those cases in which all mothers' data were missing, the fathers' data were first consulted to see whether they reported having any contact with the child. If they did not, zeros were imputed for all mother items. Among mothers who had some missing items, we imputed the respondent's mean for those items that were answered. For the remaining cases, the sample mean for the mother's index was imputed. (p. 1393)

Deleted Cases

Sometimes, you may decide that a participant's data ought to be deleted from your data set or a particular analysis. For example, you may decide to delete a participant's data from studies because it contains too many missing values. Sometimes participants have complete data, but you may decide they should be omitted from the analyses for other reasons. For example, Goldinger, He, and Papesh (2009) described six subjects who were excluded from the analyses of their first study of cross-race face learning: Two were Asian, three had excessive periods of eye-tracking failure, and one failed to complete the recognition test. In the Killeen, Sanabria, and Dolgov (2009) study on conditioning and extinction in pigeons, they wrote,

Running weights were maintained just above their 80% ad libitum weight [feed was made available at the desire of the animal]; a pigeon was excluded from a session if its weight exceeded its running weight by more than 7%. (p. 449)

Other reasons might include an indication that the participant did not understand the study's instructions. In experimental studies, researchers often include a *manipulation check* that is meant to gauge whether the manipulated conditions were attended to and believed by the subject. For example, you might ask subjects after collecting your labeling data from them whether they remembered the name of the fragrance. If they did not, you might delete the subjects' data. Or you might ask them what they thought of the name. If they said, "Didn't believe it. No one would name a perfume 'Manure'!" you might delete their data.

If you deleted data, JARS recommends that your report include (a) the number of cases of deleted data and (b) an explanation for why each case was tossed out. You should also say whether the deletion criterion was established before the experiment began or adopted post hoc, after the data were collected and a problem was discovered (e.g., include a statement such as, "We did not anticipate that participants would find the name 'Manure' implausible, but because some did [$n = x$], we excluded these participants from the analyses").

Here is how Amir et al. (2009) described why and how many trials were eliminated from their study of attention training for people with generalized social phobia:

> We first eliminated response latencies for inaccurate trials. Inaccurate trials were trials in which the probe was presented on the left side and the participant pressed the button corresponding to the right side, or vice versa. This procedure resulted in the elimination of 1% of the trials. In addition, response latencies less than 50 ms and greater than 1,200 ms were considered outliers and were also eliminated from the analysis. These ranges were determined from the inspection of the data using box plots and resulted in eliminating 1% of the trials. (p. 967)

Thus, these researchers deleted responses (not participants' entire set of data) for two specified reasons.

Adank et al. (2009) deleted participants' data (not individual responses) from their study of accent comprehension for the same two reasons:

> The data of four participants from the SE [standard English] listener group were excluded from further analysis, as they did not perform the task correctly. The data from three GE [Glasgow English] participants were excluded, as more than 20% of their responses were slower than 3.5 s. (p. 523)

Subgroups, Cells, and Null Hypothesis Significance Testing

In your Results section, for each primary and secondary outcome and for each subgroup, include a summary of

- the total sample size;
- subgroup or cell sample sizes, cell means, standard deviations or other estimates of precision, and other descriptive statistics; and the associated effect sizes and confidence intervals.

For inferential statistics (null hypothesis significance testing), include information about the direction and magnitude of the results of all inferential tests, including

- the exact p level, if null hypothesis significance testing occurred, even if no significant effect is reported, and the associated degrees of freedom (or mean square and mean square error).

The *Publication Manual* (6th ed.; APA, 2010) provides detailed descriptions of ways to present the sample sizes, cell means, standard deviations, effect sizes, confidence intervals, and the results of any null hypothesis significance tests you may have conducted. Most often, if your study included subjects in different conditions (e.g., *roses* and *manure* labels for a fragrance) and you have several dependent or outcome variables, you would present the different sample sizes, cell means, and standard deviations in a table. The first half of Chapter 5 in the *Publication Manual* (pp. 128–150) describes how to prepare tables.

Table 5.1 reproduces the table of results from Vadasy and Sanders's (2008) evaluation of a reading intervention. The table succinctly displays lots of data; it includes the cell means and standard deviations for the major outcome variables, each measured twice, as well as the gain from the first to the second measurement. Because the cell sample sizes were identical for all measures and all times, Vadasy and Sanders reported these two numbers only in the table note (along with the full definitions for all of the abbreviations in the table). Had the cell means varied for different measures or times (perhaps because of missing data), readers would expect to see additional columns with these entered. From this table, it is possible for readers to recalculate many of the inferential statistics in the report and to calculate effect sizes for any two-group comparison. This ensures that the study will be useful for researchers who want to include it in future meta-analyses. Alternatively, Norman et al.'s (2008) flowchart contains the total sample size and the cell sizes. This is an alternative way to present these data.

Effect-Size Estimates

Your Results section should include effect-size estimates and confidence intervals that correspond to each inferential test conducted, when possible.

In Chapter 3 of this volume, I introduced the three effect size metrics that are used most often by psychology researchers. JARS recommends that effect sizes and confidence intervals be reported along with the results of any null hypothesis statistical tests you may have conducted, whether or not they are significant. How to report these is covered in the *Publication Manual* (6th ed.; APA, 2010) as well, especially in Chapter 4, section 4.44, Statistics in Text (pp. 116–117).

From the viewpoint of reporting standards, the critical aspect is that this statistical information needs to be reported completely; include everything recommended in JARS. Yes, some of this information will seem redundant. After all, some effect sizes can be calculated from sample sizes, means, and standard deviations (Borenstein, 2009), and if the related null hypothesis significance test is significant, the confidence interval for an effect size will indicate this (by not containing zero). Still, you cannot expect readers to calculate these values for themselves, and you do not know which statistic will be of particular interest to different readers of your report. A complete report contains them all. You are also expected to provide a precise p value for each test, up to three decimal places, and to use the less than symbol ($<$) only when the p value is less than .001.

Primary and Secondary Hypotheses

Your Results section should include a clear differentiation between primary, secondary, and exploratory analyses and their tests or estimates.

Table 5.1. Example of a Table With Sample Sizes, Means, and Standard Deviations

Table X
Observed Pretests, Posttests, and Pretest–Posttest Gains

Measure	Treatment						Control					
	Pretest		Posttest		Gain		Pretest		Posttest		Gain	
	M	SD	M	SD	M	SD	M	SD	M	SD	M	SD
RAN	87.7	10.12					90.5	9.99				
WR accuracy	94.3	7.63	97.8	7.04	3.5	5.66	89.2	8.50	94.6	10.49	5.5	8.09
WR efficiency	87.9	9.19	94.7	10.12	6.8	7.72	89.2	8.50	94.6	10.49	5.5	9.09
PRF–U	40.0	18.35	83.1	22.27	43.2	16.53	42.3	19.91	79.0	23.76	36.7	19.56
PRF–A	37.5	16.84	68.3	26.38	30.8	18.50	39.6	17.13	62.5	26.63	22.9	18.36
Fluency rate	77.0	8.23	88.6	13.13	11.6	9.62	78.6	8.07	86.8	12.10	8.2	9.25
Comprehension	84.8	13.09	92.8	15.72	8.0	13.74	87.6	13.71	92.9	16.22	5.4	16.12

Note. Treatment group $N = 82$, control group $N = 80$. Norm-referenced standard scores (raw scores adjusted for age) were used for all measures except PRF–U and PRF–A; for these two measures, words correct per minute were used. The control group performed significantly higher on the WR accuracy pretest. RAN = Letter Naming subtest from the Rapid Automatized Naming/Rapid Alternating Stimulus tests; WR accuracy = Word Identification subtest from the Woodcock Reading Mastery Test—Revised/Normative Update; WR efficiency = Sight Word subtests from the Test of Word Reading Efficiency; PRF–U and PRF–A = words-correct-per-minute performance on uniform and alternate passages, respectively, from the Oral Reading Fluency subtests from the Dynamic Indicators of Basic Early Literacy Skills; Fluency rate = Rate subtest from the Gray Oral Reading Tests—4 (GORT); Comprehension = GORT Comprehension subtest. Adapted from "Repeated Reading Intervention: Outcomes and Interactions With Readers' Skills and Classroom Instruction," by P. F. Vadasy and E. A. Sanders, 2008, *Journal of Educational Psychology, 100,* p. 280. Copyright 2008 by the American Psychological Association.

In Chapter 3 I discussed the difference in status between measures you designate as of primary and secondary interest to you. In the Results section, you use this distinction to group your reporting and discuss what you found. Readers will expect that you have used multivariate procedures, such as multivariate analysis of variance, adjusted levels of statistical significance, or conservative post hoc means tests, when you conducted your secondary analysis. This protects you against making a false rejection of the null hypothesis because you carried out multiple tests with no firm expectation that the results might turn out one way or another.

Complex Data Analyses

In your Results section, for complex data analysis (e.g., multivariate analyses of variance, regression analyses), your results should also include

- details of the model estimated and
- the associated variance–covariance (or correlation) matrix or matrices.

If you conducted a complex data analysis, JARS recommends that you include the details of the results of the model or models—that is, the variables you included in the analyses and in what order or with what restrictions—you used. As an example, let's look at how Tsaousides et al. (2009) reported the results of the multiple regression analysis they performed to examine the relationship between perceived quality of life (PQoL) as the criterion and several predictor variables:

Regression Analyses . . .

Variables were entered in three steps: (a) injury-related variables, (b) employment status and income, and (c) employment related and general self-efficacy.
   PQoL. A hierarchical regression with PQoL as the criterion variable resulted in an overall adjusted R^2 of .22, $F(7, 268) = 12.08$, $p = .001$. The adjusted R^2 value obtained for the first block of variables was .025, $F(3, 272) = 2.36$, $p = .072$; showing that approximately 2.5% of the variance in PQoL was explained by injury-related variables. A significant increment was obtained during the next step, R^2 .058, $F(2, 270) = 8.61$, $p = .001$, increasing the adjusted R^2 to .084. The addition of employment and income accounted for an additional 5.8% of the variance in PQoL. Although employment and income were strongly related ($r = .31$), income was a stronger predictor of PQoL than employment, $\beta = .18$, $t(273) = 2.85$, $p = .005$. Another significant increment was obtained after adding the self-efficacy variables to the equation, $\Delta R^2 = .16$, $F(2, 268) = 27.50$, $p = .001$, indicating that employment-related and general self-efficacy accounted for an additional 16% of the variance in PQoL. Both variables were significant predictors of PQoL. (pp. 302–303)

Tsaousides et al. (2009) also provided a table that summarized the results of this regression analysis, which is reproduced in Table 5.2.
   JARS also suggests you include the associated variance–covariance or correlation matrix or matrices. For example, O'Neill, Vandenberg, DeJoy, and Wilson (2009) tested latent variable models in their study of anger in the workplace. They presented a table,

Table 5.2. Example of a Table Reporting a Hierarchical Regression Analysis

Table X

Hierarchical Regression Analysis Predicting Scores on the Perceived Quality of Life Measure

Predictor	Step 1			Step 2			Step 3		
	b	*SE (b)*	β	*b*	*SE (b)*	β	*b*	*SE (b)*	β
Injury severity	.062	.072	.054						
Time since injury	−.008	.016	−.034						
Age at injury	−.022	.010	.146*						
Employment				.303	.157	.122			
Current income				.224	.078	.182**			
PEM							.166	.034	.299***
IND							.100	.033	.181**
R^2 change	.025			.058			.156		
F for change R^2	2.36			8.61***			27.50***		

Note. $N = 419$. PEM = Perceived Employability subscale of the Bigelow Quality of Life Questionnaire; IND = Independence subscale of the Bigelow Quality of Life Questionnaire. Reprinted from "The Relationship Between Employment-Related Self-Efficacy and Quality of Life Following Traumatic Brain Injury," by T. Tsaousides, A. Warshowsky, T. A. Ashman, J. B. Cantor, L. Spielman, and W. A. Gordon, 2009, *Rehabilitation Psychology, 54*, p. 303. Copyright 2009 by the American Psychological Association.
$*p < .05$. $**p < .01$. $***p < .001$.

reproduced here as Table 5.3, that provided the correlation matrix on which these analyses were based. The table also contains the means and standard deviations for each variable. Again, this reporting is important for purposes of replicating your analysis and for secondary uses of your data. With this matrix, other researchers will be able to use O'Neill et al.'s data in many different ways. For example, someone doing a meta-analysis of the relationship between alcohol use and job turnover can find in the matrix the correlation between these two variables ($r = .10$). These data can contribute to this meta-analysis even though exploring this relationship was not the primary purpose of the study.

Estimation Problems

In your Results section, describe any estimation problems, regression diagnostics, or analytic anomalies you encountered and include tests that were both planned and not planned.

Estimation problems typically involve complex data analyses that for one reason or another have gone awry. Let me give you a relatively simple example. In the fragrance labeling study, you might have decided to use a logistical regression (Menard, 2002) to predict whether subjects indicated they would purchase the fragrance. Logistic regressions are used when the outcome (predicted) variable is either dichotomous or has values that range from 0 to 1, representing probability values or proportions. For each subject, the prediction equation results in a value between 0 and 1 that represents the probability that each person will buy the fragrance. Each predictor variable has a beta weight (and significance level) associated with it. In your logistic regression, the outcome variable takes on only two values (buy or not buy), and you might use as predictors of buying intention the subjects' experimental condition (roses vs. manure), sex, degree of suggestibility, and socioeconomic status.

Your logistic regression program will use an algorithm to calculate the maximum likelihood solution for the prediction equations. It will do this through an iterative process until the iterations converge on a single answer. The convergence may never be perfect, however, and your statistical program has a specified tolerance value that, when reached, stops the iterations and presents that result as the best answer. Sometimes the tolerance value is not reached, and the iterations will go on and on. Rather than do this, the computer will stop after a certain number of iterations and tell you there has been a "failure to converge." In such a case, you will need to (a) reexamine your data to see if there is an identifiable problem that you can address, (b) reset your tolerance level (if allowed), (c) choose from other procedures that alter the algorithm, or (d) abandon the analysis. Whichever option you choose, JARS recommends that you fully report the problem you encountered and your solution for it.

Statistical Software

In your Results section, describe any statistical software program and any specialized procedures used.

▦ Table 5.3. Example of a Table With a Correlation Matrix

Table X

Means, Standard Deviations, and Correlations

Variable	M	SD	1	2	3	4	5
1. Anger	1.80	.67	*.88*				
2. POS	3.03	.90	−.26	*9.4*			
3. High-risk behaviors	.30	.24	.10	−.01	—		
4. Accidents	1.80	.55	.16	−.11	.05	—	
5. Turnover intention	2.01	1.34	.18	−.39	−.01	.10	—
6. Total alcohol	18.06	44.11	.16	−.02	.14	.06	.10
7. Absence	1.76	1.09	.17	−.11	.06	.20	.12
8 Age	3.87	1.72	−.18	.03	.03	−.13	−.07
9. Supervisor/managerial responsibility	.78	.44	−.08	.03	.04	−.03	.03
10. Education	3.19	1.17	−.04	−.11	−.12	−.05	.08
11. Tenure	3.48	1.24	.11	−.24	−.02	−.02	.04
12. Gender	.692	.46	−.06	−.04	.10	.03	.09
13. White	.78	.41	.09	−.02	.04	−.01	−.04
14. Black	.08	.27	−.04	.01	−.01	.01	.01
15. Hispanic	.06	.24	−.06	.01	−.05	.01	.01
16. Inventory loss	4,391,430	611,504	.48[a]	−.86[a]	—	—	—
17. Unit turnover	.30	.09	.52[a]	−.39[a]	—	—	—
18. High involvement	3.30	.87	−.21	.63	−.01	−.09	−.36

Note. Internal consistency values are in italics. Any correlation in Rows 1 through 15 ($n = 1,136$) with an absolute value of .05 or greater is statistically significant at $p < .05$. The correlations in Rows 16 through 18 ($n = 21$) are statistically significant at $p < .05$. POS = perceived organizational support. Adapted from "Exploring Relationships Among Anger, Perceived Organizational Support, and Workplace Outcomes," by O. A. O'Neill, R. J. Vandenberg, D. M. DeJoy, and M. G. Wilson, 2009, *Journal of Occupational Health Psychology, 14,* p. 326. Copyright 2009 by the American Psychological Association.
[a]These correlations represent the relationships of the between-level index of anger and POS with the inventory loss and turnover variables. The other correlations in this column are between the pooled within-group index of anger and POS (individual level controlling for store-level variation) and the stated variables.

It is not necessary to tell readers which statistical software program you used to conduct uncomplicated and frequently used statistical tests—for example, *t* tests, analyses of variance, or multiple regressions. However, identifying the program can be important for more sophisticated and complex analyses. Different programs have different features and options, and you need to tell readers which of these you chose. On occasion, these complex programs vary significantly in the way they conduct complex analyses, which can lead to varied solutions and conclusions.

6	7	8	9	10	11	12	13	14	15	16	17	18
—												
.10	—											
−.14	—											
−.06	.05	.05	—									
−.04	−.07	.13	.05	—								
.01	−.01	.25	−.30	−.01	—							
.10	−.06	.03	−.06	.10	−.01	—						
.04	−.01	.08	−.01	.04	.05	.01	—					
−.04	−.02	−.06	−.02	−.01	−.05	−.04	−.58	—				
.01	−.02	.03	−.09	.05	−.01	−.03	.02	−.48	−.08	—		
—	—	—	—	—	—	—	—	—	—	—	—	—
—	—	—	—	—	—	—	—	—	—	—	—	—
−.08	−.05	−.02	.01	−.12	−.30	−.07	−.09	.09	.02	—	—	.93

For example, O'Neill et al. (2009) reported using the Mplus program to conduct the latent variable analyses in their study of anger in the workplace:

> We used the Mplus latent variables program (Muthén & Muthén, 2006). Mplus easily permits the control of systematic sources of between-unit variance in testing models where the primary focus is on individual differences. (p. 325)

Note the reference citation for the *Mplus User's Manual* (Muthén & Muthén, 2007), which contains information on the approach the program uses to solve the equations needed to conduct latent variable analysis.

To reiterate a point I made in Chapter 3, note that software is also used to control the introduction of stimuli and the collection of data. These are often very specialized programs, and their details should be reported.

Other and Ancillary Analyses

Your Results section should also report

- any other analyses performed, including adjusted analyses, indicating those that were planned and those that were not planned (although not necessarily in the level of detail of primary analyses),
- implications of ancillary analyses for statistical error rates, and
- any problems with statistical assumptions and/or data distributions that could affect the validity of the findings.

Adjusted analyses occur because of problems with the data, like those described earlier, but sometimes the analyses rather than the data are adjusted. For example, Taylor and James (2009), in their study of markers for substance dependence, adjusted the degrees of freedom in their analysis of electrodermal response modulation (ERM) scores rather than the scores themselves:

> As expected, ERM scores for the alcohol-dependence-only, illicit-drug-dependence-only, and combined alcohol/illicit-drug-dependence groups were significantly lower than for the control group, $t(30.234) = 1.961$, $p < .029$ (the degree of freedom was adjusted because of unequal variances between groups); $t(117) = 3.036$, $p = .002$; and $t(121) = 2.176$, $p = .016$, respectively. (p. 496)

Vinnars, Thormählen, Gallop, Norén, and Barber (2009) adjusted effect sizes because they wanted their estimate of the impact of supportive–expressive psychotherapy on personality not to reflect changes in symptoms:

> Because we were interested in the question of the degree of change in personality and dynamic variables over and beyond the change in symptoms, we also calculated effect sizes adjusted for improvement in SCL–90 [Symptom Checklist—90] for all variables. (p. 369)

The ancillary analyses that you conduct will relate to your secondary hypotheses or even to analyses for which you have no hypotheses. The more clearly these analyses are labeled *ancillary*, *exploratory*, or *secondary*, the less they will interfere with the interpretation of the study's main findings. JARS recommends that you discuss the implications of ancillary analyses for statistical error rates.

It is important for you to talk about how you might have adjusted your significance levels in null hypothesis significance testing to take into account the fact that multiple tests could lead to inflated experiment-wise error rates. For example, in your fragrance labeling study, if you looked at whether subject sex and socioeconomic status, the time of day the experiment was run, the weather, and the phase of the moon (just to highlight how exploratory some analyses can be!) were related to fragrance ratings, it would be good to clearly label these analyses as ancillary (related to exploratory hypotheses; e.g., does the fragrance labeled *manure* smell better when the moon is full?) and to adjust (downward) the *p* level the test result must reach before you will interpret the result as worthy of future attention, perhaps as a primary hypothesis in subsequent studies.

Studies With an Experimental Manipulation or Intervention

Participant flow

In your Results section, if your study included an experimental manipulation, your report should describe the number of participants as they moved through the study, including

- the total number of groups (if an intervention was administered at the group level) and the number of participants assigned to each group;
- the number of participants who did not complete the experiment or crossed over to other conditions, with an explanation of why;
- the number of participants used in primary analyses; and
- the flow of participants through each stage of the study (see Figures 5.1 and 5.2).

JARS recommends how the results of studies that used experimental manipulations should be reported. The first set of recommendations again involves the flowchart of the number of subjects progressing through the study. The diagram presented in Figure 5.1 and the example in Figure 5.2 both involve an experimental study, so I covered most of the pertinent issues earlier. The only new issue introduced here is that JARS recommends that subjects who cross over from one condition to another should be accounted for in your description. Crossover occurs when a participant starts in one condition but ends up in another condition. This happens rarely (say, when a student moves from a class with little variability in age to one with greater variability because the parents had an argument with the first teacher), but it needs to be reported, especially if it happens frequently. It might be an indication that the groups grew in nonequivalence after the study began.

Treatment fidelity

In your Results section, if your study included an experimental manipulation, your report should describe evidence on whether the treatment was delivered as intended.

Treatment fidelity relates to the degree to which a treatment is delivered to subjects in the manner in which it was intended. The term *treatment fidelity* is used most often in the context of evaluations of experimental treatments or interventions. After all, if the researchers cannot demonstrate that the intervention was implemented as intended, how can we know whether the evaluation is a fair test of its effectiveness? For example, remember that Vadasy and Sanders (2008) reported the results of an evaluation of a reading intervention. Here is how they described what they did to ensure that the intervention was delivered as intended:

> The tutors practiced the protocols during training and received immediate feedback. Following this training, coaches visited tutors biweekly to provide follow-up training and modeling and to collect data on protocol fidelity. . . .
>
> **Tutor observations**. To monitor treatment implementation fidelity, we collected data via observation forms on (a) tutor adherence to scripted *Quick Reads* protocols, (b) tutor instructional behaviors, and (c) student progress in terms of the amount of time spent actively engaged in reading passages. Tutors' fidelity to protocols was measured using a 5-point rating scale of 1 (*never*) to 5 (*always*) for each intervention step previously described. . . . Prior to onsite tutor observations, we established interobserver reliability among the five researcher–observers using five videotaped *Quick Reads* sessions. (Vadasy & Sanders, 2008, pp. 276–277)

However, treatment fidelity is not the exclusive province of applied research and intervention evaluations. Laboratory experiments also are concerned with treatment fidelity, but in these cases, it is typically referred to as a *manipulation check*. Thus, Risen and Gilovich (2008), in their study of people's desire not to tempt fate, explained their manipulation check as follows:

> In addition, participants were given a manipulation check to ensure that they had paid attention to the stories. The manipulation check consisted of one recall question for each of the stories. For the umbrella story, participants were asked, "Did Julie bring her umbrella when she packed for school?" Participants were then thanked and debriefed. (p. 299)

Earlier, I discussed manipulation checks in the context of deleting data. Typically, in laboratory contexts, experimental manipulations are pilot tested to ensure they will have the intended impact on most subjects. Therefore, it is rare to find a manipulation check in a published article that indicates that the manipulation failed. Imagine having to write of your fragrance labeling study, "No one in the manure condition believed the manipulation, but here are the results of our study anyway"! Instead, manipulation checks are used to discard the data of those few subjects who did not attend to the manipulation or misunderstood it.

Baseline data

In your Results section, if your study included an experimental manipulation, your report should describe baseline demographics and clinical characteristics of each group.

Table 5.4 displays both the baseline demographics and the clinical characteristics of subjects in Amir et al.'s (2009) study of attention training for people with generalized social phobia. Note that it does so for each of the experimental groups separately. Table 5.1, from Vadasy and Sanders's (2008) evaluation of a reading intervention, presents the baseline data for the outcome at pretest along with the posttest and gain scores. In this article, the authors presented the demographic characteristics of subjects (e.g., grade, age, minority status) in a separate table.

Intent-to-treat analysis. Another problem you can have with your study that needs to be addressed in your report involves noncompliance among subjects in a treatment condition. So, for example, in Vinnars et al.'s (2009) evaluation (of supportive–expressive therapy for people with personality disorders), the therapy was manualized, and subjects attended therapy over the course of 1 calendar year. In Amir et al.'s (2009) study (of attention training for people with generalized social phobia), the training protocol involved eight 20-min training sessions delivered over a 4-week period.

What if subjects did not attend enough sessions to allow the researchers to feel confident that the subjects received the treatment as intended? There are several approaches to data analysis, and which one is used can have critical implications for how the results can be interpreted. This is why JARS recommends that compliance be carefully reported.

Table 5.4. Example of a Table With Both Demographic and Clinical Baseline Characteristics of Subjects in More Than One Group

Table X
Patient Demographics and Clinical Characteristics

Variable	AMP	ACC
Gender (% women)	63.6	54.5
Age (years)	27.6 (8.3)	31.1 (13.2)
Ethnicity (%)		
European American	63.6	81.8
Asian American	13.6	0
Latin American	9.1	0
Other	4.5	4.5
Comorbid diagnoses (%)		
Any	50.0	40.9
Generalized anxiety disorder	22.7	13.6
Specific phobia	13.6	4.5
Past treatment for social phobia (%)	50.0	45.5

Note. Standard deviations in parentheses. AMP = attention modification program; ACC = attention control program. From "Attention Training in Individuals With Generalized Social Phobia: A Randomized Controlled Trial," by N. Amir, C. Beard, C. T. Taylor, H. Klumpp, J. Elias, M. Burns, and X. Chen, 2009, *Journal of Consulting and Clinical Psychology, 77*, p. 964. Copyright 2009 by the American Psychological Association.

First, you can do an intent-to-treat analysis. In this case, all subjects are included in the analysis, no matter how well their treatment conformed to the treatment protocol. This is what Vinnars et al. (2009) decided to do:

> Using an intent-to-treat approach, all patients were included in the statistical analyses regardless of whether or not they completed treatment. (p. 368)

When an intent-to-treat analysis is conducted, it means that the random assignment of subjects to conditions remains, but the resulting treatment effects may or may not reflect the impact of the treatment. You might say that your statistical tests relate to the causal effect of being assigned to the treatment condition and to whatever exposure to the treatment this assignment results in. That is not the same as the causal effect of the treatment itself.

Alternatively, you can decide to exclude those subjects you feel have not complied. In this approach, you have confidence that the subjects in your analysis have experienced the treatment as you intended. However, if many subjects were omitted from the analysis because of noncompliance, we again confront the possibility that the subjects in the completed-treatment group were different from subjects in the control group before the experiment began, and thus random assignment is compromised. This is what Amir et al. (2009) did:

> Analyses were conducted on treatment completers (AMP [attention modification program], $n = 22$; ACC [attention control condition], $n = 22$). We chose this approach rather than an intention-to-treat analysis given the differential dropout rate between the AMP group ($n = 0$) and ACC group ($n = 4$). However, intent-to-treat analyses did not differ from the analyses reported on treatment completers only. (p. 966)

Note that in Amir et al.'s study, noncompliers were dropouts, not people the researchers decided had not received the treatment as intended. This makes clear the relationship between complier-only analyses and the ability to draw strong causal inferences about the effectiveness of the treatment. It should also be clear why JARS calls for you to report which type of analysis you conducted.[2]

Adverse side effects

In your Results section, if your study included an experimental manipulation, your report should describe all important adverse events or side effects in each intervention group.

Needless to say, if you conduct an experiment, typically one that involves an evaluation of a treatment or an intervention, and discover that it had harmful or undesirable side effects on some subjects, you are obligated to disclose these in your research

---

[2]*Complier average causal effect* is a statistical technique for estimating the causal effect of a treatment (not treatment assignment) when noncompliance is a problem (see Little, Long, & Lin, 2009).

report and note how frequently they occurred. What constitutes an adverse side effect is a complex matter that I cannot go into here, but it is important if you are exploring the effectiveness of a new treatment that you be aware of its potential to have both helpful and harmful effects.[3]

When you request permission from your institutional review board to conduct your study, you will be asked to consider and discuss both positive and negative effects and what you will do to minimize the latter. This will require you to expand your thinking about how subjects will react to your treatment or intervention. Should any of these undesirable effects actually occur, your readers need to know about it.

Statistical methods

For studies using random assignment, your Results section should describe

- the statistical methods used to compare groups on primary outcomes;
- statistical methods used for any additional analyses, such as subgroup analyses and adjusted analyses; and
- statistical methods used for mediation analyses.

For studies using nonrandom assignment, your Results section should describe

- statistical methods used to compare study groups on primary outcomes, including complex methods for correlated data;
- statistical methods used for additional analyses, such as subgroup analyses and adjusted analyses (e.g., methods for modeling pretest differences and adjusting for them); and
- statistical methods used for mediation analyses.

Most of the items that JARS recommends you cover when reporting a study with an experimental manipulation are straightforward or have already been covered in this chapter. Again, JARS recommends that you be as comprehensive and as transparent about the reporting of statistics as you have been about your rationale for doing the study and your method in carrying it out.

More on Complex Data Analyses

Structural equation modeling. There are two additional JARS tables that relate to two types of complex statistical procedures that can be used to analyze data. The first, reproduced in Table A5.1, describes what to report when you use your data to construct structural equation models (SEMs). Structural equation modeling involves applying to the data a model based on a theory and seeing how well the model fits the data. Theory comes first; it is used to determine what variables will be included in the model, in what order, and with what hypothesized interconnections. Simplistically, you can also think of structural equation modeling as a combination of (a) a series

---

[3]If you are testing fragrance labels for a perfume company and several subjects in the manure condition pass out, readers need to know!

of multiple regression analyses ordered in such a way that the dependent variables in one set of analyses become the predictor variables in the next set of analyses (with the order of the analyses being dictated by theory) and (b) factor analyses, in that the factors, or latent variables, are the variables in the regression equations rather than the observed values on the individual measurements.

Researchers who use structural equation modeling do not claim that their models uncover causal connections (and if they do, be careful!) but instead use it to reveal how well a model fits the data, how the model might be made more efficient, and how the model compares to other alternative models (perhaps based on competing theories). Because this few-sentence description of a complex statistical approach is necessarily brief, I refer you to Hoyle (2012) for a brief introduction to structural equation modeling and to R. B. Kline (2016) for a more extensive but highly readable introduction.

As an example, O'Neill et al. (2009) used structural equation modeling to analyze their data relating anger in the workplace and perceived organization support to employees' turnover intentions, absences, and accidents. They used social exchange theory to guide their model:

> In terms of the theoretical rationale underlying the relationship of POS [perceived organizational support] and negative affect, social exchange theory (i.e., Belau, 1964; Emerson, 1976) is typically invoked to explain the association, and also points to anger as the most relevant emotion to examine in conjunction with low POS. According to social exchange theory, the relationship between employees and employers involves a series of interactions that generate obligations (Cropanzano & Mitchell, 2005). Employees' actions are contingent upon the organization fulfilling its obligations to employees (Gouldner, 1960), also known as the psychological contract (Rousseau, 1995). Employees perform at high levels and remain committed to the organization and its goals to the extent that the organization cares for its employees. On the other side, employees experience negative affect when they perceive that the organization is depriving them of something to which they feel entitled. In the case of low POS, employees perceive a lack of concern for their own well-being. Because employees feel entitled to receive support from the organization, they would naturally blame the organization for its lack of support. Following this logic, the social exchange perspective would logically result in conceptualizing low POS as a cause of anger. (O'Neill et al., 2009, pp. 319–320)

For one of their SEM analyses, O'Neill et al. (2009) proposed five hypotheses that related to the interconnections between the variables in their model:

> Hypothesis 1: The relationship between POS and anger at the individual level is negative and reciprocal. . . .
> Hypothesis 2a: The relationship of POS to turnover intentions, absences, and accidents at the individual level is partially mediated by anger. . . .
> Hypothesis 2b: The relationship of anger to turnover intentions, absences, and accidents at the individual level is partially mediated by POS. . . .
> Hypothesis 3a: The relationship of POS on alcohol consumption and high-risk health behaviors at the individual level is partially mediated by anger. . . .

Hypothesis 3b: The relationship of anger on alcohol consumption and high-risk health behaviors at the individual level is partially mediated by POS. (pp. 320–322)

They presented the path diagram reproduced in Figure 5.3 to summarize their model. The rectangular boxes represent the participants' scores on the measurements as observed, and the circles represent the latent variables the measurements were used to estimate. O'Neill et al. presented the correlations between variables and the path estimates in tables (not reproduced here; they look like the earlier example). Here is a portion of how O'Neill et al. described some of the results of their SEM:

Results indicate that POS and anger were associated with a number of work-related anger-out and anger-in behaviors. With respect to anger-out behaviors,

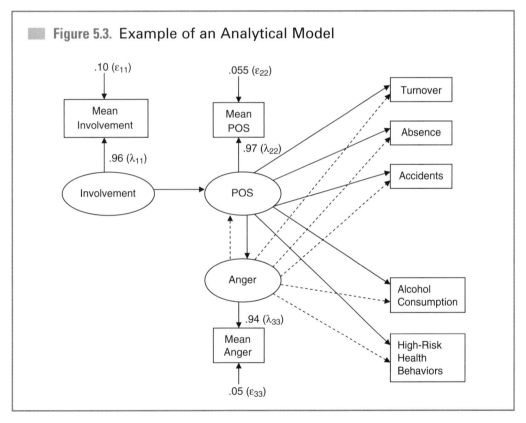

Figure 5.3. Example of an Analytical Model

Solid versus dashed arrows simply differentiate between effects because of POS (perceived organizational support) versus anger, respectively. The values for the loadings (λ) are fixed values representing the square root of the reliabilities as are the error terms (ε) representing the value 1 minus the reliability times the variance of the measure. The remaining paths were freely estimated. From "Exploring relationships among anger, perceived organizational support, and workplace outcomes," by O. A. O'Neill, R. J. Vandenberg, D. M. DeJoy, and M. G. Wilson, 2009, *Journal of Occupational Health Psychology, 14,* p. 327. Copyright 2009 by the American Psychological Association.

we found that anger partially mediated the relationship of low POS and two common measures of organizational withdrawal, namely, turnover and absenteeism. We also found that anger partially mediated the relationship of low POS and anger to a common measure of organizational safety, accidents on the job. Perhaps of greater importance to both individuals and the organization, however, are the associations of anger to anger-in behaviors, specifically, alcohol consumption and high-risk health behaviors. Although we only found an indirect relationship between POS and these behaviors, for every unit increase in anger, individuals increase alcohol consumption by 3.2 drinks per month and increase their engagement in high-risk health behaviors by 13%. (p. 330)

To briefly and simply highlight some of the JARS recommendations for reporting studies that use structural equation modeling, in their introduction researchers using structural equation modeling should describe

■ the primary model they tested and the theory or previous research that gave rise to it,
■ the most important paths in the model and the secondary paths, and
■ whether a new model will be specified if the primary model is rejected.

In the Method section, the researchers should include

■ the instruments used to collect the data (always important but especially important in structural equation modeling because they will be used to estimate latent variables),
■ the target sample size (structural equation modeling studies generally need larger samples to generate credible estimates) and a power analysis, and
■ any estimation problems the researchers encountered.

The Results section should pay careful attention to

■ missing data issues;
■ assumptions of the estimation methods used (e.g., multivariate normality);
■ the structural equation modeling approach used (e.g., an attempt to confirm the utility of a model, a comparison of alternative models, the generation of new models);
■ a full account of all models that were evaluated;
■ any assumptions that were made in the models about the measurement errors, interaction effects, and nonindependence of the data; and
■ the software program or algorithm used to generate the structural equation model estimates.

A critical part of the Results section involves the report of how well the model fit the data. There are several different statistics to help researchers describe model fit and to compare different models for how well they fit. The fit statistics, why they were chosen, and what criteria were used to accept or reject models need to be fully described. If the initial results led to respecification of a model, this should be carefully detailed. Finally, the Results section should include a description of the estimated path values, including direct paths, indirect paths, and paths involving interaction; their error; and their statistical significance.

Bayesian statistics. The second complex data analytic technique covered by JARS, reproduced in Table A5.2, relates to research that employs the Bayesian approach to statistics. Bayesian statistics start with a very different set of assumptions regarding the purpose and desired outcomes of statistical analysis.

The statistical approach you are probably most familiar with uses a frequentist statistical model. You learned how samples can be used to estimate population parameters (e.g., the population mean). You also learned how to use observed data along with some assumptions (e.g., that the data are normally distributed) to test the likelihood that multiple samples were drawn from the same population—that is, the likelihood that the null hypothesis best describes the data. You calculated a probability of getting this data given that the null hypothesis was true and used a probability cutoff, typically $p < .05$, as the decision point for when to reject it. Thus, you made a discrete decision to either (a) reject the null hypothesis (that the samples were drawn from the same population) or (b) conclude that the evidence is insufficient to reject the null hypothesis. In the fragrance labeling example, you would use the means, standard deviations, and sample sizes to test the likelihood that the two samples were drawn from the same population—that is, that the labels *roses* and *manure* made no difference in subjects' ratings of favorability.

Bayesian statistics use a very different approach. They begin with existing prior beliefs (which might or might not be the null hypothesis) and use the data gathered in the study to revise these beliefs. Thus, you might begin with the prior belief that 80% of people will rate the fragrance favorably if it is labeled *roses* but only 20% will do so if it is labeled *manure* (remember, the fragrance is actually the same). Where do the prior beliefs come from? They can come from a prediction based on a theory, from the results of past research, from what might be practically meaningful, or from your own thinking and past experience (Juliet would have a prior belief that the favorability percentages for the two labeled fragrances would be the same if the fragrance was, in fact, the same extract). After you ran your experiment, you would then use Bayes theorem to adjust your beliefs.

Because Bayesian statistical analyses require advanced training for their application, it is likely that you will have taken a specialized course in them before you put them to use. Many of the JARS reporting requirements contain specialized terms (e.g., functional forms, highest posterior density interval, triplot, utilities, conditional exchangeability, shrinkage-adjusted estimates, parameter trace plots, burn-in iterations, Bayes factors). The following are definitions of a few of the more important terms in JARS to give you a sense of what they mean and why they are important to report:

- *Systematic and stochastic parts of the model:* A Bayesian model can have parts that are systematic (involving a carefully formulated set of principles and variables) and stochastic (determined by chance or a random process).
- *Functional forms and distributions:* Functional forms are mathematical descriptions of the relation between variables (like an algebraic equation), and the related distribution is a description of how the function operates on the world of real numbers (what values you get for unknowns when you plug in different possible known values).
- *Prior distribution of model parameters:* The prior distribution is the probability distribution that expresses your beliefs about the likelihood of different outcomes before you run the experiment (sometimes just called *priors*).
- *Informative priors:* Informative priors are prior beliefs that lead to specific, precise descriptions of what you expect. For example, if you expected the fragrance to be rated neutrally if it had no label (perhaps you pretested this), you might believe that the mean favorability score would be normally distributed around 0 on a scale ranging from −5 to +5 and that the standard deviation might be 1.

■ *Posterior distribution:* Posterior distribution involves the conditional probabilities after your data have been used to adjust your prior beliefs. So, in your experiment, if your prior belief was that labels were irrelevant but you labeled the neutral fragrance *roses* and this caused more favorable ratings by subjects, you would adjust your posterior beliefs accordingly.

■ *Highest posterior density (HPD) interval:* You would choose the values for your proposed posterior distribution that occurred with the highest frequency (also called *credible intervals*). You can also construct a credible interval that leaves out an equal number of extreme values on each side of the distribution, called an *equal-tailed interval.*

■ *Normalized and nonnormalized likelihood of the prior distribution:* Likelihood of the prior distribution is a transformation of the prior distribution that expresses it under two different assumptions (normalized and nonnormalized) about the distribution of values.

■ *Triplot.* The triplot is a graphic presentation of your prior, likelihood, and posterior distributions. Figure 5.4 presents a sample triplot. In this example, the researchers wished to estimate the expected number of infections that would occur given 10,000 hospital beds. The triplot displays the posterior distribution (the dotted line) as a function of the prior expectation (the dashed line, set before the study began) and the likelihood distribution (the solid line), which is based on the evidence in the study.

■ *Bayesian factors:* Bayesian factors are used when the implications of two hypotheses are compared to one another. It gives you the ratio of the likelihood of the two probabilities. If this sounds like the kind of test you would do with frequentist statistics, it is; although the resulting statistics are quite different, the problem they tackle is related, especially when one of the two hypotheses being compared is the null hypothesis.

Other terms specified in JARS relate to other types of sampling procedures—for example, use of Markov chain Monte Carlo simulations—and procedures for more complex data analyses, including using Bayesian statistics to conduct cost–benefit analyses or models that are hierarchical in structure.

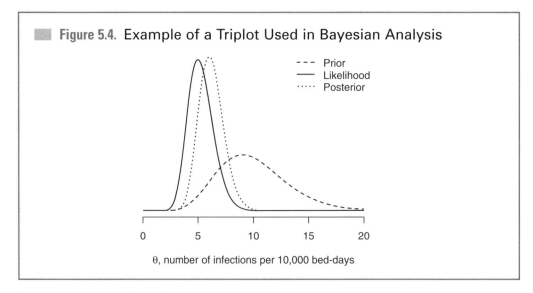

Figure 5.4. Example of a Triplot Used in Bayesian Analysis

θ, number of infections per 10,000 bed-days

From "Bayesian Statistics," by D. Spiegelhalter and K. Rice, 2009 (http://www.scholarpedia.org/article/Bayesian_statistics). CC BY-NC-SA 3.0

If you have taken a course in Bayesian statistics, the JARS standards and its terms should be familiar to you. Bayesian statistics are being applied more frequently in the social sciences (see, e.g., Bowden & Loft, 2016; Geary & vanMarle, 2016). Some good resources to help you understand whether they are most suitable for your topic of interest can be found in Dienes (2011), Jackman (2009), Kaplan (2014), and R. B. Kline (2012).

Now, with all of the details of your data analyses laid out, we are ready to pay a little more attention to a few specialized research designs.

Appendix 5.1: Additional Journal Article Reporting Standards for Studies Using Structural Equation Modeling and Bayesian Techniques

░ Table A5.1. Reporting Standards for Studies Using Structural Equation Modeling (in Addition to Material Presented in Table A1.1)

Paper section and topic	Description
Title	Mention the basic mechanism or process reflected in the primary model to which the data are fit. (*Note:* The complexity of the multivariate data analyzed in many structural equation modeling studies makes it unlikely that, in most cases, the variables under investigation and the relations between them could be concisely stated in the title.)
Abstract	Report values for at least two global fit statistics, each from a different class, and include a brief statement about local fit (residuals). State whether the interpreted model (if any model is retained) is the originally specified model.
Introduction	Describe the primary model to be fitted to the data, and include an explanation of theory or results from previous empirical studies that support the primary model.
	Point out paths that are especially important, and justify directionality assumptions, such as the claim that X causes Y instead of the reverse. Do the same for paths of secondary importance.
	State whether respecification is planned if the primary model is rejected.

Table A5.1. (*Continued*)

Paper section and topic	Description
Method	State whether the data were collected from research participants or generated by computer simulation.
	Report whether indicators of latent variables were drawn from one questionnaire or from multiple questionnaires.
	Describe, for each questionnaire, whether the indicators are items or total scores across homogeneous sets of items (scales, parcels), stating how
	• Scales were constructed, reporting their psychometrics
	• Items were treated in the analysis as continuous or categorical.
	Report how the target sample size was determined, including
	• Rule of thumb
	• Availability of resource constraints
	• Results of a priori power analysis
	• Estimates of parameter precision used to plan the number of cases with appropriate explanation.
	For a power analysis, state
	• Target level of power
	• Null and alternative hypotheses
	• Significance of key parameters
	• Fit statistics that figured in the analysis
	• Expected population effect sizes.
	Report the computer software or algorithm used if the data were generated by simulation, state and justify the sizes of generated samples, and disclose whether samples were lost because of nonconvergence or inadmissible estimates.
Results	Report data diagnostics, including
	• Percentage of missingness (if some data are missing) and how it is distributed across cases and variables
	• Empirical evidence or theoretical arguments about causes of missing data (i.e., missing completely at random, missing at random, or missing not at random)
	• Evidence that distributional or other assumptions of estimation methods are plausible.
Missing data	Indicate the statistical method used to address missingness, such as multiple imputation, full information maximum likelihood (FIML), substitution of values, or deletion of cases. For multiple imputation or FIML estimates, state whether variables not included in the model were specified as auxiliary variables.

(table continues)

■ **Table A5.1.** (*Continued*)

Paper section and topic	Description
Distributions	State whether the data were evaluated for estimation methods that assume multivariate normality. Report values of statistics that measure univariate or multivariate skewness and kurtosis that support the assumption of normal distributions. If the data were not multivariate normal, state the strategy used to address nonnormality, such as use of a different estimation method that does not assume normality or use of normalizing transformations of the scores.
Data summary	Report in the manuscript—or make available in the supplemental materials—sufficient summary statistics that allow secondary analysis, including • Covariance matrix with means, or a correlation matrix with standard deviations and means, for continuous variables • Polychoric correlation matrix, items thresholds, and the asymptotic covariance matrix for categorical variables. • Indicate whether the case-level data are archived, and provide information about how these data can be accessed by interested readers.
Specification	Indicate the general approach that best describes the application of structural equation modeling—strictly confirmatory, comparison of alternative models, or model generation. Provide the diagram for each model fitted to the data. If the diagram would be overly complex, such as when large numbers of variables are analyzed, then clearly describe the models in text. A reader should be able to translate the text description of a model into a diagram. Give a full account of the specification for all models to be evaluated, including observed variables, latent variables, fixed or free parameters, and constrained parameters. Report sufficient information, such as tabulations of the numbers of observations versus free parameters, so that the model degrees of freedom can be derived by the reader. Verify that models to be analyzed are actually identified. State the basis for this claim, including the method, rules, or heuristics used to establish identification. State the basis in theory or results of previous empirical studies if a measurement model is part of a larger model.

Table A5.1. (*Continued*)

Paper section and topic	Description
	Describe fully the specification of the mean structure if the model has a means component.
	Explain the rationale for including error correlations in the model if correlated error terms are specified.
	Explain how the effects are specified if the model includes interaction effects.
	Explain how nonindependence is accounted for in the model for nested data (e.g., occasions within persons, students within classrooms).
	Describe any comparisons of parameters to be made between groups or occasions, and indicate which parameters are to be compared if models are fitted to data from multiple groups or occasions.
Estimation	State the software (including version) used in the analysis. Also state the estimation method used and justify its use (i.e., whether its assumptions are supported by the data).
	Disclose any default criteria in the software, such as the maximum number of iterations or level of tolerance, that were adjusted in order to achieve a converged and admissible solution.
	Report any evidence of an inadmissible solution (e.g., error variances less than zero or constrained by the computer at zero; estimated absolute correlations or proportions of explained variance that exceed 1.0). Explain what was done to deal with the problem.
Model fit	Report fit statistics or indices about global (omnibus) fit interpreted using criteria justified by citation of most recent evidence-based recommendations for all models to be interpreted.
	Report information about local fit, such as covariance, standardized, normalized, or correlation residuals, that justifies retaining the model at the level of pairs of observed variables for all interpreted models.
	State the strategy or criteria used to select one model over another if alternative models were compared. Report results of difference tests for comparisons between alternative models.
	State the test and criterion for testing estimates of individual parameters. If parameter estimates were compared over groups or occasions, indicate how those comparisons were made.

(*table continues*)

■ **Table A5.1.** (*Continued*)

Paper section and topic	Description
Respecification	Indicate whether one or more interpreted models were a product of respecification. If so, then describe the method used to search for misspecified parameters. State which parameters were fixed or freed to produce the interpreted model. Also provide a theoretical or conceptual rationale for parameters that were fixed or freed after specification searching. Indicate whether models for which results are presented were specified before or after fitting other models or otherwise examining the data.
Estimates	Report both unstandardized and standardized estimates for all estimated parameters. Report the corresponding standard errors, especially if outcomes of significance testing for individual parameters are reported. State the cutoffs for levels of statistical significance if such cutoffs were used. Report estimates of indirect effects, both unstandardized and standardized. Also report values of standard errors for indirect effects if possible. State and justify the strategy for testing indirect effects. Report estimates of interaction effects and also results of follow-up analyses that clarify the underlying pattern for interpreted interactions. Also report values of standard errors for such interactions.
Discussion	Summarize the modifications to the original model and the bases, theoretical or statistical, for doing so. Address the issue of equivalent models that fit the same data as well as retained models or alternative-but-nonequivalent models that explain the data nearly as well as retained models. Justify the preference for retained models over equivalent or near-equivalent versions.

Note. Adapted from "Journal Article Reporting Standards for Quantitative Research in Psychology: The APA Publications and Communications Board Task Force Report," by M. Appelbaum, H. Cooper, R. B. Kline, E. Mayo-Wilson, A. M. Nezu, and S. M. Rao, 2018, *American Psychologist, 73*, pp. 18–19. Copyright 2018 by the American Psychological Association.

Table A5.2. Reporting Standards for Studies Using Bayesian Techniques (in Addition to Material Presented in Table A1.1)

Paper section and topic	Description
Model	Completely specify both the systematic and the stochastic parts of the analyzed model, and give the rationale for choices of functional forms and distributions.
Distributions	Describe the prior distributions for model parameters of interest. If the priors are informative, state the rationale for that choice, and conduct a sensitivity analysis to check the dependence of the results on the prior distribution.
	Describe the posterior distributions for substantive model parameters and important functions of the parameters. If feasible, report the highest posterior density interval for each parameter or function.
	Plot or describe the joint distribution if substantive parameters are correlated.
	If predictions are made for observable quantities, make available either the actual predictive distribution and parameter estimates, report summary statistics that describe the distribution, or a graphic summary.
Likelihood	Describe the unnormalized or normalized likelihood if the prior distribution is informative.
Plots	Include the prior distribution, likelihood, and posterior distribution in a single plot (i.e., a triplot) if the prior distribution is informative and plots are to be presented.
Decisions	Report the utilities, or costs and benefits, and explain how they were derived if the data are used for decision making about possible actions. Also provide a sensitivity analysis for various prior distributions or assumptions about utilities for the decision.
Special cases	Explain the rationale for assuming exchangeability (or conditional exchangeability if there are covariates) for multilevel analyses. If relevant to the research context, present plots or tables of shrinkage-adjusted estimates and their confidence intervals.
	Report forest plots or caterpillar plots that include original and shrinkage-corrected estimates of effect sizes for each study, with confidence intervals for meta-analytic summaries. If feasible for the analytic method, provide a parameter trace plot where shrinkage-adjusted estimates are shown against the standard deviation of the residual effects, combined with the posterior distribution of the residual variance.

(*table continues*)

■ **Table A5.2.** (*Continued*)

Paper section and topic	Description
	Describe the details of all decision rules, if these rules were decided (before or during the study), and the consequences (results) of each decision in adaptive designs.
Computations	Describe in detail, including the number of chains, the number of burn-in iterations for each chain and thinning if Markov chain Monte Carlo or another sampling procedure is used. Specify the methods used to check for convergence and their results.
Model fit	Describe the procedures used to check the fit of the model and the results of those checks.
Bayes factors	Specify the models being compared if Bayes factors are calculated. Report the Bayes factors and how they were interpreted. Test the sensitivity of the Bayes factors to assumptions about prior distributions.
Bayesian model averaging	State the parameter or function of parameters being estimated in Bayesian model averaging. Either plot the distribution or list the mean and standard deviation if it is near normal; otherwise, list a number of percentiles for the distribution if it is not near normal. Describe how the models were generated and, if a reduced set was used for averaging, how the selection was made and which models were used in the averaging.

Note. Adapted from "Journal Article Reporting Standards for Quantitative Research in Psychology: The APA Publications and Communications Board Task Force Report," by M. Appelbaum, H. Cooper, R. B. Kline, E. Mayo-Wilson, A. M. Nezu, and S. M. Rao, 2018, *American Psychologist, 73*, p. 20. Copyright 2018 by the American Psychological Association.

6

Reporting Other Design Features: Longitudinal Studies, Replication Studies, Studies With One Subject, and Clinical Trials

The Journal Article Reporting Standards (JARS; Appelbaum et al., 2018) contains additional recommendations for research designs that have a few other unique features. These standards relate to studies that (a) collected data on participants at more than one time; (b) are intended to be replications of previously conducted studies; (c) are conducted using only one subject or unit; and (d) are clinical trials—that is, meant to test the effectiveness of physical or mental health treatments. The flowchart in Figure 1.1 diagrams the strategy for deciding which JARS tables are relevant to your project. Here, I discuss the four additional design features in turn.

Longitudinal Studies

Table A6.1 presents the additional JARS recommendations for studies that collect longitudinal data—that is, that collect data on each participant on more than one occasion. These types of studies are most frequent in developmental psychology, when you want to see how people change over time, or in clinical and health psychology, when you want to see whether the effects of an intervention persist over time. Because these types of studies have this time dimension, the JARS table covers an aspect of design covered in none of the other tables. Therefore, you would use Table A6.1 in addition to the other tables that are relevant to your design if you collected longitudinal data.

http://dx.doi.org/10.1037/0000103-006

Reporting Quantitative Research in Psychology: How to Meet APA Style Journal Article Reporting Standards, Second Edition, by H. Cooper

Sample Characteristics

If your study involves collecting data on subjects at more than one time, your Method section should describe for each unit sampled

- the number of units per group, their age, and their sex distribution;
- their ethnic composition;
- their socioeconomic status, home language, immigrant status, education level, and family characteristics; and
- their country, region, city, and other significant geographic characteristics.

The reporting recommendation on sample characteristics is really a reiteration of a recommendation made in the general reporting standards (Table A1.1): Your report should present a complete picture of who the participants were. There are some characteristics, such as age and sex, that need to be reported universally because they so often interact with psychological phenomena. The importance of other characteristics will depend on the topic and context of the study you are conducting.

The key reason why sample characteristics are reemphasized in the JARS table for longitudinal studies is not because the characteristics that should be reported in these types of studies are different from those of other studies. Rather, it is a reminder that the composition of the sample needs to be described for each of the measurement occasions. For example, the study by Fagan, Palkovitz, Roy, and Farrie (2009) on risk factors (e.g., fathers' drug problems, incarceration, unemployment) associated with resilience factors (e.g., fathers' positive attitudes, job training, religious participation) and paternal engagement with offspring was a longitudinal study. The description of the samples is provided in Chapter 3. Remember that Fagan et al. used data drawn from the Fragile Family and Child Wellbeing Study, which followed nearly 5,000 children born in the United States between 1998 and 2000. The researchers used longitudinal data collected at a child's birth, 1-year follow-up, and 3-year follow-up. To obtain their final sample from the larger database, Fagan et al. did the following:

> We excluded married and cohabiting couples at baseline to ensure that the study focused on the most fragile families at the time of the child's birth. Next, we selected fathers who also participated at Year 1. Of the 815 eligible fathers who participated at baseline and Year 1, 130 were missing substantial data, so we removed them from the sample. These steps resulted in a sample of 685 fathers. We then excluded fathers who were not interviewed at Year 3, yielding a sample of 569 fathers. About 4% of the 569 fathers had substantial missing Year 3 data that could not be easily imputed. We omitted these fathers from the study, yielding a final sample of 549 fathers with complete data. (p. 1392)

The researchers then presented the average age of their sample at baseline and its composition by ethnic group and level of education. Also, because it was relevant to this study, they specified the relationship between the mother and father at 1-year and 3-year follow-up.

Fagan et al.'s (2009) study did not involve an experimental manipulation. One of the other examples did: Norman, Maley, Li, and Skinner's (2008) study evaluating the effectiveness of an Internet-based intervention to prevent and stop adolescents from smoking. Norman et al. took measures at baseline, postintervention, and 3-month and 6-month follow-up. After presenting a thorough description of their sampling technique and sample, they informed readers,

> The distribution of cultural groups in the smoker sample was significantly different, $t(13) = 3.105$, $p < .001$, than the nonsmoker sample, with a higher proportion of smokers identifying with Eastern European or Mediterranean cultures. Those from Central Asian or African cultural groups were the least represented in the smoker sample. (Norman et al., 2008, p. 801)

Attrition

If your study involves collecting data on subjects at more than one time, your Method section should describe for each unit sampled

- the attrition rate at each wave, breaking down reasons for attrition, and
- any differential attrition by major sociodemographic and experimental condition.

Fagan et al. (2009) told readers that the reason for *attrition*, or the exclusion of a participant's complete data, in their study was too much missing data; they began with a sample of 815 fathers who were eligible and participated at baseline. But only 549 of these fathers had complete data after the two follow-ups. This is about a 33% attrition rate. The question you must ask is whether the initial sample, if meant to be representative of a national sample of unwed fathers at baseline, would still be representative if one in three fathers were not included in the 1-year and 3-year follow-up sample. Could the missing fathers be different from the retained fathers in some way that was related to the variables of interest?

In fact, Fagan et al. (2009) looked at whether fathers who dropped out differed from ones who did not:

> We conducted attrition analyses to compare the sample of fathers who met criteria for inclusion in the present study at baseline, Year 1, and Year 3 and who were interviewed at all three times ($n = 549$) with fathers who were interviewed at baseline and Year 1 but not at Year 3 ($n = 116$). Chi-square or one-way analyses of variance were conducted on father's age, race, education, relationship with the mother of the baby, and prenatal involvement; family risk and resilience indexes at baseline; individual, family, and child risk indexes at Year 1; individual and family resilience indexes at Year 1; and whether the father resided with the child at Year 1. One significant difference was found: Fathers in the sample were more involved prenatally, $F(1, 664) = 4.7$, $p < .05$, than fathers who dropped out at Year 3. (p. 1396)

Regardless of how you answer the question of how much this difference might matter to the generalizability of the findings, the important point here is that the report gave you sufficient information to make the judgment.

Norman et al. (2008) showed the attrition rates for their different conditions in the diagram presented in Figure 5.2. For an experimental study, you are concerned about not only whether overall attrition has been appreciable, potentially threatening external validity, but also whether attrition is different for each of the conditions at each measurement, a possible threat to internal validity. If it is, the ability of the researchers to make claims about the effect of the experimental variable is compromised. If differential attrition occurs, it is possible that the composition of the groups changed, creating a plausible rival hypothesis in addition to the treatment's effect if the groups differ on subsequent tests. You can see from Figure 5.2 that attrition was less than 10% among nonsmokers in the two experimental conditions but between 15% and 30% in the two different conditions at different times for smokers. Is this difference large enough to raise your concern about whether the subjects who were smokers and completed the study were different from the smokers who did not complete the study? Regardless, JARS recommends that researchers report attrition rates for different experimental conditions so that such a determination can be made.

Additional Sample Description

If your study involves collecting data on subjects at more than one time, your Method section should describe

- any contextual changes for participants or units as the study progressed—for example,
  - school closures or mergers;
  - major economic changes; or
  - for long-term studies, major social changes that may need explanation for contemporary readers to understand the context of the study during its early years.

This reporting recommendation is pretty straightforward. People, local contexts, and larger societies change over time. The researchers should be aware of any of these changes that might influence how participants respond and should report these, along with any effort they made to adjust for or take these changes into account. For example, a new report showing that smoking is bad for your health that got widespread media attention between the baseline and 3-year follow-up waves of the Norman et al. (2008) study might have affected participants' follow-up responses. It could be a plausible rival hypothesis to a treatment effect. Researchers should make readers aware of any changes in participants and context that might affect their results.

Method and Measurement

If your study involves collecting data on subjects at more than one time, your Method section should describe the independent variables and dependent variables at each wave of data collection. It should also report the years in which each wave of data collection occurred.

This recommendation of JARS points out that measurements are sometimes not the same from one data collection time to another. For example, a revision of one of your instruments might have been developed between the posttreatment and follow-up data collections. Most researchers would be reluctant to change measurements midstream, but if the validity and reliability of the measures have improved greatly, the researchers might find that the tradeoff of quality over consistency is worth it. If you do this, you should fully detail all the measures and tell how you adjusted scores to make them as equivalent as possible (e.g., rescaling, adjustment for attenuation). Thus, just as you should mention in your report all of the measures that were taken as part of a study at only a single point in time, you should repeat this detail for every occasion of measurement, even if just to say that the measurements were the same.

Missing Data

> If your study involves collecting data on subjects at more than one time, your Method section should describe the amount of missing data and how issues of missing data were handled analytically.

This is also a reiteration of an earlier JARS recommendation. Note above how Fagan et al. (2009) removed from their sample all participants with "substantial" missing data. Did this removal mean the fathers used in the analyses were different from fathers without missing data? Fagan et al. (2009) provided the following information:

> We compared the sample of fathers who participated at all three times and who had no missing data with fathers who had substantial missing data. The fathers with no missing data were more likely to be in a romantic relationship with the mother of the baby at baseline, $\chi^2(1, N = 569) = 7.9$, $p < .01$, were less likely to have been merely friends with the mother of the baby at baseline, $\chi^2(1, N = 569) = 6.2$, $p < .05$, and experienced more individual resilience factors between baseline and Year 1, $F(1, 568) = 4.3$, $p < .05$, than fathers who had missing data. (p. 1396)

When there was missing data, but not substantially so, Fagan et al. (2009) did the following:

> The mothers' data also had missing cases that needed to be imputed. At Year 1, 19 mothers were not interviewed and 49 had missing data; at Year 3, 29 mothers were not interviewed and 82 had missing data. For those cases in which all mothers' data were missing, the fathers' data were first consulted to see whether they reported having any contact with the child. If they did not, zeros were imputed for all mother items. Among mothers who had some missing items, we imputed the respondent's mean for those items that were answered. For the remaining cases, the sample mean for the mother's index was imputed. The Cronbach alpha was .95 for Year 1 and .96 for Year 3. (p. 1393)

Throughout, these researchers used substitutions of fathers' data for missing mothers' data as well as substitutions of means when an insubstantial amount of data were missing for mothers at each time of measurement.

Norman et al. (2008) used a very different strategy for imputing missing data:

> The use of multilevel logistic regression models provided alternative strategies to deal with missing data that are comparable to estimation procedures, but rely on less data to effectively assess change over time (Little & Rubin, 1987). (p. 804)

Analysis

If your study involves collecting data on subjects at more than one time, your Method section should specify the analytic approaches used and assumptions made in performing these analyses.

Longitudinal data can be analyzed in numerous ways, from repeated measures analysis of variance to highly complex analysis strategies. For example, Fagan et al. (2009) first did a series of univariate analyses using data from each time point separately. Then they conducted a sophisticated path analysis that used the time of measurement as one variable. Thus, variables at baseline were used to predict variables at 1-year follow-up, and then both of these times of measurement were used to predict all variables at Year 3. Norman et al. (2008) used logistic growth models to analyze their data. Because these strategies require very advanced calculations (and a new set of terms), I will not describe their results here. However, the important point is that your paper needs full descriptions of all the analytic strategies in the Method or Results section.

Multiple Publication

If your study involves collecting data on subjects at more than one time, your Method section should provide information on where any portions of the data have been previously published and the degree of overlap with the current report.

You might publish a report of your data collected at baseline and immediately after treatment soon after the data are analyzed. Then perhaps years later, you might write another report covering your follow-up data. As with reports of data that have been used in more than one article published roughly at the same time, you should provide information in your later reports whenever you reuse data that were published previously, even though only part of the data in the later report are reused. Fagan et al. (2009) did this when they noted that their data were drawn from an already existing database, the Fragile Families and Child Wellbeing Study, collected in United States between 1998 and 2000. It also is not good practice to wait until the follow-up data are collected but then try to publish the longitudinal data in pieces. This is called *piecemeal publication* (see Cooper, 2016).

Replication Studies

Table A6.2 sets out reporting standards for studies that are meant to repeat earlier studies and to do so with as much fidelity as possible. The most important reporting issues concern the similarities and differences between the original study and the study meant to repeat it. Because these issues are unique to replication studies, Table A6.2 should be used with any combination of other JARS tables I have described, depending on the design of the study that is being replicated.

It will be clearest if I use as the example the hypothetical fragrance labeling study. If you are interested in reading a published replication study, look at Gurven, von Rueden, Massenkoff, Kaplan, and Lero Vie (2013) for a study examining whether the five-factor model of personality was replicable using participants from a largely illiterate society or Jack, O'Shea, Cottrell, and Ritter (2013) for an attempt to replicate the ventriloquist illusion in selective listening.

Type of Study

If your study is meant to be a replication of a previously conducted study, your report should

- include sufficient information in the report title and in the text to allow the reader to determine whether the study is a direct replication, approximate replication, or conceptual replication;
- indicate whether your study has conditions, materials, or procedures that were not part of the original study, and if so,
- describe these new features, where in the study they occur, and their potential impact on the results; and
- report indications of treatment fidelity for both the original study and your replication.

If your study is a replication of an earlier work, it is critical that the title reflects this. So, if you were replicating an earlier study by "Capulet (2018)" on the effect of labeling fragrances, you might title your study "The Effects of Labels on Subjective Evaluations: A Replication of Capulet (2018)." Note that I used part of the title of the original study (from Chapter 2) but not all of it. This way, the two studies are clearly linked but cannot be confused as the same. The fact that your study is a replication is also made clear.

The replicative nature of your experiment should also be mentioned as early in the introduction as possible, preferably the first paragraph. You should also mention as early as possible whether your study is a direct or approximate replication—that is, whether it is meant to be as operationally similar to the original study as is possible. The difference between direct and approximate replication is not black and white. For example, a replication can never be *direct*, or exact, because it will always be done at a different time, often at a different place, and with different participants, researchers, and data collectors. Still, if these are the only things that vary, the study is often called a *direct replication*. It could also be called an *approximate replication* but typically is not. The label *approximate replication* should be used if, for example, changes were made to the way measures of the pleasantness of the fragrance were constructed (e.g., a scale with a different number or type of responses) but these are expected to have little or no effect on the outcomes of the study.

A *conceptual replication* occurs when the manipulations or measures were changed but the underlying relationships between variables are expected to hold. For example, instead of using *roses* and *manure* to label your fragrances, you might want to see whether the different positive and negative labels for neutral fragrances would be rated as similarly pleasant if the labels are *lilies* and *mud*.

JARS also recommends that any additional conditions you added to the original study design be fully described. For example, you might include in your replication study an extract from roses but also one from manure, making for four conditions rather than only the two conditions with different labels for the same fragrance used in the original study by "Capulet (2018)." Thus, the two conditions using extract of roses might be a direct replication of "Capulet (2018)," but the two conditions using an extract with a less pleasant fragrance are an extension of the original research.

Describe in your introduction why you added the new conditions and your hypotheses involving them. In your Method section, detail how you created and manipulated the new conditions. In addition to new conditions, JARS recommends that any additional measures be fully described in your report. So, if "Capulet (2018)" did not include a measure of subjects' intention to buy the fragrance but you did, this needs to be detailed in your report.

Also, report any indications of the fidelity of the experimental treatments that were reported in the original study and in your study. This allows readers to assess how comparable your manipulations were to the originals. What was the rated pleasantness of the fragrances in the original studies before the labels were applied? Were your prelabeling ratings similar? Did the studies measure whether subjects remembered the label? Were the rates of recollection the same in each study?

Subjects

> If your study is meant to be a replication of a previously conducted study, your report should include
>
> - a comparison of the recruitment procedures in the original and replication studies and
> - an explanation of all major variations in how the subjects were selected, such as
>   - whether your study was conducted in a different setting (e.g., country or culture),
>   - whether the allocation of subjects to groups or conditions was different, and
>   - a description of the implications of these variations for the results.
>
> Your report should compare the demographic characteristics of the subjects in both studies. If the units of analysis are not people, such as classrooms, then you should report the appropriate descriptors of their characteristics.

These JARS recommendations allow the reader to assess whether the subjects in your study were similar to or different from those in the original study in any important ways that might relate to the labeling effect. For example, if the original study was conducted with a sample of female subjects only but your study was conducted with both female and male subjects, you need to say this in your Method section. Also, you should present any appraisal you make about whether this difference in subjects might influence the results. Might there be a difference between the sexes—might Juliet think both labels are equally sweet but Romeo think they are different? The results for female subjects might be a direct or approximate replication of the original study and the results for male subjects an extension of it, testing the generalizability of the original findings across the sexes.

In both the original labeling study and your replication, it is likely that subjects were randomly assigned to conditions. Your report should mention this. If the assignment to conditions was different in the two studies, it is critical that you report both and discuss the implications. For example, in an original school-based study of a reading intervention, the principal might have picked teachers for the new program, but in your study, teachers might have volunteered. This could create differences between the groups before the intervention began. For example, whereas the principal may have picked the teachers most in need, volunteer teachers may have been the most motivated to have their students improve, yielding two groups of teachers who would not necessarily react to the intervention in the same way.

Instrumentation

If your study is meant to be a replication of a previously conducted study, you should report

- the instruments you used, including both hardware (apparatus) and other techniques used to collect data;
- any major differences between the original and replication studies;
- whether questionnaires or psychological tests were translated to another language and the methods used, such as back-translation, to verify that the translation was accurate;
- psychometric characteristics of the scores analyzed in the replication study and a comparison of these properties with those in the original study; and
- informants and methods of administration across the two studies, including
  - the setting for testing, such as individual versus group administration, and
  - the method of administration, such as paper and pencil or online.

As noted above, any changes you made to the apparatus and instruments you used in your replication need careful documentation. Such changes might include any language translations, how these were accomplished, and how successful they were in creating equivalent instruments. Was the original fragrance labeling study conducted in Italy, with measures written in Italian, and your replication study conducted in the United States, with measures in English? If so, how were the measures translated, and what evidence do you have that the measures were equivalent?

Also, the psychometric properties of your measures and the equivalent measures used in the earlier study need to be reported. What were their reliabilities and internal consistencies? Did these differ in a way that might affect the results? You should also detail any differences in the settings and instructions to subjects. Was one study conducted in a lab and the other at a department store perfume counter? How might this difference have affected the results?

Analysis

> If your study is meant to be a replication of a previously conducted study, you should report
>
> - results using the same analytical methods (statistical or other quantitative manipulations) used in the original study;
> - results from any additional or different analyses you may have conducted;
> - whether the effect size in a power analysis was specified to equal that reported in the original study or whether power was averaged over plausible values of effect size based on an estimated standard error, which takes account of sampling error; and
> - statistical criteria you used for deciding whether the original results were replicated in the new study; and an explanation of the decision rules you used to make this determination.

The notion of replication extends not only to the methods used in the original study but to the data analysis strategy as well. It is important that when you conduct a replication, you use the same analytic strategy that was used in the original study. For example, if the original labeling study used a two-group *t* test to test the differences between labels, you should do this test as well. This also means that it is important to do a power analysis for your sample size and report it. Readers will be interested in whether the statistical power of your study roughly matches that of the original study, whether your study had a greater or lesser chance of finding statistical significance, and whether it measured parameters (e.g., means, standard deviations, effect sizes) with more or less precision.

You can also report any new ways you used to analyze the data. For example, you might do the *t* test used by the original researchers but also do a two-way analysis of variance by adding the sex of subjects to the analysis. You can improve on the original study's analyses, but only after you have reproduced them as closely as possible.

Finally, you need to spell out what criteria you used to decide whether the original results were, in fact, successfully replicated. You might use the criteria of whether the findings were statistically significant (did both you and Capulet find that the *roses* label led to significantly higher favorability ratings?), how the magnitudes of the experimental effect size compared, whether the two effect sizes were contained within each other's confidence intervals, or how the Bayesian postexperiment (a posteriori) expectations were similar or different. There are guidelines for when you might deem a replication as successful or unsuccessful (e.g., Open Science Collaboration, 2015), and Verhagen and Wagenmakers (2014) introduced a Bayesian approach and gave a brief overview of alternative methods using frequentist statistics. You can use these resources to help you pick your criteria.

Studies With One Subject or Unit (*N*-of-1 Design)

Studies that are conducted using a single subject or unit focus on trying to understand how an individual (or other type of single unit) changed over time or was affected by a treatment. This design is in contrast to those I have discussed thus far, which are concerned with what makes one group of people different from another group on average. Single-case research is used most frequently in clinical psychology, especially when a treatment is meant to help an individual who has a rare disorder or when people with the disorder are hard to find and recruit for a group study with enough power to detect a reasonable effect size. It is also used in developmental psychology, when researchers are interested in how individuals change over time, with or without an intervention. Finally, single-case designs are sometimes used in applied psychology when, say, the effects of an intervention on a large unit motivates the study. This unit might be a company, a classroom or school, or an entire city, state, or country rather than the individuals who make up the unit. In this case, the average or sum of the individual scores of everyone in the unit (e.g., a factory's productivity, the percentage of a school's students scoring below grade level) represents the "behavior" of the single unit.

Table A6.3 will be of interest if your study is being conducted on a single individual or other type of unit. The single-case design is a unique type of research, not just because of the question it asks. You would complete Table A6.3 along with Table A1.1 and any other JARS tables that are relevant (see especially the section below on clinical trials).

The material called for in the introduction and Discussion sections of Table A1.1 applies to all types of designs. So, does much of the material reported in the Method section, including participant characteristics and sampling procedures (in the case of single-case research, this would constitute the individual's demographic characteristics and how the unit was recruited). However, some of the material in the Method and Results sections would look quite different. For example, in a study with a single subject, the sample size and total number of participants is 1, and that is the intended sample size. Power analysis is irrelevant for an *N*-of-1 design, but a complete description of the characteristics of the measures is no less important. Similarly, you should examine the entries in Table A1.1 relating to results. You will see that most are relevant to *N*-of-1 designs, but they would be reported in a different way.

I will not use the hypothetical fragrance labeling study as an example of a single-case design. If you were conducting a labeling study, you might be able to use the two label conditions as a within-subjects factor, perhaps by exposing subjects to the same fragrance twice but once labeling it *roses* and once *manure*. But *N*-of-1 designs require numerous measurements, sometimes hundreds, over time, so this would not be the design of choice where labeling of fragrances is concerned. A subject would be incredulous if asked to sniff the fragrances too many times with the same two labels used over and over again. Also, if done too quickly, the subject's sense of smell would change. You could ask the subject to return day after day, but this likely would be impractical.

So instead, I will use a hypothetical example in which you wish to test the effectiveness of a drug to help a smoker cut down on the number of cigarettes smoked each day or to eliminate smoking entirely. I will also introduce another example drawn from the literature involving the effectiveness of a video modeling treatment meant to improve how well an 8-year-old child with autism can perceive different emotions (happy, sad, angry, and afraid). It was conducted by Corbett (2003) and appeared in *The Behavior Analyst Today*. Video modeling was described by Corbett as follows:

> Video modeling is a technique that has been developed to facilitate observational learning. It generally involves the subject observing a videotape of a model showing a behavior that is subsequently practiced and imitated. The child is typically seated in front of a television monitor and asked to sit quietly and pay attention to the video. The child is praised for attending and staying on task. Following the presentation of a scene showing a target behavior, the child is asked to engage in or imitate the behavior that was observed. This procedure is then repeated across examples and trials. (p. 368)

Corbett went on to say that video modeling had been used successfully with children with autism to teach them a variety of skills and that there were some instances in which it was shown to be more effective than live modeling. Can video modeling be used to teach a child with autism how to better recognize the emotions expressed on other peoples' faces, a skill that is notably difficult for these children?

Design

> If your study was conducted on a single subject, your report should describe
>
> - the design type—for example, withdrawal–reversal, multiple-baseline, alternating-treatments, changing-criterion, some combination thereof, or adaptive design—and
> - the treatment phases, the phase sequence and whether it was determined a priori or data driven, and the criteria for phase change, if applicable.

Single-case designs can take many forms. When an experimental manipulation is examined in the study (such as the autism study), the most general variations in design relate to (a) whether the intervention is introduced but then withdrawn or reversed after a time, (b) whether more than one treatment is used and the treatments are introduced individually or in combination, (c) whether multiple measures are taken and whether these were meant to be affected differently by the treatment, and (d) what criteria will be used to decide when an intervention should be introduced or changed. Single-case studies without an intervention can be less complicated, but the researchers still need to decide whether multiple different measures will be taken and what length of time to allow between measures. JARS recommends that these basic design features be described in the report, and it would be odd, indeed, if they were not. Two excellent books for studying up on single-case research designs are Barlow, Nock and Hersen (2008) and Kazdin (2011).

JARS also specifies that the length of the phases used in the study be described and the method of determining these lengths. Sometimes the length of phases is preset before the experiment begins. Other times phase length is determined by the subject's pattern of behavior once the study begins. For example, in single-case studies with interventions, it is important to achieve a stable baseline for the behaviors of interest before the intervention is introduced; if you do not have a good estimate of how the subject was behaving before the intervention begins, how can you tell whether the intervention had an effect? Once the intervention starts, it might last for a preset amount of time, or it might be withdrawn or changed when a preset criterion is met. For example, if a drug meant to help people stop smoking reduces the number of cigarettes smoked in a day from 30 to 20, this might lead you to increase the drug dosage to test whether the rate of smoking can be reduced yet further.

Corbett (2003) described the phases of the video modeling treatment as follows:

> The video modeling treatment consisted of the participant observing brief (3 to 15 seconds) videotaped scenes showing the target behavior of happy, sad, angry or afraid performed by typically developing peer models. The videotape consisted of five examples of each emotion for a total of twenty different social or play situation scenes. Each scene was shown only once per day resulting in a total intervention time of 10 to 15 minutes per day. The videotape was shown five days per week in the participant's home generally at the same time and in the same location. (p. 370)

She reported the baseline conditions as follows:

> The baseline condition consisted of the child being seated in front of the television monitor. The therapist instructed the child to "Pay attention." The first scene was played for the child. The therapist asked, "What is he/she feeling?" The therapist presented the child with a laminated sheet of four primary emotions with cartoons and words representing the four emotion categories. The child could provide a verbal response or point to the word or picture on the sheet. The therapist documented a "1" for correct responding or a "0" for incorrect responding for each scene across the four emotion categories. In order to establish a stable trend, a minimum of two days of baseline data was obtained. (Corbett, 2003, p. 371)

Her treatment conditions were described as follows:

> The treatment condition consisted of the child being seated in front of the television. Again, the therapist said, "Pay attention." After the first scene, the participant was asked: "What is he/she feeling?" referring to the primary emotion conveyed in the scene. If the child answered correctly, social reinforcement was given. If the child answered incorrectly, then corrective feedback was provided and the therapist said, "The child is feeling (Emotion)." Next, the therapist enthusiastically responded, "Let's do what we saw on the tape. Let's do the same!" The therapist then initiated the interaction observed on the tape. The therapist interacted with the child in a role-play using imaginary materials to simulate the social and play situations. This interaction was intended to be enjoyable and was not rated or scored. The child was encouraged to imitate and display the feeling that he observed. The emotion response was scored 1 or 0 and the next scene was introduced. (Corbett, 2003, p. 371)

In sum, Corbett described her design as a

> multiple-probe-across-behaviors design. The treatment involved providing the subject with the fewest probes and modifications needed followed by more supportive intervention, as required. (p. 371)

Procedural Changes

> If your study was conducted on a single subject, your description of the research design should include any procedural changes that occurred during the course of the investigation after the start of the study.

You would need to document in your report of a single-case study any changes that occurred to your procedures once the study began. Corbett (2003) had no such procedural change:

> The participant's mother, who was familiar with basic behavioral principles, was trained and supervised weekly on the procedure by the author. The child observed the tapes in a structured, supportive environment that was devoid of extraneous visual and auditory stimuli during video watching and rehearsal periods. (p. 370)

In the hypothetical smoking cessation study, a change in procedure would need to be reported if, say, after a short period of time the original dosage of the drug proved ineffective and you decided to increase it.

Replication

> If your study was conducted on a single subject, your report should include a description of any planned replications.

Although a single-case study, by definition, is conducted on only a single unit, it is not uncommon for the same report to include multiple replications of the same study using different units. Thus, Corbett (2003) might have reported the effects of video modeling separately for five different children with autism. If she did this, she would present the data for each child individually and then consider the similarities and differences in results in the Discussion.

Randomization

> If your study was conducted on a single subject, your report should
>
> ■ state whether randomization was used, and if so,
> ■ describe the randomization method and the elements of the study that were randomized (e.g., during which phases treatment and control conditions were instituted).

Randomization can occur in single-case research but, obviously, not by randomly assigning subjects to conditions. Instead, randomization can occur by randomly deciding the phases in which the different conditions of the experiment will appear. For example, in the antismoking drug experiment, you might decide that each phase will be a week long. After establishing a baseline (How many cigarettes does the subject smoke per day before the drug is introduced?), you flip a coin to decide whether the subject will or will not get the drug during each of the next 10 weeks. Note that the subject might then get the drug for some consecutive weeks and get no treatment for other consecutive weeks. This randomization helps you rule out numerous threats to the validity of your assertion that the drug was the cause of any change in smoking behavior (especially history or other events that are confounded with your treatment).

If you used randomization in your single-case study, you should be sure to report it: It is a positive feature of your study that you will want readers to know about. In Corbett's (2003) description of her phases of treatment above, she did not say explicitly whether the presentation of the emotions on the faces of the video models was randomized. In this type of experiment, it is not clear that randomization is necessary; the treatment was administered fairly quickly (over 3 weeks) and introducing and withdrawing the treatment would likely only diminish its effectiveness.

Sequence Completed

If your study was conducted on a single subject, your description of the research design should report

- the sequence actually completed, including the number of trials for each session for each case, and
- when a subject who did not complete the sequence stopped and the reason for stopping.

Corbett (2003) reported that the full sequence was completed and that there were 15 trials. She reported no incomplete replications. All reports of single-case designs include this information.

Outcomes and Estimation

If your study was conducted on a single subject, your description should include the results for each participant, including raw data for each target behavior and other outcomes.

Analyses of the data from single-case research designs can be conducted using techniques that vary from simple to highly complex. Highly complex techniques have been developed specifically for data that are interdependent because of time. A compendium of these techniques can be found in Kratochwill and Levin (2014). What is also unique about reporting results of single-case designs is that the raw data should be presented, which often occurs in the form of a graph. Corbett (2003) presented her results in the graph shown in Figure 6.1. She described her results without conducting

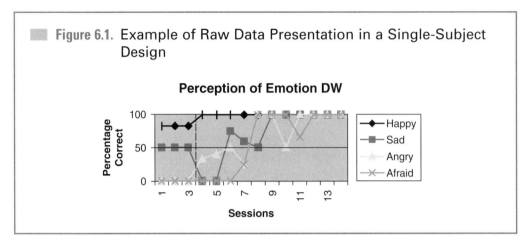

Figure 6.1. Example of Raw Data Presentation in a Single-Subject Design

Daily percentage of emotion perception. Adapted from "Video Modeling: A Window Into the World of Autism," by B. A. Corbett, *The Behavior Analyst Today, 4,* pp. 371–372. Copyright 2003 by the American Psychological Association.

any formal statistical analysis, a procedure that is not uncommon in simple single-case studies when the data are clear and irrefutable:

> Video modeling resulted in the rapid acquisition of the perception of the four basic emotions. As can be observed in Figure 1, D.W. quickly mastered the identification of happy, which was already somewhat established in his repertoire. Subsequently, D.W. showed gradual improvement across the remaining emotion categories. D.W. showed rapid, stable acquisition and maintenance of all the emotion categories. (Corbett, 2003, p. 372)

Clinical Trials

When studies evaluate a specific type of experimental treatment, namely the effects of health interventions, these are called *clinical trials.* To briefly revisit what I wrote in Chapter 1, clinical trials can relate to mental health or physical health interventions. In psychology, clinical trials often examine the psychological components of maintaining good physical health—for example, interventions meant to motivate people to comply with drug regimens or the implications of maintaining good physical health for good mental functioning, such as the effects of exercise programs on cognitive abilities in older adults. Clinical trials may involve manipulated interventions introduced by the experimenters. Or they can be used to evaluate an intervention that was introduced by others, perhaps administrators at a hospital who want to know whether a program they have begun is working. A clinical trial may use random or nonrandom assignment.

There are other types of interventions or treatments for which you might consider completing Table A6.4 even though health issues are not involved. For example, reports on studies like that by Vadasy and Sanders (2008) examining the effects of a reading intervention might benefit from completing this table. In these cases, many of the questions on standards in Table A6.4 will help you make your report as useful to others as possible.

The example I will use to illustrate the reporting of a clinical trial is from an article by Vinnars, Thormählen, Gallop, Norén, and Barber (2009) titled "Do Personality Problems Improve During Psychodynamic Supportive–Expressive Psychotherapy? Secondary Outcome Results From a Randomized Controlled Trial for Psychiatric Outpatients With Personality Disorders," published in *Psychotherapy Theory: Research, Practice, Training*.[1] In this study, two treatments for personality disorder were compared. The experimental treatment was a manualized version of supportive–expressive psychotherapy (SEP), and the control condition was nonmanualized community-delivered psychodynamic treatment (CDPT). Thus, this was a simple one-factor between-subjects design with two experimental conditions.

Participant Characteristics and Sampling Procedures

If you are reporting a clinical trial, your report should

- state the methods of ascertaining how participants met all inclusion and exclusion criteria, especially if assessing clinical diagnoses, and
- provide details regarding similarities and differences in data collection locations if a multisite study.

Vinnars et al. (2009) described their inclusion and exclusion criteria for participants and how they recruited them in the same paragraph:

> Participants were consecutively recruited from two community mental health centers (CMHCs) in the greater Stockholm area. They had either self-applied for treatment or were referred, mainly from primary health care. In general, participants asked for nonspecific psychiatric help, although a few specifically asked for psychotherapy. The inclusion criteria consisted of presence of at least one *DSM–IV* [*Diagnostic and Statistical Manual of Mental Disorders*, fourth edition; American Psychiatric Association, 1994] PD [personality disorder] diagnosis, or a diagnosis of passive–aggressive or depressive PD from the *DSM–IV* appendix. Exclusion criteria included age over 60 years, psychosis, bipolar diagnosis, severe suicidal intent, alcohol or drug dependence during the year before intake, organic brain damage, pregnancy, or unwillingness to undergo psychotherapy. Participants also needed to be fluent in Swedish. (p. 364)

This description gives readers a good idea about who was included and excluded from treatment so that researchers who want to replicate the results or extend them to different populations will know how to do so.

---

[1] Is this title too wordy according to JARS recommendations outlined in Chapter 2? Can you make it shorter? Does the descriptor *randomized controlled trial* need to be in the title or could this be mentioned in the abstract?

Measures

If you are reporting a clinical trial, you should state

- whether clinical assessors were involved in providing treatment for studies involving clinical assessments and
- whether they were aware or unaware of assignment to condition at posttreatment and follow-up assessments; if they were unaware, how was this accomplished?

From the description of subjects, it appears that in the Vinnars et al. (2009) clinical trial, people had been diagnosed with any personality disorder or specifically with passive–aggressive or depressive personality disorder. It also suggests that this clinical diagnosis happened before the study began (because subjects self-nominated or were referred). So the clinical assessors prior to treatment were not involved in providing treatment.

With regard to posttreatment assessments, Vinnars et al. (2009) told readers that clinical assessments for the study were taken at three time points: pretreatment, 1 year after treatment, and 1 additional year later. They stated that "Clinical psychologists with extensive clinical experience conducted the Structural Clinical Interview for *DSM–IV* II [as well as other clinical assessment instruments]" (p. 366). Thus, we can assume that the clinicians taking treatment-related assessments (the outcome variables) were not the same clinicians who administered the treatment. The researchers did not say whether the assessors were unaware of the subjects' experimental condition (and it would have been nice if they did so), but I think it is safe to assume they were.

Experimental Intervention

In your report of a clinical trial, include

- whether the study protocol was publicly available (e.g., published) prior to enrolling subjects and if so, where and when;
- how the intervention in your study differed from the "standard" approach in order to tailor it to a new population (e.g., differing age, ethnicity, comorbidity); and
- any materials (e.g., clinical handouts, data recorders) provided to subjects and how information about them can obtained (e.g., URL address).

Vinnars et al. (2009) used a manualized version of the psychotherapy manipulation, so we should not be surprised to find that their description of it begins with reference to where the manuals can be found:

> The SEP in this study followed Luborsky's treatment manual (Barber & Crits-Christoph, 1995; Luborsky, 1984). The treatment consisted of 40 sessions delivered, on average, over the course of 1 calendar year. (p. 365)

Vinnars et al. sent us elsewhere to find the details of their experimental treatment. This is a perfectly appropriate reporting approach, as long as (a) the document referred to is easily available (e.g., has been published, is available on the Internet), (b) the conceptual underpinnings of the treatment were carefully detailed (as they were in the introduction to Vinnars et al., 2009), and (c) any details are reported regarding how the treatment was implemented that might be different from the manual description or not be contained therein. Vinnars et al.'s description also contains information on the exposure quantity (40 treatment sessions) and the time span of the treatment (about 1 calendar year).

Equally important is the researchers' description of the comparison group:

> The comparison group was intended to be a naturalistic treatment as usual for PD patients. The basic psychotherapeutic training of these clinicians was psycho-analytically oriented, and they received supervision from a psychoanalyst during the study period. They were not provided with any clinical guidelines on how to treat their patients. They chose their own preferred treatments and had the free-dom to determine the focus of the treatment, its frequency, and when to termi-nate treatment. However, it was quite clear that the predominant orientation of all but one therapist was psychodynamic. This reinforced our conclusion that this trial involved the comparison of two psychodynamic treatments, one manualized and time limited and one nonmanualized. (Vinnars et al., 2009, p. 365)

In much evaluation research conducted in naturalistic settings, the comparison group often receives "treatment as usual." Many times, this creates a problem for readers and potential replicators of the study findings because they have no way of knowing exactly what the comparison treatment was. The revealed effect of a treatment—the differences between it and its comparator on the outcome variables—is as much dependent on what it is being compared to as on what effect the treatment had. After all, even the effect of different perfume labels depends on both labels (*roses* vs. *manure* as opposed to *roses* vs. *daisies*). If your control group receives treatment as usual, consider in your research design how you will collect information on what usual treatment is. This may involve observing the control group and/or giving treatment deliverers and control group mem-bers additional questions about what they did or what happened to them. The important point is that just collecting the outcome variables from control group members typically will not be enough for you (and your readers) to interpret the meaning of any group differences you find. To address this problem, JARS explicitly asks for descriptions of the control groups and how they were treated. Vinnars et al. (2009) described this; be sure to do the same.

Vinnars et al. (2009) told readers that the aim of their study was "to explore the extent to which SEP can improve maladaptive personality functioning in patients with any PD from the *Diagnostic and Statistical Manual of Mental Disorders* (4th ed.; *DSM–IV*)" (p. 363). Thus, we might conclude that their aim was to gather data on the generalizability of the treatment's effectiveness.

Treatment Changes and Safety Monitoring

In your report of a clinical trial, include

- a description of any changes to the protocol during the course of the study, including all changes to the intervention, outcomes, and methods of analysis;
- a description of the data and safety monitoring board; and
- a description of any stopping rules.

It appears that in the Vinnars et al. (2009) study, there were no changes to the protocol once the study began. If there were, these would be reported in this section.

A *data and safety monitoring board* is an independent group of experts whose job it is to monitor the clinical trial to ensure the safety of the participants and the integrity of the data. The National Institutes of Health (NIH; 1998) have a policy about when and how a formal monitoring board should function:

> The establishment of the data safety monitoring boards (DSMBs) is required for multi-site clinical trials involving interventions that entail potential risk to the participants. The data and safety monitoring functions and oversight of such activities are distinct from the requirement for study review and approval by an Institutional Review Board (IRB).

The policy goes on to say that although all clinical trials need to be monitored, exactly how they are to be monitored depends on (a) the risks involved in the study and (b) the size and complexity of the study:

> Monitoring may be conducted in various ways or by various individuals or groups, depending on the size and scope of the research effort. These exist on a continuum from monitoring by the principal investigator or NIH program staff in a small phase I study to the establishment of an independent data and safety monitoring board for a large phase III clinical trial.

NIH also has rules regarding how monitoring boards should operate and when they are needed. Because the Vinnars et al. (2009) study was conducted in Sweden, they would have had to meet their country's requirements for safety and data integrity. We might conclude, because this was a relatively small study with minimal risk to participants, that the establishment of an independent group of experts to monitor the trial was not necessary. It is also the case that if your study is being conducted through a research center or institute, the organization may have an independent board that oversees many projects done under its auspices.

Stopping Rules

Clinical trials are instances in which stopping rules can play an important role in ensuring the safety of participants. If too many instances of defined adverse effects occur, the trial should be stopped. Similarly, if the treatment is showing strong and clear benefits to people, stopping the trial early may facilitate getting the treatment to people in need as soon as possible.

Treatment Fidelity

If your study involved a clinical trial, your report should include a description of

- the method and results regarding treatment deliverers' (e.g., therapists') adherence to the planned intervention protocol (e.g., therapy manual),
- the treatment deliverers' competence in implementing the planned intervention protocol, and
- whether participants followed treatment recommendations (e.g., Did they complete homework assignments if given? Did they practice activities assigned?).

Treatment fidelity refers to how reliably the treatment was administered to subjects. If the treatment was not administered the way it was intended—"by the book"—then it is hard to interpret what the active ingredients in the treatment were. The same is true if there was lots of variation in administration from one treatment deliverer to the next. Vinnars et al. (2009) took care to provide details on how the fidelity of their treatment administration was monitored and with what reliability:

> All therapy sessions were videotaped, and two trained raters evaluated adherence to the SEP method using an adherence/competence scale (Barber & Crits-Christoph, 1996; Barber, Krakauer, Calvo, Badgio, & Faude, 1997). The 7th session for each patient for whom we had recordings available was rated. The raters had a training period of 2 years and completed roughly 30 training tapes during this period. The scale includes three technique subscales: general therapeutic (non–SEP-specific interventions), supportive (interventions aimed at strengthening therapeutic alliance), and interpretative–expressive (primarily CCRT [Core Conflictual Relationship Theme] specific interventions). Intraclass correlations for the two independent raters' adherence ratings were calculated and found to be good in the current sample (general therapeutic techniques .81, supportive techniques .76, and expressive techniques .81). (p. 365)

Treatment Deliverers

In the Vinnars et al. (2009) study, the experimental and comparison interventions were delivered by psychotherapists. So as JARS recommends, the researchers paid careful attention in their Method section to the professional training of these treatment deliverers:

> Six psychologists conducted the SEP, and 21 clinicians performed the CDPT treatment. Three senior SEP therapists, with more than 20 years of experience in psychiatry and dynamic psychotherapy, had trained the remaining SEP therapists, whose experience varied from 1 to 10 years. The three senior SEP therapists had received their training in both SEP and the use of the adherence/competence rating scale . . . by the developers of the treatment. The training cases of these three·therapists were translated into English and rated by adherence raters at the University of Pennsylvania Center for Psychotherapy Research until they reached acceptable adherence levels to start training the other SEP therapists and adherence raters in Sweden.
>
> The CDPT clinicians had a mean experience of 12.5 years in psychiatry and dynamic psychotherapy. All therapists except one had at least 1 year of full-time formal postgraduate training in dynamic psychotherapy consistent with a psychotherapist certification. They all received weekly psychodynamic psychotherapy supervision prior to and during the study. Within the public health care system, dynamic therapists tend to emphasize supportive techniques when dealing with patients with severe pathology. The CDPT group included two psychiatrists who had three patients in treatment, six psychologists who had 13 patients in treatment, five psychiatric nurses who had 42 patients in treatment, six psychiatric social workers who had 16 patients in treatment, and two psychiatric nurses' assistants who had two patients in treatment. All therapists were unaware of the specific hypotheses. (p. 365)

Vinnars et al. (2009) discussed the training of therapists in the comparison group when they described the treatment itself:

> Although the manualized SEP was time limited, CDPT was open ended. That is, the research team did not determine the length of treatment in the CDPT group. However, this did not mean that all CDPT patients received long-term therapy. In fact, the mean number of total treatment sessions attended between pretreatment and the 1-year follow-up assessment did not differ between the two groups (Mann–Whitney $U = 2,994.00$, $p < .87$). On average, SEP patients received 26 sessions ($SD = 15.2$, $Mdn = 30$, range $= 0–78$) and CDPT patients received 28 sessions ($SD = 23.7$, $Mdn = 22$, range $= 0–101$). Even when one focuses only on the time between the pretreatment and posttreatment assessments, the SEP patients had a mean of 25 ($SD = 13.0$, $Mdn = 30$, range $= 0–40$) sessions in contrast to 22 sessions for the CDPT patients ($SD = 15.5$, $Mdn = 21$, range $= 0–61$), respectively (Mann–Whitney $U = 2,638.00$, $p < .19$). (pp. 365–366)

Activities to Increase Compliance or Adherence

Vinnars et al. (2009) said that subjects were recruited from two community mental health centers and had either applied to take part themselves or been referred for treatment. They had a compliance issue because subjects in the SEP condition entered into contracts before the treatment began but CDPT subjects did not. Here is how they reported on the problem:

> Treatment Attendance
>
> As the nonmanualized treatment, by its nature, did not have a protocol on which treatment contracts were agreed, the definition of dropouts for this condition was complicated. To solve the attendance issue, we collected session data from patients' medical records. Treatment attendance was classified into (a) regular once a week (SEP = 52, 65.0%; CDPT = 43, 56.6%); (b) irregular, that is, less frequent than once a week, including an inability to keep regular appointments scheduled once a week (SEP = 16, 20.0%; CDPT = 17, 22.4%); or (c) no treatment, that is, not attending more than two sessions after randomization (SEP = 12, 15.0%; CDPT = 16, 21.1%). No significant difference was found between the two treatments in terms of attendance, $\chi^2(2) = 1.35$, $p < .51$. (Vinnars et al., 2009, p. 366)

Methods of Concealment

If you were enrolling subjects in Vinnars et al.'s (2009) study of SEP therapy versus treatment as usual, you would not want to steer people in or out of one group or the other on the basis of whether you felt the subject would benefit from the experimental treatment. This is why Vinnars et al. reported both that "patients were randomized using a computerized stratification randomization procedure" (p. 368) and that "participants were consecutively recruited from two community mental health centers" (p. 364). The word *consecutively* indicates that subjects were screened only on whether they had a personality disorder and the other prespecified inclusion and exclusion criteria; the enroller had no personal leeway in deciding whom to invite into the study and into which condition. Similarly, who generates the assignment sequence, who enrolls subjects, and who assigns subjects to groups needs to be reported in experiments in which some form of bias in recruiting and assignment might creep into the process at each of these time points.

Research Design

> If you are reporting a clinical trial, your report should provide a rationale for the length of follow-up assessment.

Vinnars et al. (2009) did not provide an explicit rationale for their timing of measurements. However, the intervals they chose are easily defended on the basis of the type of clinical intervention they were testing. Interestingly, these researchers encountered an ethical issue with regard to treatment and assessments that deserves mention:

> Because the comparison condition was not a time-limited treatment, patients could still conceivably be in treatment at the time that SEP patients were in posttreatment and follow-up. The questionnaires were filled out at the CMHCs in connection with the assessment interviews. Twenty-nine patients (38.2%) in the CDPT condition and 13 patients (16.3%) in the SEP group were still in treatment during the follow-up phase. Ethical protocols for this study allowed patients who were still under considerable distress to continue SEP treatment. As a result, there were still a number of patients in SEP treatment during follow-up. (p. 366)

Thus, for ethical reasons, the treatment for subjects with personality disorders did not stop when the clinical trial was over.

Now that we have covered the major research designs and statistical analyses that psychological researchers use, we need to look at what your readers will need you to report in your Discussion section so they can make sense of your findings.

Appendix 6.1:
Additional Journal Article Reporting Standards for Longitudinal Studies, Replication Studies, Studies With One Subject or Unit, and Clinical Trials

■ **Table A6.1.** Reporting Standards for Longitudinal Studies (in Addition to Material Presented in Table A1.1)

Paper section and topic	Description
General reporting expectation	
Sample characteristics (when appropriate)	Describe reporting (sampling or randomization) unit—individual, dyad, family, classroom: • *N* per group, age, and sex distribution • Ethnic composition • Socioeconomic status, home language, immigrant status, education level, and family characteristics • Country, region, city, and geographic characteristics.
Sample recruitment and retention methods	
Attrition	Report attrition at each wave, breaking down reasons for attrition. Report any differential attrition by major sociodemographic characteristics and experimental condition.
Additional sample description	Report any contextual changes for participants (units) as the study progressed (school closures or mergers, major economic changes; for long-term studies, major social changes that may need explanation for contemporary readers to understand the context of the study during its early years).
Method and measurement	Specify independent variables and dependent variables at each wave of data collection. Report the years in which each wave of the data collection occurred.

■ **Table A6.1.** (*Continued*)

Paper section and topic	Description
Missing data	Report the amount of missing data and how issues of missing data were handled analytically.
Analysis	Specify analytic approaches used and assumptions made in performing these analyses.
Multiple publications	Provide information on where any portions of the data have been previously published and the degree of overlap with the current report.

Note. Adapted from "Journal Article Reporting Standards for Quantitative Research in Psychology: The APA Publications and Communications Board Task Force Report," by M. Appelbaum, H. Cooper, R. B. Kline, E. Mayo-Wilson, A. M. Nezu, and S. M. Rao, 2018, *American Psychologist*, *73*, p. 14. Copyright 2018 by the American Psychological Association.

■ **Table A6.2.** Reporting Standards for Replication Studies (in Addition to Material Presented in Table A1.1)

Paper section and topic	Description
Study type	Report sufficient information both in the study title and, more important, in the text to allow the reader to determine whether the study is a direct (exact, literal) replication, approximate replication, or conceptual (construct) replication. Indicate whether a replication study has conditions, materials, or procedures that were not part of the original study. Describe these new features, where in the study they occur, and their potential impact on the results. Report indications of treatment fidelity for both the original study and the replication study.
Participants	Compare the recruitment procedures in the original and replication studies. Note and explain major variations in how the participants were selected, such as whether the replication study was conducted in a different setting (e.g., country or culture) or whether the allocation of participants to groups or conditions was different. Describe implications of these variations for the results. Compare the demographic characteristics of the participants in both studies. If the units of analysis are not people (cases), such as classrooms, then report the appropriate descriptors of their characteristics.

(table continues)

▨ **Table A6.2.** (*Continued*)

Paper section and topic	Description
Instrumentation	Report instrumentation, including both hardware (apparatus) and soft measures used to collect data, such as questionnaires, structured interviews, or psychological tests. Clarify in appropriate subsections of the Method section any major differences between the original and replication studies.
	Indicate whether questionnaires or psychological tests were translated to another language, and specify the methods used, such as back-translation, to verify that the translation was accurate.
	Report psychometric characteristics of the scores analyzed in the replication study and compare these properties with those in the original study.
	Specify and compare the informants and methods of administration across the two studies. The latter includes the setting for testing, such as individual versus group administration, and the method of administration, such as paper and pencil or online.
Analysis	Report results of the same analytical methods (statistical or other quantitative manipulations) used. Results from additional or different analyses may also be reported.
	State the statistical criteria for deciding whether the original results were replicated in the new study. Examples of criteria include statistical significance testing, effect sizes, confidence intervals, and Bayes factors in Bayesian methods.
	Explain decision rules when multiple criteria, such as significance testing with effect size estimation, are employed. State whether the effect size in a power analysis was specified to equal that reported in the original study (conditional power) or whether power was averaged over plausible values of effect size on the basis of an estimated standard error (predictive power), which takes account of sampling error.

Note. Adapted from "Journal Article Reporting Standards for Quantitative Research in Psychology: The APA Publications and Communications Board Task Force Report," by M. Appelbaum, H. Cooper, R. B. Kline, E. Mayo-Wilson, A. M. Nezu, and S. M. Rao, 2018, *American Psychologist, 73*, p. 17. Copyright 2018 by the American Psychological Association.

▓ **Table A6.3.** Reporting Standards for *N*-of-1 Studies (in Addition to Material Presented in Table A1.1)

Paper section and topic	Description
Design	Describe the design, including • Design type (e.g., withdrawal–reversal, multiple baseline, alternating treatments, changing criterion, some combination thereof, or adaptive design) • Phases and phase sequence (whether determined a priori or data driven) and, if applicable, criteria for phase changes.
Type of design	
Procedural changes	Describe any procedural changes that occurred during the course of the investigation after the start of the study.
Replication	Describe any planned replication.
Randomization	State whether randomization was used, and if so, describe the randomization method and the elements of the study that were randomized (e.g., during which phases treatment and control conditions were instituted).
Analysis	
Sequence completed	Report for each participant the sequence actually completed, including the number of trials for each session for each case. State when participants who did not complete the sequence stopped and the reason for stopping.
Outcomes and estimation	Report results for each participant, including raw data for each target behavior and other outcomes.

Note. Adapted from "Journal Article Reporting Standards for Quantitative Research in Psychology: The APA Publications and Communications Board Task Force Report," by M. Appelbaum, H. Cooper, R. B. Kline, E. Mayo-Wilson, A. M. Nezu, and S. M. Rao, 2018, *American Psychologist*, *73*, p. 16. Copyright 2018 by the American Psychological Association.

Table A6.4. Reporting Standards for Studies Involving Clinical Trials (in Addition to Material Presented in Table A1.1)

Paper section and topic	Description
Title page	State whether the trial was registered prior to implementation.
Abstract	State whether the trial was registered. If so, state where and include the registration number.
	Describe the public health implications of trial results.
Introduction	State the rationale for evaluating specific interventions for a given clinical problem, disorder, or variable.
	Describe the approach, if any, to assess mediators and moderators of treatment effects.
	Describe potential public health implications of the study.
	State how results from the study can advance knowledge in this area.
Method	
Participant characteristics	State the methods of ascertaining how participants met all inclusion and exclusion criteria, especially if assessing clinical diagnoses.
Sampling procedures	Provide details regarding similarities and differences in data collection locations if a multisite study.
Measures	State whether clinical assessors were
	• Involved in providing treatment for studies involving clinical assessments
	• Aware or unaware of assignment to a condition at post-treatment and follow-up assessments; if unaware, how was this accomplished?
Experimental interventions	Report whether the study protocol was publicly available (e.g., published) prior to enrolling participants and if so, where and when.
	Describe how intervention in this study differed from the "standard" approach in order to tailor it to a new population (e.g., differing age, ethnicity, comorbidity).
	Describe any materials (e.g., clinical handouts, data recorders) provided to participants and how information about them can obtained (e.g., URL address).
	Describe any changes to the protocol during the course of the study, including all changes to the intervention, outcomes, and methods of analysis.
	Describe involvement of the data and safety monitoring board.
	Describe any stopping rules.

■ **Table A6.4.** (*Continued*)

Paper section and topic	Description
Treatment fidelity	Describe method and results regarding treatment deliverers' (e.g., therapists') adherence to the planned intervention protocol (e.g., therapy manual).
	Describe method and results regarding treatment deliverers' competence in implementing the planned intervention protocol.
	Describe (if relevant) method and results regarding whether participants (i.e., treatment recipients) understood and followed treatment recommendations (e.g., did they comprehend what the treatment was intended to do, complete homework assignments if given, and/or practice activities assigned outside of the treatment setting?).
	Describe any additional methods used to enhance treatment fidelity.
Research design	Provide rationale for length of follow-up assessment.
Results	Describe how treatment fidelity (i.e., therapist adherence and competence ratings) and participant adherence were related to intervention outcome.
	Describe method of assessing clinical significance, including whether the threshold for clinical significance was prespecified (e.g., as part of a publicly available protocol).
	Identify possible differences in treatment effects attributable to intervention deliverers.
	Describe possible differences in treatment effects attributable to the data collection site if a multisite study.
	Describe results of analyses of moderation and mediation effects, if tested.
	Explain why the study was discontinued, if appropriate.
	Describe the frequency and type of adverse effects that occurred (or state that none occurred).
Discussion	Describe how this study advances knowledge about the intervention, clinical problem, and population.

Note. Adapted from "Journal Article Reporting Standards for Quantitative Research in Psychology: The APA Publications and Communications Board Task Force Report," by M. Appelbaum, H. Cooper, R. B. Kline, E. Mayo-Wilson, A. M. Nezu, and S. M. Rao, 2018, *American Psychologist, 73*, pp. 12–13. Copyright 2018 by the American Psychological Association.

7

Interpreting Your Results: The Discussion Section

Now that you have provided your readers with a thorough rendering of the mechanics of your study and the results of your statistical analyses, it is time to tell them what you think it all means. The Journal Article Reporting Standards (JARS; Appelbaum et al., 2018) recommends including several important elements. First, you must summarize what you found by telling readers which results were most important and which were secondary. You do not need to label them in this way (e.g., by having subsections called Primary Findings and Secondary Findings), although it would be OK to do so. You make the importance of your different results clear by when, how, and in what depth you choose to discuss them. In your fragrance labeling study, if your interest was primarily theoretical, you might spend considerable time detailing and interpreting what you found on the measures related to the fragrance's pleasantness, but you might mention only briefly how the label affected buying intentions. If you had more applied motives for doing the study, the two types of measures might get equal attention. Some secondary findings (reported in the Results section) might hardly be mentioned, however compelled you may feel to explain everything.

Also, in the Discussion section you interpret your findings in light of the issues that motivated you to do the study in the first place, as described in your introduction. State how you think your study advances knowledge on these issues. For example, in the fragrance labeling study, what do you know about labeling effects that you did not know before? If you cannot answer this question, your study may not be of great interest to others.

Finally, cast an evaluative eye on your own work, taking a step back and looking at both its strengths and weaknesses. This permits you to propose the next steps that will advance the field.

http://dx.doi.org/10.1037/0000103-007

Reporting Quantitative Research in Psychology: How to Meet APA Style Journal Article Reporting Standards, Second Edition, by H. Cooper

It is typical for the Discussion section to begin with a recap of the rationale for the study. You should be able to return to the introduction, find the sentences you wrote there, and rephrase these at the beginning of the Discussion. For example, O'Neill, Vandenberg, DeJoy, and Wilson (2009) began their Discussion section with two simple sentences meant to remind readers of the broad agenda that motivated their research:

> The goal of the current study was to extend organizational support theory through an examination of anger in the workplace. We first examined whether anger was an antecedent or a consequence of employees' perceptions of conditions or events in the workplace. (p. 330)

Adank, Evans, Stuart-Smith, and Scott (2009) did the same:

> The purpose of the present study was to determine the relative processing cost of comprehending speech in an unfamiliar native accent under adverse listening conditions. As this processing cost could not always be reliably estimated in quiet listening conditions . . ., we investigated the interaction between adverse listening conditions and sentences in an unfamiliar native accent in two experiments. (p. 527)

A quick summary serves as a simple reminder of your purpose. After the detailed Method and Results sections, it is good to draw your readers' attention back to the big issues. That said, you should realize that readers will have different levels of interest in your article and will read different sections with different levels of care and attention. Do not feel insulted if I suggest that some readers will skip the Method and Results sections entirely (after you worked on them so hard!) or just skim them quickly and move directly from reading your introduction to reading your Discussion section. For these readers, the brief summary at the beginning of the Discussion section will sound a lot like what they read at the end of your introduction. That is OK. If you consider that different readers will read different chunks of your article, it makes sense to help keep them all on track.

Statement About the Primary Hypotheses

In your report, your Discussion section should include a statement of

- support or nonsupport for all original hypotheses distinguished by primary and secondary hypotheses and
- the implications of exploratory analyses, including
  - substantive findings and
  - potential error rates.

After the restatement of the goals for your research, JARS recommends that you provide a summary statement of your principal findings. Not every finding should be included, just the ones that support or refute your major hypotheses. These findings should be the focus of the discussion that follows. You can return to findings that help you explain your principal findings or that are of secondary interest later in the Discussion section. For example, O'Neill et al. (2009) immediately followed their two-sentence restatement of goals with a two-sentence recap of what they considered to be their major finding:

> Although a negative reciprocal relationship between anger and POS [perceived organizational support] was hypothesized, only the negative relationship from POS to anger was supported. The relationship of POS and anger lends support to the social exchange perspective; anger seems to result from employees' negative perceptions of workplace conditions rather than anger serving as a filter for negative perceptions of the organization, as suggested by affect-as-information and mood congruency theories. (p. 330)

Note that O'Neill et al. pointed out that they had hypothesized a reciprocal relationship but did not find it. They also said that their finding supported one theoretical interpretation of the data but not two others. This is a perfect way to set up the more detailed discussion that follows.

Fagan, Palkovitz, Roy, and Farrie (2009) were also relatively brief in summing up their findings:

> The findings of this study are consistent with our hypothesis suggesting that risk and resilience factors of low-income, urban fathers who are unmarried and not residing with the mother and baby at birth, later nonresidence with the child, and mother–father relationship quality are significant components of an ecological model of paternal engagement with young children. (pp. 1398–1399)

This simple categorical statement of support is then followed by three pages of summary and interpretation of the findings.

Risen and Gilovich (2008) also began with a succinct summary of their findings:

> Despite explicit knowledge that tempting fate does not change the likelihood of a broad range of negative outcomes, participants gave responses that reflected the intuitive belief that it does. Thus, even if they rationally recognized that there is no mechanism to make rain more likely when they leave behind an umbrella . . . participants reported that they thought these particular negative outcomes were indeed more likely following such actions. (p. 303)

However, two sentences are not the limit for how long the summary should be. Goldinger, He, and Papesh (2009) went into a bit more detail about their findings regarding other-race bias (ORB) in their opening summation:

> Having observed the ORB in recognition, we, as our primary goal, sought to examine information-gathering behavior during learning. Considering first eye movements, widespread differences emerged between own- and cross-race face processing. In quantitative terms, when participants studied own-race faces, their eye fixations were brief and plentiful. Relative to cross-race trials, own-race trials elicited more fixations to facial features, briefer gaze times per

> fixation, more fixations to unique features, and fewer regressions. All these findings were reflected in an index of total distance traveled by the eyes during encoding, which we used for most analyses. The differences in eye movements were not an artifact of recognition accuracy: The same patterns were observed in subsets of learning trials leading only to eventual hits. In qualitative terms, participants favored different features across races (see Figures 2 and 8). (p. 1120)

Goldinger et al. (2009) chose to mention each of their primary measures in the summary, whereas authors of the earlier examples chose more general statements of support and nonsupport. Which approach you take should be determined by how consistent findings are across measures (can you quickly mention them in groups, or will you lose readers in the details?) and how much attention you intend to pay to each outcome measure separately.

These four examples present the happy news that the authors' primary hypotheses largely were confirmed by the data. But the opening summary is not always a bed of roses; sometimes the manure is evident. Evers, Brouwers, and Tomic (2006) had to contend with a deeper level of nonsupport for their primary hypotheses. First, though, they also began with a brief restatement of purpose and research design:

> In the present article, we examined the question of whether management coaching might be effective. To this end, we conducted a quasi-experiment in which we compared an experimental group of managers with a control group at Time 1 and Time 2. We measured hypothesized outcome expectations and self-efficacy beliefs on three domains of behavior, for example, acting in a balanced way, setting one's own goals, and mindful living and working. (Evers et al., 2006, p. 179)

However, things did not turn out exactly as they had hoped:

> We found a significant difference between the experimental and the control group on only outcome expectations and not on self-efficacy beliefs regarding the domain "acting in a balanced way." (Evers et al., 2006, p. 179)

Thus, Evers et al. did not get exactly the results they had expected. Still, they provided a reasonable post hoc explanation for why this might have been the case; the intervention simply did not have time to effect all the changes they had expected:

> These objectives clearly show that improving existing skills and developing new ones precede new beliefs, convictions, and judgments, which may explain the nonsignificance of differences between the experimental and the control groups with respect to the variable "to act in a balanced way." In the short time between measuring the variable at Time 1 and Time 2, self-efficacy beliefs with respect to "acting in a balanced way" may not have developed yet. It may also be that managers have come to the conviction that some specific type of behavior will be advantageous but that they still experience some inner feelings of resistance toward getting rid of their old behavior. (Evers et al., 2006, p. 180)

Adank et al. (2009) delved a bit deeper into the nuances of their listening comprehension findings and the relationship of these findings to past research. Of their primary hypotheses, they wrote the following:

> The results for the GE [Glasgow English] listener group in Experiment 1 showed that they made an equal number of errors and responded equally fast for both accents. The finding that the performance of the GE listeners was not affected by the accent of the speaker confirms that the processing delay for the GE sentences by the SE [Standard English] listener group was due to the relative unfamiliarity of the SE listeners with the Glaswegian accent. SE listeners thus benefited from their relative familiarity with SE. (p. 527)

In summary, your Discussion section should commence with a restatement of your goals and a summary of your findings that relate to those goals. You do not have to list every finding. However, JARS recommends that you present a complete picture of the findings that relate to your primary hypotheses, regardless of whether they were supportive. If you found unsupportive results, try to explain why.

Finally, the introductory paragraphs to your Discussion section can also briefly mention the results of any exploratory analyses you might have conducted. It would be OK for you to use these results to flesh out any theoretical explanations you have for why you obtained the results you did. Of course, because these were exploratory analyses, ones for which you had no explicit predictions, these results need to be labeled as such and readers alerted to interpret them with caution; they are more likely to have appeared by chance. It is also not unusual for authors to return to the results of exploratory analyses when they discuss directions for future research (discussed below) and suggest that the findings need replication and more precise testing in the next round of research.

Comparisons With the Work of Others

> In your Discussion section, delineate similarities and differences between your results and the work of others.

Adank et al. (2009) highlighted the importance of an interaction between listening comprehension and amount of background noise. This led them directly into a discussion of how their work compared with the work of others:

> No effects were found for processing the unfamiliar native accent in quiet. This result shows again that the cognitive processing cost cannot easily be estimated in quiet conditions (cf. Floccia et al., 2006). However, in both experiments, an interaction was found between the unfamiliar accent and moderately poor SNRs [signal-to-noise ratios] . . . listeners slow down considerably for these SNRs for the unfamiliar accent. A similar interaction has been found in experiments comparing the processing speed for synthetic versus natural speech (e.g., Pisoni et al., 1985). In conclusion, it seems justified to assume

that processing an unfamiliar native accent in noise is delayed compared with processing a familiar native accent in noise. (Adank et al., p. 527)

Note that Adank et al. compared their results with the work of others in two different ways, both of which were consistent with their findings. Their first reference to another study is used to suggest that others' research confirms their finding. Essentially, Adank et al. replicated this earlier result. The second reference to another study also suggests a replication, but here the earlier study varied from their study in an important way in that it compared processing speed between natural and synthetic speech rather than two accents of the same language.

Of course, your comparison with past research will not always indicate congruency between your results and the interpretations of other studies. Indeed, you might have undertaken your study to demonstrate that a past finding was fallacious or cannot be obtained under certain circumstances. Adank et al. (2009) pointed out an inconsistency of the former type between their results and past findings:

On the basis of Evans and Iverson's results, one could hypothesize that familiarity with a native accent does not come from being exposed to it through the media alone but that interaction with speakers of that accent (or even adapting one's own speech to that accent) is also required. However, our results do not provide support for this hypothesis, as GE listeners were equally fast for GE and SE. The GE listeners had been born and raised in Glasgow, and although they were highly familiar with SE through the media, they had had little experience of interacting with SE speakers on a regular basis. (p. 527)

Risen and Gilovich (2008) also pointed out how their findings contradicted some explanations for superstitious behavior:

Although most traditional accounts of superstition maintain that such beliefs exist because people lack certain cognitive capacities (Frazer, 1922; Levy-Bruhl, 1926; Piaget, 1929; Tylor, 1873), the work presented here adds to accumulating evidence of magical thinking on the part of people who, according to traditional accounts, should not hold such beliefs. (p. 303)

In summary, JARS recommends that you place your work in the context of earlier work. You can cite work that your study replicates and extends, but you should also include work with results or predictions at odds with your own. In this regard, if your fragrance labeling study showed that when the fragrance was labeled *rose* it was rated as more pleasant than when labeled *manure*, it would be perfectly appropriate for you to point out that this finding was in conflict with the assertion by Juliet Capulet.[1] When you do this, you should propose reasons why the contradictions may have occurred.

---

[1]Sorry, Juliet (see Collins, 1977; Kohli, Harich, & Leuthesser, 2005).

Interpretation of Results

In your Discussion section, your interpretation of the results should take into account

- sources of potential bias and other threats to internal and statistical validity,
- imprecision of measures,
- overall number of tests or overlap among tests, and
- adequacy of sample sizes and sampling validity.

JARS focuses its prescription for what to include in the interpretation of results on aspects of the research design and analyses that limit your ability to draw confident conclusions from your study. This is not because your Discussion section should focus on only the study's limitations but because you may be tempted to disregard these and to promote your research by discussing only its strengths. Typically, this strategy does not work. Your manuscript will get a careful reading once it has been submitted for peer review. If you do not point out your study's weaknesses, the peer reviewers will. Those who will read your work know every study has flaws; it is impossible to conduct a flawless study. By being transparent about what you know was not perfect, you convey to the reader a scientific posture that puts your article in a better light. By turning a critical eye on your own work, you instill confidence in your readers that you know what you are doing.

Strengths of the Study

That said, even though JARS focuses on weaknesses, do not forget to point out your study's strengths. For example, Taylor and James (2009) began their discussion of biomarkers for substance dependence (SD) with a positive assertion about their findings:

> SD is a common and costly disorder, and efforts to uncover its etiology are under way on several fronts. . . . Other work has shown promise for ERM [electrodermal response modulation] as an independent marker for SD, and the present study provides initial evidence of the possible specificity of ERM as a putative biomarker for SD. This could enhance the search for underlying genetic factors and neural pathways that are associated not with externalizing disorders generally but with SD more specifically. (p. 496)

Moller, Forbes-Jones, and Hightower (2008), who studied the effects of the age composition of classrooms on preschoolers' cognitive, motor, and social skills, began their General Discussion section with a strong statement of what was best about their work:

> This investigation represents a unique and important contribution to the literature on preschool classroom age composition in a number of respects. First, the study included a sample far larger than that in any previously conducted research. . . . Second, this research is among the first to use a well-validated assessment of early childhood development (i.e., the COR [Child Observation Record]) in a

variety of domains (social, motor, and cognitive) and to include assessments at two time points (spaced approximately 6 months apart). (p. 748)

So "This study was the first . . . the biggest . . . the best" are all good ways to think about your study's strengths. But neither Taylor and James (2009) nor Moller et al. (2008) stopped there. They also described some of the less positive aspects of their work.

Limitations or Weaknesses of the Study

If your study drew its inspiration from theories or problems that posited causal relationships among variables but your research design had some limitations in allowing such inferences, JARS recommends that this be acknowledged. For example, Moller et al. (2008) included the following acknowledgment in their discussion:

> Another limitation of this research involves the correlational nature of these data. Empirical investigations that manipulate the age composition of preschool classrooms, with random assignment to condition, are warranted. (p. 750)

Fagan et al. (2009) put this same concern about internal validity in proximity to their strongest interpretation of their study:

> Our findings suggest that as time passes, risk and resilience factors continue to play a significant role in relation to paternal engagement. Furthermore, our findings reveal that the patterns of interrelatedness between risk, resilience, and engagement (direct and mediating effects) are the same when the child is 3 years old as they are when the child is 1. Although causal relationships cannot be inferred from our analyses, our approach to measuring risk and resilience in fathers is an improvement to previous research. (p. 1399)

O'Neill et al. (2009) acknowledged a similar weakness in internal validity that was due to their research design:

> The design of the study precludes drawing causal inferences at the individual level of analysis. Hence, a stronger test of these relationships is needed, particularly in light of potential reciprocity between POS and anger. (p. 330)

If your research design did not allow for strong causal inferences, it is also critical that you avoid the use of causal language in the interpretation of your results. For example, if you correlated the positivity of people's reactions to perfume names with their evaluation of the fragrance itself, avoid using terms such as *caused*, *produced*, or *affected* that suggest your study uncovered a causal connection between labels and fragrance evaluations. It is easy to slip up on this matter because we all use causal language in everyday conversation without being consciously aware of doing so.

In addition to their caution about internal validity, O'Neill et al. (2009) alerted their readers to some concerns about their measurements:

> A final limitation is that our anger measure did not capture feelings of anger specifically directed toward the organization or its members. In this way,

our conceptual model is not perfectly aligned with the operational definitions of the variables. (p. 331)

Generalizability

In your Discussion section, your interpretation of your results should discuss the generalizability (external validity) of the findings, taking into account

- the target population (sample validity) and
- other contextual issues, such as the settings, measurement characteristics, time, or ecological validity

---

JARS addresses limitations related to internal validity, measurement, and statistics in one section. It gives a separate treatment to concerns about the generalization of findings. Evaluating the generalizability of your study's findings involves you in at least three different assessments.

First, you need to consider the people or other units involved in the study in comparison with the larger target population they are meant to represent—the validity of the sample. I discussed the importance of circumscribing these boundaries in Chapter 3. Now it is time to address the issue head on and attempt to answer the questions I set out: Are the people in the study in some way a restricted subsample of the target population? If they are, do the restrictions suggest that the results pertain to some but not all members of the target population?

Second, generalization across people is only one domain you must consider. As noted in JARS, other contextual variations should be considered. If your study involved an experimental manipulation, you need to ask how the way the manipulation was operationalized in your study might be different from how it would be experienced in a natural setting. Was there something unique about the settings of your study that suggests similar or dissimilar results might be obtained in other settings? Could being in a psychology lab while choosing between two fragrances with different labels lead to a greater focus on the fragrance name than would making the same choice while standing at a perfume counter with dozens of fragrances in a large department store?

A third assessment involves considering whether the outcome variables you used in your study are a good representation of all the outcomes that might be of interest. For example, if you measured only subjects' preference for a fragrance, does this preference generalize to buying intentions?

Our example studies provide instances in which the researchers grappled with each of these types of generalizations. Taylor and James (2009) provided the following cautions regarding the generalization of their findings across people:

> Although the present study holds promise in helping move research into biological factors associated with SD forward, it had limitations that warrant mention. First, the PD [personality disorder]-only group was difficult to fill given the high comorbidity of PD with SD, and the results for that relatively small group should not be overinterpreted. Second, the sample comprised college

students, and it is possible that a clinical sample with more extreme presentations of PD and SD could produce different results. (p. 497)

Here, Taylor and James expressed two concerns about generalization across people. First, they wanted readers to know that people with PD but without SD were rare—the sample was small, so be careful in drawing conclusions about them. Second, they pointed out that the study used only college students, so even the people who were identified as having SD or PD were probably less extreme on these characteristics than were people seeking clinical treatment, and thus, making generalizations to more extreme populations should be done with caution.

Amir et al. (2009) addressed the issues of generalization of their attention training intervention to combat social phobia across people and settings:

> The finding that similar treatment outcomes were obtained within the current study at separate sites with differing demographic profiles, as well as in an independent laboratory . . ., supports the generalizability of the attention modification program across settings. (p. 969)

However, the stimuli used in their attention training also led them to appraise the generalizability of results:

> Although the training stimuli used in the current study included faces conveying signs of disgust, there is evidence to suggest that disgust-relevant stimuli activate brain regions also implicated in the processing of other emotional stimuli such as fear. (Amir et al., 2009, p. 969)

Even Killeen, Sanabria, and Dolgov (2009), whose study focused on as basic a process as response conditioning and extinction and used pigeons as subjects, had to grapple with the issue of generalization, in this case across behaviors:

> A limitation of the current analysis is its focus on one well-prepared response, appetitive key pecking in the pigeon. The relative importance of operant and respondent control will vary substantially depending on the response system studied. (p. 467)

As a final example, Fagan et al. (2009) pointed out a limitation of their study related to generalization across time:

> Although the . . . data provide one of the most comprehensive views of this population over time, the operationalized measures provide snapshots of fathers at the time of measurement, and we are attempting to understand the processes and development of father–child relationships across time. (p. 1403)

The overall message to be taken from my discussion of the JARS recommendations about treatment of the limitations of your study is that you should not be afraid to state what these limitations are. Here, I have only sampled from the example studies; there were many more mentions of flaws and limits I did not reproduce. Still, all of these studies got published in top journals in their field. Again, adopting a critical posture toward your own work speaks well of you and instills confidence in readers that you understood what you were doing. The advancement of knowledge was your first priority.

Implications

> In your Discussion section, your interpretation of the findings should discuss your study's implications for future research, program development and implementation, and policy making.

Your final task in the Discussion section involves detailing what you think are the implications of your findings for theory, practice, policy, and future research. Which of these areas is emphasized most depends on the purposes of your study. However, it is not impossible that all four will deserve mention. For example, Moller et al. (2008) included a Theoretical Implications subsection in their Discussion section:

> The findings from the present investigation strongly support the theory-based predictions offered by Piaget (1932) and others, who argued that interacting with peers who are close in age and ability will result in optimal learning. At the same time, these findings are not entirely inconsistent with predictions offered by Vygotsky (1930/1978) and others, who argued for mixed-age interaction principally on the basis of the merits implicit for younger children in these contexts. (p. 749)

Moller et al. (2008) were equally if not more interested in the practical implications of their work. They began their discussion by stating the strong message of their study for how classroom age grouping should be carried out:

> We consistently observed a significant main effect at the classroom level for classroom age composition, which suggested that a wide range in children's ages within a classroom (and high standard deviations in terms of age) was negatively related to development. . . . In this context, the present research strongly suggests that reconsideration of the issue of classroom age composition in early childhood education is warranted. (Moller et al., 2008, p. 749)

O'Neill et al. (2009) thought their findings had an important lesson for organizations' policies and practices:

> The good news is that if an organization successfully influences employees' perceived organizational support, anger, withdrawal behaviors, accidents, and high-risk behaviors will decline. Anger reduction is particularly important for the organization, as highlighted by the costs in terms of employee turnover and loss of inventory. (p. 331)

Future Research

Researchers often joke that concluding a study with the call for more research is a requirement, lest the public lose sight of the value of their enterprise and the need to keep researchers employed. In fact, a study that solves a problem, whether theoretical or practical, once and for all is a rare occurrence indeed. The call for new research is always justified, and now you can cite JARS as giving you license to do so.

The limitations of a study will lead to suggestions for new research with improvements in design. So Moller et al. (2008) called for future experimental research, as noted earlier, because their study on classroom age grouping was correlational in design. Or the results of the study will suggest new questions that need answering. For example, Fagan et al. (2009) stated the agenda for future research in the form of questions in a subsection titled Future Research:

> The study raises questions regarding the importance of early adaptations of fathers during the transition to fatherhood. Why do some men experience impending fatherhood as a wake-up call to improve their lives by reducing risk and increasing developmental resources, whereas others seem to eschew the development of personal resources that would position them to be more engaged fathers? What are the specific meanings of fathering for men in challenging circumstances, and what are the processes and conditions that allow some men to make positive adjustments to their lives and become involved fathers? What is the role of birth mothers in facilitating and discouraging men's transitions within fathering? Are there interventions or policies that would increase the proportion of men who reduce risk and increase resilience during various transitions within fathering? (pp. 1403–1404)

Conclusions

Finally, you might consider ending your Discussion section with yet another recap of the study. For example, Tsaousides et al. (2009) finished their discussion with a conclusion section, which reads in its entirety as follows:

> The present findings highlight the importance of domain-specific and general self-efficacy in perceptions of QoL [quality of life]. Both study hypotheses were supported, as both employment-related and general self-efficacy were associated with perceptions of QoL and need attainment, and both were better predictors than traditionally important contributors such as income and employment. These findings were consistent with Cicerone and Azulay (2007) in terms of the importance of self-efficacy on well-being, and with Levack et al. (2004), Opperman (2004), and Tsaousides et al. (2008) in terms of the importance of subjective self-appraisals of employment in evaluating quality of life post-TBI [traumatic brain injury]. The clinical implications for professionals working in the field of rehabilitation are that increasing confidence in

work-related abilities and enhancing self-efficacy among individuals with TBI may facilitate return to work and will certainly have an impact on perceptions of well-being. (pp. 304–305)

This statement hits on almost all of the recommendations included in JARS, and it serves as a nice complement to the study's abstract for readers who do not wish to delve too deeply into the details.

Discussion of Studies With Experimental Manipulations

If your study involved an experimental manipulation, your Discussion section should include

- a summary of the results, taking into account the mechanism by which the manipulation or intervention was intended to work (causal pathways) or alternative mechanisms;
- the success of and barriers to implementing the experimental manipulation;
- the fidelity of how the manipulation was implemented;
- generalizability (external validity) of the findings, taking into account
  - the characteristics of the experimental manipulation,
  - how and what outcomes were measured,
  - the length of the follow-up if any,
  - incentives provided to subjects, and
  - compliance rates; and
- the theoretical or practical significance of outcomes and the basis for these interpretations.

If your study involved an experimental manipulation, JARS makes some other recommendations regarding issues that should be addressed in the Discussion section. First, JARS suggests you discuss the mechanisms that mediate the relationship between cause and effect. For example, how is it that different labels lead to different ratings of the same fragrance? Does it trigger positive or negative memories? Does it alter the length of time subjects inhale?

Amir et al. (2009) found evidence for the following causal mechanisms in their study of attention training:

Although accumulating evidence suggests that computerized attention training procedures are efficacious in reducing symptoms of anxiety in treatment-seeking samples, little is known about the attentional mechanisms underlying clinical improvement. . . . The results suggested that the AMP [attention modification program] facilitated participants' ability to disengage their attention from social threat cues from pre- to posttraining. (p. 970)

Thus, they suggested the AMP training made it easier for subjects to ignore cues of social threats (the mediating mechanism), which in turn led to reduced anxiety. However, they were careful to point out the limitations of their proposed explanation:

> The results of the mediation analysis, however, should be interpreted with caution, given that change in the putative mediator (attention bias) and change in social anxiety symptoms were assessed at the same time, and temporal precedence was therefore not established. Thus, although causal inferences can be made about change in attention resulting from the AMP, we cannot make such claims about the relation between change in attention and symptom change. (Amir et al., 2009, p. 970)

In addition, they used this limitation to call for future research:

> In future research, investigators should administer assessments of attention at multiple points during the course of treatment to better address these issues. (Amir et al., 2009, p. 970)

When your study involves the evaluation of an intervention, there can be unique aspects of the study related to the generalizability of the findings that need to be addressed in the Discussion section. For example, Amir et al. (2009) highlighted their use of a 4-month follow-up:

> Assessments completed approximately 4 months after completion of the postassessment revealed that participants maintained symptom reduction after completing the training, suggesting that the beneficial effects of the AMP were enduring (see also Schmidt et al., 2009). However, follow-up data should be interpreted with caution because assessors and participants were no longer blind to participant condition. Future research should investigate the long-term impact of the attention training procedure, including an assessment of symptoms as well as attention bias. (p. 969)

Vadasy and Sanders (2008) provided a discussion of the limitations of their study that almost directly paralleled the recommendations of JARS. First, the summary:

> The present study evaluated the direct and indirect effects of a supplemental, paraeducator-implemented repeated reading intervention (*Quick Reads*) with incidental word-level instruction for second and third graders with low fluency skill. Results show clearly that students benefited from this intervention in terms of word reading and fluency gains. Specifically, our models that tested for direct treatment effects indicated that tutored students had significantly higher pretest–posttest gains in word reading accuracy and fluency. (Vadasy & Sanders, 2008, pp. 281, 286)

Then, they addressed how their findings related to the work of others. Note how this excerpt also addresses some of the JARS recommendations regarding discussions of generalization (e.g., multiple outcomes, characteristics of the intervention including treatment fidelity), but here the authors pointed out the strengths of their study in this regard:

> This study specifically addressed limitations in previous research on repeated reading interventions. First, students were randomly assigned to conditions. (Vadasy & Sanders, 2008, p. 287)

They used multiple outcomes:

> Second, we considered multiple outcomes, including word reading accuracy and efficiency as well as fluency rate and comprehension outcomes. (Vadasy & Sanders, 2008, p. 287)

Their treatment was implemented with high fidelity, using the types of professionals likely to be used in real life and in the real-life setting:

> Third, because this was an efficacy trial, the intervention was implemented with a high degree of fidelity by paraeducators who were potential typical end users, and in school settings that reflected routine practice conditions. (Vadasy & Sanders, 2008, p. 287)[2]

Their treatment was well specified:

> Fourth, the 15-week intervention was considerably more intense than the repeated reading interventions described in many previous studies. Fifth, the particular repeated reading intervention, *Quick Reads*, is unusually well specified in terms of text features and reading procedures often hypothesized to influence fluency outcomes. (Vadasy & Sanders, 2008, p. 287)

Finally, they discussed some limitations. First, for theoretical interpretation, the intervention might not have involved reading instruction only:

> Findings from this study should be considered in light of several limitations. First, although the intervention used in this study was primarily characterized as repeated reading, a small portion (up to 5 min) of each of the tutoring sessions included incidental alphabetic instruction and word-level scaffolding. (Vadasy & Sanders, 2008, p. 287)

The characteristics of students may have been unique:

> Second, students entered this study with a wide range of pretest fluency levels that reflected teacher referral patterns; nevertheless, students ranged from the 10th to the 60th percentiles on PRF [passage reading fluency] performance, similar to students served in repeated reading programs. (Vadasy & Sanders, 2008, p. 287)

---

[2]An *efficacy trial* is an experiment that is undertaken to demonstrate that a particular intervention can have its intended effect. These are typically followed by *effectiveness trials* that are meant to show that the intervention effect can be produced under real-world conditions.

Note that Vadasy and Sanders here raised a possible shortcoming of their study that they then provided evidence to refute. This can be an important strategy for you to use: Think of concerns that might occur to your readers, raise them yourself, and provide your assessment of whether they are legitimate and why.

The classroom observations may have limited the researchers' ability to describe the causal mediating mechanisms:

> Third, we observed classroom instruction only twice during the intervention. As others have demonstrated . . . dimensions of classroom instruction that our coding system did not capture, such as individual student engagement or quality of instruction . . ., may have influenced student outcomes. (Vadasy & Sanders, 2008, p. 287)

Some teachers refused to participate, so some results may apply only to teachers who were open to full participation:

> Fourth, our findings on classroom literacy instruction are based on data excluding six teachers (and their students). It is possible that these teachers' refusal to participate reflects a systematic difference in their literacy instruction; however, outcomes of students within these classrooms did not reliably differ from outcomes of students whose teachers were observed. (Vadasy & Sanders, 2008, p. 287)

Finally, some important variables may have gone unmeasured:

> A final limitation of this study is that many variables expected to contribute to comprehension gains were not accounted for in this study, including vocabulary knowledge, strategy skills, and general language skills. (Vadasy & Sanders, 2008, p. 287)

It is especially important when reporting the results of an evaluation of an intervention to delve into the clinical or practical significance of the findings. In the case of Amir et al.'s (2009) evaluation, the practical implications were most evident because of the short duration of the treatment:

> These findings speak to the utility of the AMP, given the brevity of the intervention (eight sessions over 4 weeks, 20 min each) and absence of therapist contact. Although empirically supported treatments for SP [social phobia] already exist, many people do not have access to therapists trained in CBT [cognitive–behavioral therapy], and others opt not to take medication for their symptoms. . . . The ease of delivery of the current intervention suggests that the AMP may serve as a transportable and widely accessible treatment for individuals with SP who are unable to or choose not to access existing treatments. (p. 970)

Likewise, Vadasy and Sanders (2008) drew some clear practice implications for reading instruction:

> Findings support clear benefits from the opportunities students had to engage in oral reading practice during the classroom reading block. When students read aloud, teachers have opportunities to detect student difficulties, including poor

prosody, decoding errors, and limited comprehension reflected in dysfluent reading. Teachers can use this information to adjust instruction for individual students and provide effective corrections and scaffolding. (p. 287)

Discussion of Studies With No Experimental Manipulation

If your study contained no experimental manipulation, your Discussion section should describe the potential limitations of the study. As relevant, describe

- the possibility of misclassification,
- any unmeasured confounding, and
- changing eligibility criteria over time.

Each of the examples of study reports with nonexperimental designs includes a discussion of potential limitations of the results. In fact, three of them have a subsection in the Discussion section titled Limitations. Although the three potential limitations mentioned in JARS are just examples of limitations that might be described, they are broad issues that should generally be considered when interpreting the results of a nonexperimental study. In addition to these, it is good practice to mention in the Discussion the fact that causal interpretations of nonexperimental data must always be done with caution, if at all. To be more complete, the STROBE guidelines for the Discussion section of an observational study make this point nicely:

> The heart of the discussion section is the interpretation of a study's results. Over-interpretation is common and human: even when we try hard to give an objective assessment, reviewers often rightly point out that we went too far in some respects. When interpreting results, authors should consider the nature of the study on the discovery to verification continuum and potential sources of bias, including loss to follow-up and non-participation. . . . Due consideration should be given to confounding . . ., the results of relevant sensitivity analyses, and to the issue of multiplicity and subgroup analyses. . . . Authors should also consider residual confounding due to unmeasured variables or imprecise measurement of confounders. (Vandenbroucke et al., 2014, p. 1519)

As I mentioned when I discussed the reporting of methods of measurement, misclassification of people into the wrong group is a problem with nonexperimental designs that deserves careful attention and should be returned to in the Discussion. If the process of assignment to conditions was accomplished through a procedure other than random assignment, you should consider in the Discussion (a) how the people in different conditions might have differed in ways other than your classification variable (which you identified in the methods), (b) whether participants switched groups in the course of the experiment (called *unintended crossover*), and (c) whether these differences might have been related to the outcome variable of interest. In the hypothetical example of workplace support I used in the discussion of methods, following the JARS recommendation I suggested you would need to take special care to determine that absenteeism, turnover, and perceived organizational support were measured in comparable ways in the two intact groups (the retail stores). In the Discussion section, you would need to revisit any differences you discussed in the Method section and consider whether these might be plausible rival hypotheses to the conclusion you want to make. Otherwise, readers will not be able to assess the importance of any potential sources of bias in the measures.

Another example of discussing the possibility of misclassification was provided in Fagan et al.'s (2009) study of risk and resilience in nonresident fathers' engagement with their child. In their Limitations section, they noted differences in how risk and resilience were measured:

> We also note measurement issues in regard to the risk and resilience variables reflecting temporality and centrality. Specifically, the risk index taps items that reflect ongoing or past behaviors that deleteriously influence men's ability to actively engage as fathers, such as incarceration, substance use, and mental health problems. In contrast, more of the items on the resilience scale represent factors with the potential to positively position men for fathering. (p. 1403)

Although the researchers do not say so explicitly, the concern is that the trustworthiness of the two measures might be different and that this could lead to more misclassification of fathers for one construct of interest than the other.

You also need to discuss the possibility that your measured variables were confounded, or confused, with other variables. For example, Fagan et al. (2009) wrote,

> The prenatal involvement measure is limited to five overlapping items pooled across mother and father reports of three very broad indicators of paternal involvement. In actuality, it is not clear whether the prenatal measure is an indicator of father engagement with the child, the paternal role, the mother, or a combination of these. (p. 1403)

In this way the researchers cautioned that their measure may have confounded multiple aspects of parenting (i.e., the father's engagement, the father's role, and characteristics of the mother) into a single score and that it was not clear which might be the specific aspect of parenting that was related to the other variables in the study.

Finally, JARS suggests you address whether the criteria for eligibility in the study changed over time. For example, the Taylor and James (2009) study of differences in electrodermal response modulation to aversive stimuli in people who are and are not substance dependent used subjects from two studies conducted between 2001 and 2006. Although the measure of substance disorder was the same in both studies, the measure of personality disorder was different:

> Trained clinical graduate students administered the Structured Clinical Interview for *DSM–IV* Axis I Disorders (SCID–I; First, Spitzer, Gibbon, & Williams, 1995) to assess lifetime occurrence of substance use disorders for alcohol, cannabis, sedatives, stimulants, cocaine, opioids, hallucinogens, and "other" substances (e.g., inhalants). Antisocial PD and borderline PD were assessed with the Structured Interview for *DSM–IV* Personality (SIDP–IV; Pfohl, Blum, & Zimmerman, 1994) in the earlier study and the Structured Clinical Interview

for *DSM–IV* Axis II Personality Disorders (SCID–II; First et al., 1997) in the later study. These interviews are functionally equivalent and assess the same criteria. (Taylor & James, 2009, p. 494)

Thus, the researchers assured us that although the criteria used to assess whether participants had personality disorders (clinical interviews) were different in the two studies, they were "functionally equivalent." This is important because changes in diagnostic criteria (e.g., duration of symptoms, number of symptoms present) could change the types of people diagnosed with psychiatric disorders. In experimental studies, subjects are assigned to different groups at the same time; subsequent changes in diagnostic criteria could affect external validity (generalizability) but not internal validity (i.e., bias). In nonexperimental studies, differences over time could affect both external validity and internal validity. Taylor and James (2009) addressed this issue in their Method section, but it could also have been addressed in the Discussion.

If you are interested in examples of all of the items that should be included in reports of nonexperimental designs, these can be found in the article by Vandenbroucke et al. (2014), which contains examples and explanations of the STROBE guidelines.

Discussion of Studies With Structural Equation Modeling

In your Discussion section, if your research includes the use of a structural equation model, your discussion should

- summarize any modifications to the original model and the bases, theoretical or statistical, for doing so;
- address the issue of equivalent models that fit the same data just as well as retained models or alternative but nonequivalent models that explain the data nearly as well as retained models; and
- justify the preference for retained models over equivalent or near-equivalent versions.

If you used a structural equation model in your study, you need to discuss the explanatory value of the model or models you tested, how they compared to one another, and why you favored one or more models over others. If you altered models because of what the data revealed, you need to state this and what the implications of the changes might be.

Discussion of Clinical Trials

If you are reporting a clinical trial, your report should describe how the study advances knowledge about the intervention, clinical problem, and population.

As described in Chapter 6, a *clinical trial* is a study that evaluates the effects of one or more health-related interventions on health outcomes. It involves assigning individuals or groups to different conditions. Thus, the Vadasy and Sanders (2008) study on reading instruction would be considered a controlled trial that compares different approaches to reading instruction, the Amir et al. (2009) study a controlled trial of attention training, the Norman et al. (2008) study an evaluation of a program for smoking prevention in adolescents, and the Vinnars et al. (2009) study an examination of different psychotherapies for personality disorders. All would be considered clinical trials.

For example, Norman et al.'s (2008) smoking intervention proved to be generally successful:

> This study demonstrates that an intervention designed around a website supported by additional motivational components can be integrated into schools to support smoking cessation and prevention in an engaging manner. Through the use of multiple learning channels, the *Smoking Zine* was able to significantly reduce the likelihood that an adolescent would take up smoking over 6 months when compared with similar students in the control condition, especially with regard to adoption of heavy smoking. (p. 807)

However, the way the researchers chose to introduce the intervention might have placed limits on their ability to generalize to other means of implementation:

> School-based trials typically randomize classes; we chose to randomize participants at the individual level because of the personalized nature of the intervention. Doing so introduced the possibility that students would share lessons learned with their peers. . . . Integrating the intervention into regular classroom activities potentially reduced its novelty and the likelihood of extramural discussion. (Norman et al., 2008, p. 807)

Norman et al.'s (2008) first concern, often referred to as *treatment diffusion*, would reduce the effect of the intervention because students in the treatment condition shared what they learned with students in the control condition. Their second concern would limit the impact of the treatment. In addition, Norman et al. pointed out a concern about compliance rates:

> Another area worthy of consideration is the fact that fewer smokers completed the 6-month trial compared with nonsmokers. A potential reason could be attributed to complications arising from increased engagement in risk behaviors among the smokers. . . . These risk behaviors may have contributed to an increased absenteeism rate at school, making follow-up more difficult. (pp. 807–808)

Perhaps one of the most interesting discussions of limitations was by Vinnars et al. (2009). They found that their experimental treatment for people with personality disorder did not outperform the control treatment:

> This study explored the extent to which manualized psychodynamic psychotherapy was superior to ordinary clinical treatment as conducted in the community

in Scandinavia in improving maladaptive personality functioning in patients with any *DSM–IV* [*Diagnostic and Statistical Manual of Mental Disorders,* fourth edition; American Psychiatric Association, 1994] PD diagnosis. We did not find any significant difference between the two treatments, suggesting perhaps that the format of treatment (i.e., whether it was manualized psychodynamic or ordinary clinical treatment) did not seem to differentially affect change in personality. The one exception was for neuroticism, and this was only during follow-up. (p. 370)

So what do we learn from this study?

In summary, the results from these studies indicate that improvement in interpersonal problems is possible. However, it is hard to predict in advance what specific treatment, what treatment length, or for what specific sample of patients these interpersonal problems will improve. (Vinnars et al., 2009, p. 372)

Ordering Material in the Discussion

One of the more difficult chores I had in writing this book was taking apart the Discussion sections of the example reports so that I could illustrate the items in JARS; it was difficult because the various elements of each Discussion were intertwined with one another. Other than the placement of the restatement of goals and summary of findings, what elements of a Discussion section should go where is a matter of the individual authors' preferences and the unique demands of the topic and findings. Therefore, do not get hung up on preparing your Discussion in the same sequence I have here. Just be sure to include discussion of the elements called for in JARS. Where in the Discussion section you cover each and in what depth should be dictated by what order will help your readers make sense of your findings and make your message clear. Clarity and completeness rule the day.

There is one more table to be considered. This table involves the reporting of research syntheses and meta-analyses, which I discuss in Chapter 8.

8

Reporting Research Syntheses and Meta-Analyses

The same concerns that have led to more detailed reporting standards for new data collections have led to similar efforts to establish standards for the reporting of other types of research. Particular attention has been focused on the reporting of research syntheses and meta-analyses (Cooper, 2017). A *research synthesis* attempts to summarize, integrate, and draw conclusions from a set of studies that explore the same problem or hypotheses. A *meta-analysis* is a research synthesis that uses quantitative techniques to integrate the results of the studies. The American Psychological Association Working Group that developed Journal Article Reporting Standards (JARS) also developed Meta-Analysis Reporting Standards (MARS) for quantitative research syntheses (Appelbaum et al., 2018; see Table A8.1). (For reporting standards for qualitative research syntheses, see Levitt, in press; Levitt et al., 2018.)

In this chapter, I do not try to explain each of the items in MARS. That would take another book, and many books already exist for learning how to conduct research syntheses and meta-analyses (e.g., Borenstein, Hedges, Higgins, & Rothstein, 2009; Cooper, 2017; Cooper, Hedges, & Valentine, 2009). Many of the items are also analogous to items you have read about in previous chapters. Instead, I focus on the most important items that are unique to the MARS.[1]

---

[1]How did I know which items to pick? In the course of preparing a book chapter, Amy Dent and I (Cooper & Dent, 2011) conducted a survey of the 74 members of the Society for Research Synthesis Methodology. The society's members were asked to rate the importance of each MARS item on a scale from 1 (*generally, it is unnecessary in my field for researchers to report this information*) to 10 (*generally, it would be considered unethical in my field not to include this information in the report*). Of the society's members, 42 (57%) responded to the survey. I discuss those items that received a score of 10 from 50% or more of the society's members.

http://dx.doi.org/10.1037/0000103-008

Reporting Quantitative Research in Psychology: How to Meet APA Style Journal Article Reporting Standards, Second Edition, by H. Cooper

Introduction

The introduction to your meta-analysis should include a statement of the question or relation under investigation, including

- populations to which the question or relation is relevant,
- types of predictor and outcome measures used and their psychometric characteristics, and
- types of study designs.

It is important to address three sets of items in your meta-analysis introduction that relate to the question under investigation. These items call for a clear statement of the research problem. The statement should include (a) a description of the population to which the question is relevant, (b) a description of the predictor (independent) and outcome (dependent) variables of primary interest, and (c) a rationale for the choice of what study designs to include, as well as the other characteristics of studies that will be gathered from the study reports. These items are akin to those most important to include in the introduction to a report based on new data. The MARS items simply reiterate how critical a clear problem statement is to any scientific endeavor.

As a running example for this chapter, I refer to a research synthesis by Grabe, Ward, and Hyde (2008). These authors reported the results of a meta-analysis on the role of mass media in the body image concerns of women. They stated their research question plainly and simply:

> Why is it that so many girls and young women are dissatisfied with their bodies, regardless of size? (Grabe et al., 2008, p. 460)

This statement also makes clear what population (girls and young women, operationally defined by age in the Method section by the inclusion of studies on female participants who averaged between 7.5 and 32.7 years of age) was relevant to the question. Media, the researchers' conceptual independent variable, was defined as "movies, magazines, and television" (Grabe et al., 2008, p. 460). The conceptual definition for their outcome variable was not as simple:

> What is perhaps the greatest challenge to drawing sound conclusions from this large and growing literature is that results may vary depending on the particular dimension of body image or related eating behavior that is being measured. (Grabe et al., 2008, p. 462)

Grabe et al.'s (2008) problem highlights an important difference between meta-analysis and primary research and why these conceptual definitions are so critical. Researchers collecting new data typically gather or manipulate only one or two operational definitions of the same construct. For example, they may expose women to images of thin people in a film and then ask them how satisfied they are with their own bodies: one manipulation of the conceptual variable—media—and one measure of body image concerns. Meta-analysts, however, may come across numerous operational definitions of the variables of interest. In addition to satisfaction measures, Grabe et al. discovered measures of body image based on preoccupation with the body, internalization of thin ideals, and behaviors related to eating. They had to provide a multidimensional scheme for measures of body image and then examine the effects of media on four different clusters of body image concerns. Their intention to do this and the rationale for it were clearly laid out in their introduction.

In addition to these characteristics of the problem you are interested in, the introduction to your research synthesis needs to include the same background information you find in reports of primary data collections: the problem's historical background, its theoretical underpinnings, and issues of policy and practice that make the topic interesting. You also need, as in primary research, to state your hypotheses and give a broad overview of your strategy for analyzing the data, especially if you are going to perform a meta-analysis.

Method
Inclusion Criteria

If you are reporting a research synthesis or meta-analysis, your report of the *inclusion criteria*, or the criteria used to decide which studies to include in your synthesis, should include

- operational characteristics of independent (predictor) and dependent (outcome) variables,
- eligible participant populations,
- eligible research design features (e.g., random assignment only, minimal sample size),
- time period in which studies needed to be conducted, and
- any other study characteristics that might have been used to determine whether a study would be included (e.g., geographic location).

The four items on the MARS most critical to criteria for including and excluding studies are (a) the operational definitions of the independent (predictor) and (b) the dependent (outcome) variables, (c) a description of the eligible participant populations, and (d) the features of eligible research designs.[2] It is not surprising that the most important inclusion and exclusion criteria correspond to the conceptual issues laid out in the introduction.

For measures of body image, Grabe et al. (2008) mentioned 14 standardized measures (plus a catchall category) used to assess women's dissatisfaction with their bodies. For each measure, they provided a reference so that readers could find more information about it:

> In the category of body dissatisfaction we focused on measures that assess the evaluative component of body image, that is, satisfaction or dissatisfaction with

---

[2]These were followed closely in the survey by the need to include any time-period restrictions. For example, Grabe et al. (2008) reported that they included studies published between 1975 and January 2007.

the body. The following scales were classified as measures that assessed dis-satisfaction with the body and were included in the current review: (a) the Visual Analogue Scales (Heinberg & Thompson, 1995) . . . and (n) the Body Esteem Scale (Mendelson & White, 1985). In addition to these scales, a variety of scales that were not standardized but were specifically described as measuring global body dissatisfaction were included. (Grabe et al., 2008, p. 463)

Providing these references is good practice and permits you to spend less space describing each measure, instrument, or procedure included in the meta-analysis. Grabe et al. (2008) used the same approach to report the measures of preoccupation with the body, internalization of body image ideals, and eating behaviors. For media use, they included correlational studies that asked women about media use or media exposure but left out studies that simply asked participants how influenced they were by the media.

When conducting a meta-analysis (or any research synthesis, for that matter), you will find much more variety in the data collection procedures than in any report of a single new study. This is why spelling out the inclusion criteria is so important. Grabe et al. (2008) included all of the body image measures they found. For media exposure, however, they drew the line at indirect measures:

Because our goal was to test directly the association between the use of media and women's body image and related concerns, we included only those studies that investigated media use or media exposure, as opposed to self-report of media influence (i.e., perceived pressure from media to change exercise or eating patterns). (Grabe et al., 2008, p. 463)

The important thing, from the point of view of the MARS, is that the authors told readers why studies were included in the analysis. With this information, readers can agree or disagree with their decision.

Meta-analysts also must tell readers the characteristics of participants who were and were not considered relevant to the research question. Grabe et al. (2008) did not explicitly define "girls and young women" (p. 460), but their table containing the characteristics of studies included in the meta-analysis has a column that provides the median age of the samples. Also, because issues with body image are culture bound, they explained that they included only studies conducted in four English-speaking countries. This placed a geographic as well as cultural restriction on studies included in the research synthesis:

Search limits restricted the results to articles published in English between 1975 and January 2007 and included studies conducted in English-speaking countries (i.e., the United States, Canada, Great Britain, and Australia). Appearance ideals can vary widely across cultures, yet little research has been conducted in other cultures. We therefore restricted ourselves to these four closely related cultures in which there is substantial research and often shared media. (Grabe et al., 2008, p. 464)

Without this information, readers could not assess to whom the results apply, nor could they argue that participants who were included or excluded should not have been.

Grabe et al. (2008) first addressed the issue of eligible research designs in the introduction to their meta-analysis. They devoted nearly a whole page to telling readers that two designs had been used in media and body image studies. Experimental studies manipulated whether girls and young women were exposed to thin media models (or other images) and then tested to see whether subjects exposed to thin images felt worse about their bodies. Correlational studies used naturalistic data to test the relationship between exposure to media and body image. Grabe et al. then used research design as a moderator variable in their meta-analysis. As in new data collections, a clear description of methods allows the reader to gauge the fit among the research designs, how the design was implemented, and the inferences drawn by the meta-analysts.

Information Sources

If you are reporting a research synthesis or meta-analysis, your description of your information sources should include

- reference and citation databases searched and
- treatment of unpublished studies.

Reference and citation databases searched. Your first step in finding studies relevant to the topic of your meta-analysis likely will be to search computerized reference databases and citation indexes. MARS calls for a full accounting of which databases you consulted and the keywords and keyword combinations you used to enter them. This is important because different reference databases cover different journals and other sources of documents. Also, some reference databases contain only published research, whereas others contain both published and unpublished studies, and others include only unpublished research. It will be difficult for readers to consider what studies you might have missed if they do not know which databases you used. Equally important, without this information, it would be difficult for others to reproduce the results of your meta-analysis.

Grabe et al. (2008) described their search of reference databases as follows:

> A computerized database search of PsycINFO and the Web of Science was conducted to generate a pool of potential articles. To identify all articles that investigated the link between media use and body image concerns, the words *body image, media, television, advertising*, and *magazines* were used as key terms in the literature search. These broad terms were selected to capture the wide range of research that has been conducted. Search limits restricted the results to articles published in English between 1975 and January 2007. (p. 464)

A host of other literature retrieval strategies are available (see Atkinson, Koenka, Sanchez, Moshontz, & Cooper, 2015; Cooper, 2017). Some will be more relevant to your search than others. MARS recommends that you list them all. Note as well that Grabe et al. (2008) explicitly stated the key terms they used to search the databases and two other restrictions on their search.

Treatment of unpublished studies. Your decision to include or exclude unpublished research in your literature search is of critical importance because unpublished studies typically reveal smaller effect sizes than do published ones, on average by about one third (Lipsey & Wilson, 1993). So, including only published studies can make relationships appear stronger than they would if all of the studies were included.

Meta-analysts who exclude unpublished research often say they do so because these studies have not undergone the peer review process and therefore may be of lesser quality. However, there is good evidence that publication is often not the final stop for much research, regardless of its quality (cf. Cooper, DeNeve, & Charlton, 1997). For example, if you completed the hypothetical study of fragrance labeling effects as a master's thesis or doctoral dissertation and you then went to work for a perfume company, you might never submit the study for publication. Likewise, a report for a government agency might appear in a reference database but never be submitted for publication (even if it underwent peer review before the agency released it). Also, studies are often turned down by journals for reasons other than quality. Journals sometimes use the novelty of the contribution as a criterion for publication, and this is of no concern to meta-analysts. Finally, a report submitted for publication may be turned down because the statistical test failed to reject the null hypothesis. Sometimes authors interested in publication do not even submit reports for publication when the null hypothesis is not rejected. To meta-analysts, the statistical significance of the individual finding is irrelevant; they want all of the evidence.

Summary Measures: Effect Sizes

If you are reporting a meta-analysis, your description of the effect sizes should include

- formulas used to calculate effect sizes (e.g., means and standard deviations, use of univariate F to r transform),
- corrections made to effect sizes (e.g., small sample bias, correction for unequal sample sizes), and
- effect size averaging and weighting methods, including how studies with more than one effect size were handled.

Effect size metrics. In Chapter 5, I discussed what an effect size estimate is and the different effect size metrics. In a meta-analysis, it is especially critical that you tell readers what formulas you used to calculate effect sizes and whether you applied any corrections. Some day, every primary researcher will report effect sizes, and this will become less of an issue. Today, meta-analysts often have to calculate the effect sizes themselves. They use a host of formulas; the most prominent of these require access to means and standard deviations so meta-analysts can calculate d indexes. In many instances, however, they must estimate effect sizes from inference test values (e.g., t tests or F tests) and sample sizes or degrees of freedom (for many approaches to estimating effect sizes, see Borenstein, 2009; Fleiss & Berlin, 2009). Sometimes, meta-analysts can plug these numbers into software programs that do the calculations for them. If you had to estimate effect sizes in your meta-analysis, it is important to describe the formulas or the name of the program that you used. Grabe et al. (2008) described their effect size calculations as follows:

> Formulas for the effect size *d* were taken from Hedges and Becker (1986). When means and standard deviations were available, the effect size was computed as the mean body image score for the control group minus the mean body image score for the experimental group, divided by the pooled within-groups standard deviation. Therefore, negative effect sizes represent a more negative outcome (e.g., more body dissatisfaction) for women exposed to thin-ideal media than women in the control condition. Means and standard deviations were available for 74 (93%) of experimental studies. When means and standard deviations for experimental studies were not available, the effect size was calculated from reported *t* or *F* tests. (p. 468)

Corrections to effect sizes. Sometimes, effect sizes are adjusted to remove some form of bias in estimation. Most frequently, this is small-sample bias, but you can also remove biases attributable to artifacts, such as the reliability of a measure or a restriction on the range of scores in the sample. Grabe et al. (2008) wrote the following:

> Because effect sizes tend to be upwardly biased when based on small sample sizes, effect sizes were corrected for bias in the estimation of population effect sizes using the formula provided by Hedges (1981). (p. 468)

Effect-size averaging and weighting methods. Once each effect size has been calculated, meta-analysts next average the effects that estimate the same relationship. Grabe et al. (2008) averaged 20 effect sizes relating media exposure to eating disorder symptoms. It is generally accepted that the individual effect sizes should be weighted by the inverse of their variance (on the basis of the number of participants in their respective samples) before they are averaged. Sometimes, however, unweighted effect sizes are presented. Weighted and unweighted effect sizes can differ in magnitude, sometimes by a lot.[3] For this reason, MARS recommends that the procedures you used to average effect sizes be included in your meta-analysis report. Grabe et al. (2008) reported this as follows:

> All effect size analyses were weighted analyses (i.e., each effect size was weighted by an inverted variance). (p. 468)

How studies with more than one effect size were handled. Related to the weighting of studies is the issue of what to do when researchers give multiple measures of the same

---

[3]The difference between a weighted and an unweighted average effect size depends on the strength of the relationship between the effect size and the sample size. Therefore, if larger effects are associated with smaller sample sizes (a not uncommon occurrence in meta-analysis because of a reporting bias against the null hypothesis), the unweighted average effect size would be larger than the weighted average.

construct to the same sample of participants and then report multiple effect-size estimates. For example, suppose you found a correlational study with three measures of media exposure (movies, television, and magazines) and three measures of body satisfaction. You might find in the report nine effect sizes, even though the effects all relate to the same underlying constructs and were collected from the same people. These effect sizes are not statistically independent and therefore cannot be treated as such when you combine the effect sizes across all studies in your meta-analysis (some studies might have reported only one effect size and therefore would get only one ninth the weight of the study with multiple measures). Unless you take this into account, studies with more measures would influence the average effect size more, and the assumption that effect-size estimates are independent will be violated when you calculate a confidence interval for the average effect size.

Meta-analysts use several approaches to handle dependent effect sizes. Some meta-analysts use the study as the unit of analysis by taking the mean or median effect size to represent the study. Others use a shifting unit of analysis (Cooper, 2017).[4] Finally, there are sophisticated statistical approaches to solving the problem of dependent effect-size estimates that weight them when the average effect sizes are calculated (Tanner-Smith & Tipton, 2014).

Which techniques you use can have a large impact on (a) the estimated average magnitude of the effect size, (b) the estimated variance in effect sizes, and (c) the power of tests to uncover moderators of effects. For this reason, a clear and complete description of how nonindependent estimates of effect were handled should be part of your description of the weighting procedures.

Variation among effect sizes. The assumptions meta-analysts make about the sources of variance in effect sizes require them to grapple with some fairly complex issues. In a nutshell, you have three choices: a fixed-effect model, a random-effects model, or a mixed-effects model. A *fixed-effect model* assumes that each effect size's variance reflects sampling error of participants only—that is, error solely attributable to participant differences. In a *random-effects model*, other features of studies, such as their location, measures, experimenters, and so on, are assumed to be sampled as well, creating additional random influences. Hedges and Vevea (1998) stated that a fixed-effect model should be used when your goal is "to make inferences only about the effect size parameters in the set of studies that are observed (or a set of studies identical to the observed studies except for uncertainty associated with the sampling of subjects)" (p. 487). Use the random-effects model when you want to make inferences about a broader population of people and studies.

---

[4]Here, each effect size associated with a study is coded as if it were independent. These are averaged prior to entry into the analysis when estimating the overall effect size. This way, each study contributes one value. However, in analyses that examine moderators, each study could contribute one effect size to the estimate of each moderator grouping's average effect size. Therefore, in the media and eating disorder example, all nine correlations would be averaged before entering it into the estimation of the overall relationship strength. Three correlations would be averaged (across measures of eating disorder symptoms) within the three types of media when the influence of media type on the relationship is examined and reaveraged across media types when eating disorder symptoms are examined.

The results produced by random-effects models are typically more conservative than those of fixed-effect models. Random-effects models typically estimate more variability around average effect sizes and, therefore, are less likely to reveal statistically significant effects. Finally, the two models also can generate different average effect sizes, again depending on the relationship between the size of effects and the size of samples. In a *mixed-effects model,* some variance is assumed to be systematic (that associated with the moderator variable) and some is assumed to be random (attributable to truly chance factors).

For these reasons, MARS states that it is essential that you report whether you used a fixed-effect, random-effects (or its cousin, robust variance estimation; Tanner-Smith & Tipton, 2014), or mixed-effects model when you (a) averaged your effect sizes, (b) calculated their variance, and (c) conducted moderator analyses. Without knowing this information, it is impossible for readers (and the meta-analysts themselves!) to interpret the results. For example, Grabe et al. (2008) wrote the following:

> We used mixed-effects models, which assume that effect size variance can be explained by both systematic and random components. . . . Mixed-effects models assume that the effects of between-study variables are systematic but that there is a remaining unmeasured random effect in the effect size distribution in addition to sampling error. As is done in random-effects models, a random-effects variance component (derived from the residual homogeneity value after the moderators are taken into account) is estimated and added to the standard error associated with each effect size, and inverted variance weights are calculated. (pp. 468–469)

Although this description is very technical and requires considerable knowledge of meta-analysis to decode, it provides a complete description of what was done and why.

Results

Flowchart of Study Selection

The first subsection of your Results section will report the outcome of your literature search and the application of your inclusion criteria. It tells how you found studies to consider for exclusion and then how you winnowed these down to the ones that were ultimately included in your review. This is the research synthesis analog to the flow of participants through a study with a new data collection. A succinct and visual way to do this is through the use of a flowchart. Grabe et al. (2008) did not use this device, but Ottaviani et al. (2016) did. Their flowchart is reproduced in Figure 8.1. Read their diagram beginning at the top of the first column, "Records identified through database." The second column then gives the documents excluded at each stage of the screening process. Note that adding the number of studies in the excluded boxes plus those in the meta-analysis equals the total number of studies retrieved (i.e., in the top box; 3,616 + 213 = 2,116 + 1,548 + 105 + 60).

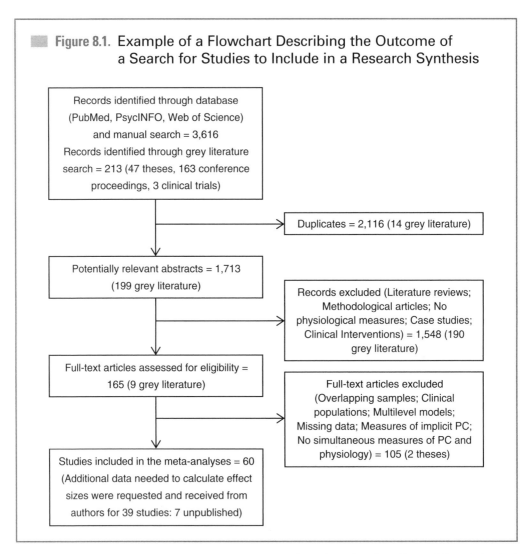

Figure 8.1. Example of a Flowchart Describing the Outcome of a Search for Studies to Include in a Research Synthesis

PRISMA flowchart describing search results and study selection. From "Physiological Concomitants of Perseverative Cognition: A Systematic Review and Meta-Analysis," by C. Ottaviani, J. F. Thayer, B. Verkuil, A. Lonigro, B. Medea, A. Couyoumdjian, and J. F. Brosschot, 2016, *Psychological Bulletin, 142,* p. 234. Copyright 2016 American Psychological Association.

Tables

If you are reporting a meta-analysis, your report should include

- the overall characteristics of the database (e.g., number of studies with different research designs);
- the overall effect-size estimates, including measures of uncertainty (e.g., confidence and credibility intervals);
- the results of moderator and mediator analyses (analyses of subsets of studies), including
  - the number of studies and total sample sizes for each moderator analysis and
  - the assessment of interrelations among variables used for moderator and mediator analyses; and
- a description of the characteristics of each included study, including effect size and sample size.

It is not surprising that a table that summarizes the results of the meta-analysis is de rigueur. In most cases, a table listing the results for the individual studies going into the analyses may also be called for. A table with information on your tests of moderator variables is also needed. This table would include, at the least, the number of studies in each moderator category and effect sizes and confidence intervals for each category. However, space limitations may dictate that these tables not be included in the published version of the article.

Grabe et al. (2008) presented a table listing characteristics of each study. It spanned three and a half double-columned pages. I do not reproduce that here. Suffice it to say that the columns of the table presented the following:

- first author and year of appearance of the study,
- effect size,
- sample size (experimental and control group separately or total sample for correlational studies),
- mean age of the sample,
- study design,
- media type,
- type of control, and
- measurement instrument.

Table 8.1 presents Grabe et al.'s table for their overall findings, and Table 8.2 presents one of their tables reporting moderator analyses. Details of how to construct these tables in your manuscript can be found in the *Publication Manual of the American Psychological Association* (APA, 2010, pp. 128–150, sections 5.07–5.19, Tables).

Table 8.1. Example of a Table Reporting Overall Findings of a Meta-Analysis

Table X

Summary of Mean Effect Sizes for Mixed-Effects Analyses

Measure type	No. of studies	d	95% CI	Q_T
Body image dissatisfaction	90	−.28	−.21 to −.35	100.34
Internalization	23	−.39	−.33 to −.44	66.15*
Eating behaviors and beliefs	20	−.30	−.24 to −.36	46.30***

Note. A negative *d* indicates that the control group scored higher than the experimental group on negative body image. CI = confidence interval; Q_T = total heterogeneity. From "The Role of Media in Body Image Concerns Among Women: A Meta-Analysis of Experimental and Correlational Studies," by S. Grabe, L. M. Ward, and J. S. Hyde, 2008, *Psychological Bulletin, 134*, p. 469. Copyright 2008 by the American Psychological Association.
*$p < .05$. ***$p < .001$.

Table 8.2. Example of a Table Reporting Moderator Analyses in a Meta-Analysis

Table X

Variables Potentially Moderating the Link Between Media Exposure and Eating Behaviors and Beliefs

Variable	Between-groups Q	No. of studies	d	Within-group Q
Study design	0.94			
Experimental		8	−.36	21.91**
Correlational		12	−.28	28.46**
Age group in years	6.43*			
Adolescent (ages 10–18)		4	−.20	4.38
Young adult/adult (ages 19–32)		16	−.35	40.40***
Media type	4.0*			
Television		7	−.29	22.42***
Magazines		11	−.26	24.70**
Generalized media		2	−.50	0.09
Publication status	11.42**			
Published		17	−.27	37.72**
Not published		3	−.99	2.07
Publication year	0.09			
1990–1999		8	−.30	25.81***
2000–2005		12	−.28	25.31**

Note. Q = heterogeneity. From "The Role of Media in Body Image Concerns Among Women: A Meta-Analysis of Experimental and Correlational Studies," by S. Grabe, L. M. Ward, and J. S. Hyde, 2008, *Psychological Bulletin, 134*, p. 470. Copyright 2008 by the American Psychological Association.
*$p < .05$. **$p < .001$.

Discussion

If you are reporting a research synthesis or meta-analysis, your interpretation of the results (i.e., Discussion section) should include

- a statement of main results, including results of all preplanned analyses;
- assessment of the quality of the evidence and the strengths and limitations of the meta-analysis;
- consideration of alternative explanations for observed results;
- generalizability of conclusions (e.g., to relevant populations, treatment variations, dependent [outcome] variables, research designs);
- implications for theory, policy, practice; and
- guidelines for future research.

Similar to the elements of the introduction, the items on MARS stating what is needed in the Discussion section look much like the items recommended for reports of new primary research. Grabe et al. (2008) began their Discussion by stating the following:

> This meta-analysis represents a systematic inquiry into the overall associations of thin-ideal media exposure and three main areas of women's body image and related concerns. The results show consistent associations across both experimental and correlational designs and across multiple measures of women's body image and eating behaviors and beliefs. Thus, these findings provide strong support for the notion that exposure to mass media depicting the thin-ideal body is related to women's vulnerability to disturbances related to body image. (p. 470)

Concerning alternative explanations, Grabe et al. (2008) appealed to the fact that the finding was consistent across both experimental and correlational evidence. This suggests that alternative explanations are not many:

> The finding from the experimental literature in the current review (57% of studies) provides evidence of a link between exposure to thin-ideal media images and body dissatisfaction in women. The similar outcome found in the correlational literature supports this finding and suggests that this phenomenon also operates outside a laboratory context. Prospective studies will be important in fully assessing the role of the media in women's vulnerability to disturbances related to body image. (Grabe et al., 2008, p. 470)

This final sentence indicates that Grabe et al. thought future studies would be most valuable if they included longitudinal measures, a design feature rarely used in past research. Implicitly, they were acknowledging that experimental studies were of short duration and that this might influence the impact of their media images on women.

How should we interpret the findings?

> The current findings can be interpreted in the context of other, more well established areas of media research. For example, researchers have focused extensively on the influence of violent media on the aggressive behavior of youth. . . . Experimental studies demonstrated that brief exposure to violent video games led to an immediate increase in aggressive behavior, whereas the correlational studies linked repeated exposure to violent video games to a variety of types of real-world aggressive behavior. . . . Thin-ideal media research is much newer and inferences must therefore be more modest, but the media violence research provides a roadmap for ways in which research can proceed. (Grabe et al., 2008, p. 471)

What does it all mean?

> The findings from this study can inform prevention and intervention efforts particularly in the areas of education and advertising. With respect to education, media literacy can be used to teach girls and women to become more active, critical consumers of appearance-related media. . . . Perhaps of greater benefit would be to reduce the emphasis on an unrealistically thin ideal that is perpetuated through the objectification of women's bodies in the media. (Grabe et al., 2008, pp. 471–472)

However, Grabe et al. were careful not to claim too much:

> Despite the contributions of the present study, there are limitations that future research may want to address. First, much of what is known about women's body dissatisfaction is based largely on White samples. . . . Second, although we believe that the correlational data enhanced the validity of the experimental findings by providing data on actual media diets, the nature of correlational data do not permit identification of the prospective contributions of media to the development of negative body image. . . . Third, research on the potential consequences of thin-ideal media need to be extended to include other outcomes, such as obesity and body self-consciousness. . . . Finally, it is interesting to note that in a small percentage of studies there was a positive effect of media on women's body image concerns, suggesting that some women actually feel better about themselves after viewing media images. . . . It is possible that women who are consciously addressing their body image (e.g., restricting calories) or are already satisfied with their bodies feel elevated satisfaction in the presence of the appearance-related cues provided by the media. However, given that the number of studies in this area were few, interpretations of this finding are tentative. (Grabe et al., 2008, p. 472)

Finally, what are the policy implications?

> New policies adopted in Spain and Italy, and more tentatively by the Council of Fashion Designers of America, that exclude hyperthin women from modeling

may be helpful not only to the models themselves but also to millions of girls and women who view these images. (Grabe et al., 2008, p. 472)

In sum, then, the MARS recommends that the introduction and Discussion sections of a meta-analysis contain information not unlike their counterparts in reports of primary research. Where the two forms of research differ is "up the middle" in their descriptions of methods and results, where the methodologies are unique.

Appendix 8.1:
Meta-Analysis Reporting
Standards (MARS)

Table A8.1. Meta-Analysis Reporting Standards (MARS): Information Recommended for Inclusion in Manuscripts Reporting Research Syntheses and Meta-Analyses

Paper section and topic	Description
Title	State the research question and type of research synthesis (e.g., narrative synthesis, meta-analysis).
Author note	List all sources of monetary and in-kind funding support; state the role of funders in conducting the synthesis and deciding to publish the results, if any.
	Describe possible conflicts of interest, including financial and other nonfinancial interests.
	Give the place where the synthesis is registered and its registry number, if registered.
	Provide name, affiliation, and e-mail address of corresponding author.
Abstract	
Objectives	State the research problems, questions, or hypotheses under investigation.
Eligibility criteria	Describe the characteristics for inclusion of studies, including independent variables (treatments, interventions), dependent variables (outcomes, criteria), and eligible study designs.
Methods of synthesis	Describe the methods for synthesizing study results, including • Statistical and other methods used to summarize and to compare studies • Specific methods used to integrate studies if a meta-analysis was conducted (e.g., effect size metric, averaging method, model used in homogeneity analysis).

■ **Table A8.1.** (*Continued*)

Paper section and topic	Description
Results	State the results of the synthesis, including • Number of included studies and participants and their important characteristics • Results for the primary outcomes and moderator analyses • Effect sizes and confidence intervals associated with each analysis if a meta-analysis was conducted.
Conclusion	Describe strengths and limitations of the evidence, including evidence of inconsistency, imprecision, risk of bias in the included studies, and risk of reporting biases.
Introduction	
Problem	State the question or relation under investigation, including • Historical background, including previous syntheses and meta-analyses related to the topic • Theoretical, policy, and practical issues related to the question or relation of interest • Populations and settings to which the question or relation is relevant • Rationale for choice of study designs, selection and coding of outcomes, and selection and coding of potential moderators or mediators of results • Psychometric characteristics of outcome measures and other variables.
Objectives	State the hypotheses examined, indicating which were pre-specified, including • Question in terms of relevant participant characteristics (including animal populations), independent variables (experimental manipulations, treatments, or interventions), ruling out of possible confounding variables, dependent variables (outcomes, criteria), and other features of study designs • Methods of synthesis and, if meta-analysis was used, specific methods used to integrate studies (e.g., effect size metric, averaging method, model used in homogeneity analysis).
Protocol	List where the full protocol can be found (e.g., supplemental materials) or state that there was no protocol. State that the full protocol was published (or archived in a public registry) or that it was not published before the review was conducted.

(table continues)

■ **Table A8.1.** (*Continued*)

Paper section and topic	Description
Method	
Inclusion and exclusion criteria	Describe the criteria for selecting studies, including • Independent variables (e.g., experimental manipulations, types of treatments or interventions, predictor variables) • Dependent variable (e.g., outcomes in syntheses of clinical research including both potential benefits and potential adverse effects) • Eligible study designs (e.g., methods of sampling or treatment assignment) • Handling of multiple reports about the same study or sample, describing which are primary, and handling of multiple measures used for the same participants • Restrictions on study inclusion (e.g., by study age, language, location, report type) • Changes to the prespecified inclusion and exclusion criteria and when these changes were made • Handling of reports that did not contain sufficient information to judge eligibility (e.g., lacked information about study design) and reports that did not include sufficient information for analysis (e.g., did not report numerical data about outcomes).
Information sources	Describe all information sources, including • Search strategies for electronic searches such that they could be repeated (e.g., search terms used, Boolean connectors, fields searched, explosion of terms) • Databases searched (e.g., PsycINFO, ClinicalTrials.gov), including dates of coverage (i.e., earliest and latest records included in the search), and software and search platforms used • Names of specific journals searched and volumes checked • Explanation of rationale for choosing reference lists if examined (e.g., other relevant articles, previous research syntheses) • Documents for which forward (citation) searches were conducted, stating why these documents were chosen • Number of researchers contacted if study authors or individual researchers were contacted to find studies or to obtain more information about included studies, criteria for making contact (e.g., previous relevant publications), and response rate

▒ **Table A8.1.** (*Continued*)

Paper section and topic	Description
	• Dates of contact if other direct contact searches were conducted (e.g., corporate sponsors or mailings to distribution lists) • Search strategies in addition to those above and the results of these searches.
Study selection	Describe the process for deciding which studies to include in the synthesis and/or meta-analysis, including • Document elements (e.g., title, abstract, full text) used to make decisions about inclusion or exclusion from the synthesis at each step of the screening process • Qualifications (e.g., training, educational or professional status) of those who conducted each step in the study selection process, stating whether each step was conducted by a single person or in duplicate and explaining how reliability was assessed if one screener was used or how disagreements were resolved if multiple screeners were used.
Data collection	Describe methods of extracting data from reports, including • Variables for which data were sought and the variable categories • Qualifications of those who conducted each step in the data extraction process, stating whether each step was conducted by a single person or in duplicate and explaining how reliability was assessed if one screener was used or how disagreements were resolved if multiple screeners were used • Location of data coding forms, instructions for completion, and data (including metadata) if available (e.g., public registry, supplemental materials).
Methods for assessing risk to internal validity	Describe any methods used to assess risk to internal validity in individual study results, including • Risks assessed and criteria for concluding risk exists or does not exist • Methods for including risk to internal validity in the decisions to synthesize the data and the interpretation of results.
Summary measures	
Methods of synthesis	Describe the statistical methods for calculating effect sizes, including the metrics (e.g., correlation coefficients, differences in means, risk ratios) and formulas used.

(table continues)

▓ **Table A8.1.** (*Continued*)

Paper section and topic	Description
	Describe narrative and statistical methods used to compare studies. If meta-analysis was conducted, describe the methods used to combine effects across studies and the model used to estimate the heterogeneity of the effect sizes (e.g., fixed-effect or random-effects model, robust variance estimation), including • Rationale for the method of synthesis • Methods for weighting study results • Methods to estimate imprecision (e.g., confidence or credibility intervals) both within and between studies • Description of all transformations or corrections (e.g., to account for small samples or unequal group numbers) and adjustments (e.g., for clustering, missing data, measurement artifacts, construct-level relationships) made to the data and justification for these • Additional analyses (e.g., subgroup analyses, meta-regression), including whether each analysis was pre-specified or post hoc • Selection of prior distributions and assessment of model fit if Bayesian analyses were conducted • Name and version number of computer programs used for the analysis • Statistical code and where it can be found (e.g., supplemental materials).
Publication bias and selective reporting	Address the adequacy of methods used (e.g., contacting authors for unreported outcomes) to identify unpublished studies and unreported data. Describe any statistical methods used to test for publication bias and selective reporting or address the potential limitations of the synthesis's results if no such methods were used.
Results	
Study selection	Describe the selection of studies, ideally with a flowchart, including • Number of citations assessed for eligibility • Number of citations and number of unique studies included in the synthesis • Reasons for excluding studies at each stage of screening. Include a table with complete citations for studies that met many but not all inclusion criteria, with reasons for exclusion (e.g., effect size was not calculable).

Table A8.1. (*Continued*)

Paper section and topic	Description
Study characteristics	Summarize the characteristics of included studies. Provide a table showing, for each included study, the principal variables for which data were sought, including • Characteristics of the independent and outcome or dependent variables and main moderator variables • Important characteristics of participants (e.g., age, sex, ethnicity) • Important contextual variables (e.g., setting, date) • Study design (e.g., methods of sampling or treatment assignment). Report where the full data set is available (e.g., from the authors, supplemental materials, registry).
Results of individual studies	Report the results for each study or comparison (e.g., effect size with confidence intervals for each independent variable). If possible, present this information in a figure (e.g., forest plot).
Synthesis of results	Report a synthesis (e.g., meta-analysis) for each study result (e.g., weighted average effect sizes, confidence intervals, estimates of heterogeneity of results). Describe risks of bias that different design features might introduce into the synthesis results.
Assessment of internal validity of individual studies	
Publication and reporting bias	Describe risk of bias across studies, including • Statement about whether (a) unpublished studies and unreported data or (b) only published data were included in the synthesis and the rationale if only published data were used • Assessments of the impact of publication bias (e.g., modeling of data censoring, trim-and-fill analysis) • Results of any statistical analyses looking for selective reporting of results within studies.
Adverse and harmful effects	Report any adverse or harmful effects identified in individual studies.
Discussion	
Summary of the evidence	Summarize the main findings, including • Main results of the synthesis, including all results of prespecified analyses • Overall quality of the evidence

(*table continues*)

■ Table A8.1. (*Continued*)

Paper section and topic	Description
	• Strengths and limitations of findings (e.g., inconsistency, imprecision, risk of bias, publication bias, selective outcome reporting) • Alternative explanations for observed results (e.g., confounding, statistical power) • Similarities to and differences from previous syntheses.
Generalizability	Describe the generalizability (external validity) of conclusions, including • Implications for related populations, intervention variations and dependent (outcome) variables.
Implications	Interpret the results in light of previous evidence. Address the implications for further research, theory, policy, and/or practice.

Note. Adapted from "Journal Article Reporting Standards for Quantitative Research in Psychology: The APA Publications and Communications Board Task Force Report," by M. Appelbaum, H. Cooper, R. B. Kline, E. Mayo-Wilson, A. M. Nezu, and S. M. Rao, 2018, *American Psychologist, 73*, pp. 21–23. Copyright 2018 by the American Psychological Association.

How the Journal Article Reporting Standards and the Meta-Analysis Reporting Standards Came to Be and Can Be Used in the Future

In the preceding chapters, I have discussed why researchers need the Journal Article Reporting Standards (JARS; Appelbaum et al., 2018), how to use the JARS tables, and how to address the tension between complete reporting and space limitation. In each chapter, I have defined and discussed most items and have presented a rationale for their inclusion. I have also provided examples of both good and not-so-good ways to present information recommended in JARS and in the Meta-Analysis Reporting Standards (MARS; Appelbaum et al., 2018). In this final chapter, I describe in more detail how JARS and MARS came to be and consider how JARS can be used in the future.[1]

Those of us in the first Journal Article Reporting Standards Working Group (JARS Working Group) found that in the past 2 decades, developments in the social, behavioral, and medical sciences had motivated researchers to provide more details when they reported their investigations. In the arenas of public and health policy and practice, we found a growing call for use of evidence-based decision making. This call placed a new importance on understanding how research was conducted and what it found. Policymakers and practitioners who were making decisions based at least partly on social science evidence wanted to know how reliable the information was and in what context the data had been collected. In 2006, the American Psychological Association (APA) Presidential Task Force on Evidence-Based Practice (2006) said that "evidence-based practice requires that psychologists recognize the strengths and limitations of evidence obtained from different types of research" (p. 275).

---

[1]Much of what follows, including some sentences and phrases, is taken from the JARS Working Group report (APA P&C Board Working Group on Journal Article Reporting Standards, 2008). This material is used with the permission of the APA P&C Board and the JARS Working Group members.

http://dx.doi.org/10.1037/0000103-009
Reporting Quantitative Research in Psychology: How to Meet APA Style Journal Article Reporting Standards, Second Edition, by H. Cooper

In medicine, members of the JARS Working Group found the movement toward evidence-based practice to be pervasive (see Sackett, Rosenberg, Gray, Haynes, & Richardson, 1996). Two events impressed us most. First was the establishment in 1993 of the Cochrane Collaboration (http://www.cochrane.org), an international consortium of medical researchers. This organization has adopted guidelines for conducting and reporting research syntheses and has produced thousands of reviews examining the cumulative evidence on everything from public health initiatives to surgical procedures. Their documents reveal much discussion of reporting standards. The other event, on the primary research side, was the adoption by the International Committee of Medical Journal Editors (2007) of a policy requiring registration of all medical trials in a public trials registry as a condition of consideration for publication. This indicated a new level of reporting accountability in medical research.

Other developments also have motivated stricter requirements for reporting. In education, the No Child Left Behind Act of 2001 (2002) and the Every Student Succeeds Act, which replaced it in 2015, required the policies and practices adopted by schools and school districts to be based on scientific evidence. In public policy, a consortium similar to the Cochrane Collaboration was formed: The Campbell Collaboration (http://www.campbellcollaboration.org) is dedicated to promoting high-quality research syntheses and, along with other organizations (e.g., the Laura and John Arnold Foundation Initiation in Evidence-Based Policy and Innovation; http://www.arnoldfoundation.org/initiative/evidence-based-policy-innovation/), was meant to promote government policy-making based on rigorous evidence of program effectiveness. The developers of previous reporting standards (discussed later in this chapter) were often the same individuals who were instrumental in forming these organizations. Collectively, they argued that new transparency in reporting was needed so that accurate judgments could be made about the appropriate inferences and applications derivable from research findings.

The basic research domain within the social and behavioral science disciplines was not without its own calls to action. This was a development close to my own area of interest. As evidence about specific hypotheses and theories accumulates, greater reliance is placed on syntheses of research, especially meta-analyses (Cooper, Hedges, & Valentine, 2009). As described in Chapter 8, research syntheses attempt to summarize cumulative knowledge. New synthesis techniques, in particular meta-analysis, allow researchers to integrate different findings relating to a specific question. However, through either planned or naturally occurring circumstances, varying research designs and contexts are used across studies. Meta-analysts use this variation to find clues to the mediation of basic psychological, behavioral, and social processes uncovered in the individual studies. In meta-analysis, these clues emerge when studies are grouped on the basis of distinctions in their methods and settings and then their results are compared. This synthesis-based evidence is then used to guide the next generation of problems and hypotheses studied in new data collections. Meta-analysts need detailed descriptions of what the primary researchers did. The JARS Working Group agreed that without complete reporting of methods and results, the utility of studies for purposes of research synthesis and meta-analysis is diminished.

Those of us in the JARS Working Group viewed these spurs to action as positive developments for the psychological sciences. We wrote,

> The first [use of evidence] provides an unprecedented opportunity for psychological research to play an important role in public and health policy. The second

[meta-analysis of basic research] promises a sounder evidence base for explanations of psychological phenomena and a next generation of research that is more focused on resolving critical issues. (APA Publication and Communication Board [P&C Board] Working Group on Journal Article Reporting Standards, 2008, p. 840)

The State of the Art Before JARS

The development of the first JARS began in 2007 with the collection of reporting standards that had been developed by other social science and health organizations. Three efforts quickly came to the attention of the JARS Working Group.

The first is called the Consolidated Standards of Reporting Trials (CONSORT; http://www.consort-statement.org). CONSORT was developed by an ad hoc group primarily composed of biostatisticians and medical researchers. The CONSORT standards are specific to the reporting of studies that carried out random assignment of participants to conditions. These standards also use language that is most familiar to medical researchers. CONSORT comprises a checklist of study characteristics that should be included in research reports and a flowchart that provides readers with a description of the number of participants as they progress through the study—and by implication the number who drop out—from the time they are deemed eligible for inclusion until the end of the investigation. The use of CONSORT is now required by top medical journals and many other biomedical journals. The JARS Working Group found that some APA journals had adopted the CONSORT guidelines as well.

The second effort, developed through an initiative of the Centers for Disease Control and Prevention (CDC), is called Transparent Reporting of Evaluations with Nonrandomized Designs (TREND; CDC, 2016; Des Jarlais, Lyles, & Crepaz, 2004). The CDC brought together a group of editors of journals related to public health, including several journals in psychology. TREND contains a 22-item checklist, similar to the checklist in CONSORT but with a specific focus on reporting studies that use quasi-experimental designs—that is, group comparisons in which the groups were established through procedures other than random assignment to place participants in conditions.

In the social sciences, the American Educational Research Association (AERA, 2006) published "Standards for Reporting on Empirical Social Science Research in AERA Publications." These standards encompass a broad range of research designs, including both quantitative and qualitative approaches. AERA divided the standards into eight general areas, including problem formulation; design and logic of the study; sources of evidence; measurement and classification; analysis and interpretation; generalization; ethics in reporting; and title, abstract, and headings. These standards contain about two dozen general prescriptions for the reporting of studies as well as separate prescriptions for quantitative and qualitative studies.

The JARS Working Group also examined previous editions of the *Publication Manual of the American Psychological Association*. We discovered that, for the past half century, the *Publication Manual* has played an important role in the establishment of reporting standards. The first edition was published in 1952 as a supplement to *Psychological Bulletin* (APA, Council of Editors, 1952). It contained 61 pages printed on 9-in. × 6-in. paper (and cost $1—ah, the good old days). The principal divisions of manuscripts were Problem, Method, Results, Discussion, and Summary.

Here is what the first *Publication Manual* suggested should be included in each section: The Problem section was to include

- the questions asked and the reasons for asking them and
- when experiments were theory driven, the theoretical propositions that generated the hypotheses, along with the logic of their derivation.

The Method section was to include

- "enough detail to permit the reader to repeat the experiment unless portions of it have been described in other reports which can be cited" (APA, Council of Editors, 1952, p. 9),
- the design and logic of relating the empirical data to theoretical propositions, the subjects, sampling and control devices, the techniques of measurement, and any apparatus used.

The Results section was to include

- enough data to justify the conclusions, with special attention to tests of statistical significance and the logic of inference and generalization.

The Discussion section was to include

- limitations of the conclusions,
- the relation of conclusions to other findings and widely accepted points of view, and
- implications for theory or practice.

Also, authors were encouraged to use good grammar and to avoid jargon: "Some writing in psychology gives the impression that long words and obscure expressions are regarded as evidence of scientific status" (APA, Council of Editors, 1952, pp. 11–12; maybe the good old days weren't so good after all).

These descriptions suggest that little has changed over the past half century in the basic structure and function of a psychology journal article. Of interest, we found two other policy decisions made by the first drafters of the *Publication Manual* that have particular resonance today. First, the APA Council of Editors (1952) advised that negative or unexpected results were not to be accompanied by extended discussions: "Long 'alibis,' unsupported by evidence or sound theory, add nothing to the usefulness of the report" (p. 9). Second, this edition of the *Publication Manual* also stated that "sometimes space limitations dictate that the method be described synoptically in a journal, and a more detailed description be given in auxiliary publication" (APA, Council of Editors, 1952, p. 9). This practice has rarely been used by journals but is now coming back into favor, as discussed in Chapter 1 in this volume.

In later editions of the *Publication Manual*, the APA Style recommendations for reporting became more detailed and specific. Of special note was the report of Wilkinson and the Task Force on Statistical Inference (1999), which presented guidelines for statistical reporting in APA journals. This report informed the content of the fifth edition of the *Publication Manual* (APA, 2001). Although the fifth edition did not contain an aggregated set of reporting standards, this does not mean that it was devoid of standards. Instead, prescriptions for reporting were embedded in various sections of the text. In the *Publication Manual*'s description of the parts of a manuscript, members of the JARS Working Group found statements regarding how to report and what to report in the Method and Results sections of a study (APA, 2001, pp. 10–29). For example, when discussing who participated in a study, the fifth edition stated, "When humans participated as the subjects of the study, report the procedures for selecting and assigning them and the agreements and payments made" (APA, 2001, p. 18). With regard to the Results section, the fifth edition stated, "Mention all relevant results, including those that run counter to the hypothesis" (APA, 2001, p. 20), and it provided descriptions of "sufficient statistics" (p. 23) that need to be reported.

Thus, members of the JARS Working Group found that although reporting standards and requirements were not highlighted in the past editions of the *Publication Manual*, they appeared in it nonetheless. In that context, we concluded that the proposals we offered could be viewed not as breaking new ground for psychological research reporting but rather as systematizing, clarifying, and somewhat expanding standards that already existed. The intended contribution of our effort became one of increased emphasis as much as of increased content.

Drafting, Vetting, and Refining JARS

After these initial explorations of existing reporting standards, members of the JARS Group canvassed the APA Council of Editors to find out the degree to which the CONSORT and TREND standards were already used in APA journals and to learn about other reporting standards. Then, we compared the content of the CONSORT, TREND, and AERA standards with one another and developed a combined list of nonredundant elements contained in any or all of the three sets of standards. Finally, we examined the combined list, rewrote some items so that they would better apply to the work of psychologists, and added a few suggestions of our own.

This combined list was then shared with the APA Council of Editors, the *Publication Manual* Revision Task Force, and the APA P&C Board. These groups were asked to react to the list. After receiving their comments and anonymous reactions from reviewers chosen by the *American Psychologist*, we revised our report and arrived at the list of recommendations contained in Table A1.1, Table A4.1, Tables A4.2a and 4.2b, and Figure 5.1. The report was then approved again by the P&C Board. The full report of the JARS Group was published in 2008 in the *American Psychologist* (APA Publications and Communications Board Working Group on Journal Article Reporting Standards, 2008).

Development of the MARS

Members of the JARS Working Group did the work of developing the MARS in much the same way as they developed JARS. We began by contacting the members of the Society for Research Synthesis Methodology and asking them to share what they thought were the critical aspects of conducting a meta-analysis that needed to be reported so that readers could make informed, critical judgments about the appropriateness of the methods used for the inferences drawn. This query led to the identification of four other efforts to establish reporting standards for meta-analyses. These included the Quality of Reporting of Meta-Analysis Statement (Moher et al., 1999) and its revision, Preferred Reporting Items for Systematic Reviews and Meta-Analyses (PRISMA; Moher, Liberati, Tetzlaff, & Altman, 2009), as well as the Meta-Analysis of Observational Studies in Epidemiology

(Stroup et al., 2000) and the Potsdam Consultation on Meta-Analysis (Cook, Sackett, & Spitzer, 1995).

Next, members of the JARS Working Group compared the content of the four sets of standards with one another and developed a combined list of nonredundant elements. We then examined the combined list; rewrote some items for maximum applicability to the fields of psychological, social, and behavioral science; and added a few suggestions of our own. We shared the resulting recommendations with a subgroup of members of the Society for Research Synthesis Methodology who had experience writing and reviewing research syntheses in the discipline of psychology. After their suggestions were incorporated into the list, the items were shared with members of the APA P&C Board. We arrived at the list of recommendations contained in Table A8.1. These recommendations were then approved by the Publications and Communications Board.

The Revision: JARS for Quantitative Studies

The JARS Working Group for revision, referred to as the JARS–Quant Working Group to distinguish it from the group working on guidelines for qualitative research, began working in 2015. The JARS–Quant Working Group was tasked with updating JARS and adding modules for additional research designs. We found that in at least one way the landscape for reporting standards had changed dramatically: there was a growing recognition of the need for greater transparency in reporting. In fact, we found an organization called the Equator Network (Enhancing the Quality and Transparency of Health Research; http://www.equator-network.org/) that had compiled a library of literally dozens of research reporting standards. These standards related to research designs of many types, including experiments, observational studies, research syntheses, case reports, qualitative research, diagnosis and prognosis, and economics, to name a few. Still, because most of these had a medical bent to them, we felt a JARS for psychology was in order so that our unique problem and analysis issues could be highlighted and so the terminology fit that used in our field.

The JARS–Quant Group followed the same steps established by the original JARS Working Group: (a) collect related reporting standards, (b) examine them for items relevant to research in psychology that were not included in the original JARS, and (c) vet our product with the APA Council of Editors, the P&C Board, and other specialized groups with particular interest in a specific type of research design (e.g., the Society for Research in Child Development for the JARS module on longitudinal data collections). The full report of the JARS–Quant Group was published in 2018 in the *American Psychologist* (Appelbaum et al., 2018).

Other Issues Related to Reporting Standards

A Definition of *Reporting Standards*

The JARS Group struggled with the issue of how prescriptive our effort should be. We recognized that our standards could be taken at least three different ways: as recommendations, standards, or requirements. We were indeed recommending that certain information be reported in the research write-up. We also thought these recommendations could be viewed as standards, or at least as a beginning effort at developing standards, because we thought researchers who followed them more closely would produce documents of greater value or quality. The recommendations set a standard based on an integration of efforts by authoritative groups of researchers and editors.

However, we did not want the proposed standards to be viewed as requirements. The methods used in the subdisciplines of psychology vary greatly. The critical information needed to assess the quality of research and to integrate it successfully with other related studies varies from method to method and by the context of the topic under consideration. We felt that calling these guidelines *standards* rather than *requirements* would give them the weight of authority while retaining flexibility for authors and editors to use them in the most efficacious fashion.

Benefits and Drawbacks of Reporting Standards

The general principle that guided the establishment of JARS and MARS was to promote sufficient and transparent descriptions of a study's design, implementation, and findings. Complete reporting allows readers to make a clearer assessment of the strengths and weaknesses of a study. This permits the users of the evidence to judge more accurately the appropriate inferences and applications derivable from research findings.

Further, the existence of reporting standards could have a positive effect on the way research is conducted. For example, by setting a standard that attrition rates should be reported (see Figures 5.1 and 5.2), researchers may begin considering more concretely what acceptable levels of attrition might be and feel compelled to implement procedures meant to maximize the number of participants who complete a study.

Finally, reporting standards can make it easier for other researchers to design and conduct replications and related studies. Standards help by providing more complete descriptions of previous study recipes. Complete reporting of the critical aspects of design and results enables researchers to figure out what caused the difference in outcomes when new studies do not replicate the results of older ones.

The JARS Working Groups also thought it was important to point out that reporting standards also can have a downside. Both groups tried to highlight the relationship between standards and standardization and why we were not interested in calling our effort "requirements." For example, standardized reporting could fill articles with details of methods and results that are inconsequential to interpretation. The critical facts about a study can get lost in an excess of minutiae. Also, a forced consistency can lead a researcher to ignore important uniqueness. We thought that reporting standards that appeared comprehensive might lead researchers to believe that if it is not asked for or does not conform to criteria specified in the standards, it is not necessary to report. This was not our intent. The standards you encounter in this book may appear exhaustive, but they should not lead you to omit information critical to understanding what was done in a study and what was found.

Again, the JARS Working Groups noted that different methods are required for studying different psychological phenomena. What needs to be reported to evaluate the correspondence between methods and inferences is highly dependent on the research question and approach and the context in which the study is being conducted. Inferences about the neuroscience of text processing, for example, require attention to aspects of research design and analysis that are different from those important for inferences about influences on conformity. This context dependency pertains not only to topic-specific considerations but also to research designs. Thus, an experimental study of the determinants of well-being analyzed with analysis of variance raises different reporting needs than does a study on the same topic that involves to establishment of a new measure of well-being.

Obstacles to Developing Standards

The first obstacle we ran into while developing JARS was that differing taxonomies of research approaches exist and that different terms are used within different subdisciplines to describe the same research procedures. For example, researchers in health psychology typically refer to studies that use experimental manipulations of treatments conducted in naturalistic settings as *randomized clinical trials*, whereas similar designs are referred to as *randomized field trials* in educational psychology. As a further example, the terms *multilevel modeling, hierarchical linear modeling*, and *mixed-effects modeling* all are used to identify a similar approach to data analysis. To address the problem of terminology differences across the disciplines of social and behavioral sciences and the subdisciplines of psychology, we attempted to use the simplest descriptions possible and to avoid jargon in the JARS tables.

A second obstacle we encountered was that certain research topics and methods reveal different levels of consensus regarding what is and is not important to report. Generally, the newer and more complex the method, the less agreement there is about reporting standards. For example, although there are many benefits to reporting effect sizes, there are certain situations (e.g., multilevel designs) in which no clear consensus exists on how best to conceptualize or calculate effect size measures. In a related vein, reporting a confidence interval with an effect size is sound advice. However, calculating confidence intervals for effect sizes is often difficult given the current state of software. For this reason, the JARS Working Groups avoided developing reporting standards for research designs about which a professional consensus had not yet emerged. As consensus emerges, the JARS tables can still be expanded with new modules.

Finally, the rapid pace of developments in methodology dictates that any standards have to be updated frequently to remain relevant. For example, the state of the art for reporting various analytic techniques is in a constant state of flux. Although some general principles (e.g., reporting the estimation procedure used in a structural equation model) can incorporate new developments easily, other developments can involve fundamentally new types of data for which standards must, by necessity, evolve. New and emerging methods used in psychological research, such as functional neuroimaging and molecular genetics, may require frequent revision of standards to ensure that the current standards are covering what researchers in the field think is important.

Future Uses of JARS

Members of the JARS–Quant Working Group recognize that our work is incomplete because we have included only a few families of research designs. In the future, we plan to add new modules for other research designs that can be used in conjunction with Table A.1.1. Also, additional standards could be adopted for any of the parts of a report, and new areas of research, perhaps research involving the use of archival records and the development of new psychological tests, can be added, to name just two. Perhaps these will be added to future revisions of JARS (and this book).

APPENDIX
Abstracts of the 16 Articles Used as Examples in Text

Journal of Experimental Psychology:
Human Perception and Performance
2009, Vol. 35, No. 2, 520–529

© 2009 American Psychological Association
0096-1523/09/$12.00   http://dx.doi.org/10.1037/a0013552

Comprehension of Familiar and Unfamiliar Native Accents Under Adverse Listening Conditions

Patti Adank
Radboud University Nijmegen

Bronwen G. Evans
University College London

Jane Stuart-Smith
University of Glasgow

Sophie K. Scott
University College London

This study aimed to determine the relative processing cost associated with comprehension of an unfamiliar native accent under adverse listening conditions. Two sentence verification experiments were conducted in which listeners heard sentences at various signal-to-noise ratios. In Experiment 1, these sentences were spoken in a familiar or an unfamiliar native accent or in 2 familiar native accents. In Experiment 2, they were spoken in a familiar or unfamiliar native accent or in a nonnative accent. The results indicated that the differences between the native accents influenced the speed of language processing under adverse listening conditions and that this processing speed was modulated by the relative familiarity of the listener with the native accent. Furthermore, the results showed that the processing cost associated with the nonnative accent was larger than for the unfamiliar native accent.

Keywords: speech comprehension, native accents, nonnative accents, adverse listening conditions

Journal of Consulting and Clinical Psychology
2009, Vol. 77, No. 5, 961–973

© 2009 American Psychological Association
0022-006X/09/$12.00   http://dx.doi.org/10.1037/a0016685

Attention Training in Individuals With Generalized Social Phobia: A Randomized Controlled Trial

Nader Amir
San Diego State University

Courtney Beard
Brown University

Charles T. Taylor
San Diego State University

Heide Klumpp
University of Michigan

Jason Elias
McLean Hospital

Michelle Burns
University of Georgia

Xi Chen
San Diego State University

The authors conducted a randomized, double-blind placebo-controlled trial to examine the efficacy of an attention training procedure in reducing symptoms of social anxiety in 44 individuals diagnosed with generalized social phobia (GSP). Attention training comprised a probe detection task in which pictures of faces with either a threatening or neutral emotional expression cued different locations on the computer screen. In the attention modification program (AMP), participants responded to a probe that always followed neutral faces when paired with a threatening face, thereby directing attention away from threat. In the attention control condition (ACC), the probe appeared with equal frequency in the position of the threatening and neutral faces. Results revealed that the AMP facilitated attention disengagement from threat from pre- to postassessment and reduced clinician- and self-reported symptoms of social anxiety relative to the ACC. The percentage of participants no longer meeting *Diagnostic and Statistical Manual of Mental Disorders* (4th ed.; American Psychiatric Association, 1994) criteria for GSP at postassessment was 50% in the AMP and 14% in the ACC. Symptom reduction in the AMP group was maintained during 4-month follow-up assessment. These results suggest that computerized attention training procedures may be beneficial for treating social phobia.

Keywords: socialphobia, attention, treatment, information processing

The Behavior Analyst Today
2003, Vol. 4, No. 3, 367–377

© 2003 by the American Psychological Association
http://dx.doi.org/10.1037/h0100025

Video Modeling: A Window into the World of Autism

Blythe A. Corbett. Ph.D.
M.I.N.D. Institute
Department of Psychiatry and Behavioral Sciences

Video modeling is a well-validated behavioral intervention documented in the behavioral sciences. The methodology appears particularly beneficial for children with autism. The underlying theoretical explanations are posited and discussed. A single case study is presented using video modeling to improve the perception of emotion in a child with autism and mild mental retardation. The subject was shown a series of video tapes of typically developing children engaged in a variety of play and social scenarios showing four basic emotions: happy, sad. angry and afraid. The preliminary results, based on behavioral and neuropsychological data, demonstrated video modeling to be an efficacious intervention for the attainment and generalization of emotion perception. The acquisition of skills using video modeling is often very rapid compared to other methods of intervention and requires limited time and personal resources to implement. The skill is then maintained with careful behavioral programming, which includes stable attainment of mastery and built-in generalization conditions (e.g.. multiple exemplars). Further, video modeling appears to be particularly useful in eliciting generalized responses across behaviors and stimuli that is corroborated by improvement on neuropsychological instruments. Implications for current and future research are discussed.

Keywords: autism, video modeling, behavioral treatment

A Quasi-Experimental Study on Management Coaching Effectiveness

Will. J. G. Evers, André Brouwers, and Welko Tomic
The Open University

Coaching has become an important managerial instrument of support. However, there is a lack of research on its effectiveness. The authors conducted a quasi-experimental study to figure out whether coaching really leads to presupposed individual goals. Sixty managers of the federal government were divided in 2 groups: one group followed a coaching program, the other did not. Before the coaching program started (Time 1), self-efficacy beliefs and outcome expectancies were measured, linked to 3 central domains of functioning: setting one's own goals, acting in a balanced way, and mindful living and working. Four months later (Time 2), the same variables were measured again. Results showed that the coached group scored significantly higher than the control group on 2 variables: outcome expectancies to act in a balanced way and self-efficacy beliefs to set one's own goals. Future examination might reveal whether coaching will also be effective among managers who work at different management levels, whether the effects found will be long-lasting, and whether subordinates experience differences in the way their manager functions before and after the coaching.

Keywords: management coaching, quasi-experiment, outcome experiences, self-efficacy

Copyright 2006 by the American Psychological Association and the Society of Consulting Psychology, 1065-9293/06/$12.00
DOI: 10.1037/1065-9293.58.3.174
Consulting Psychology Journal: Practice and Research, Vol. 58, No. 3, 174–182

Developmental Psychology
2009, Vol. 45, No. 5, 1389–1405

Pathways to Paternal Engagement:
Longitudinal Effects of Risk and Resilience on Nonresident Fathers

Jay Fagan
Temple University

Rob Palkovitz
University of Delaware

Kevin Roy
University of Maryland

Danielle Farrie
Temple University

This article assesses the longitudinal effects of risk and resilience on unmarried nonresident fathers' engagement with children across the first 3 years of their lives. The authors used a subsample of 549 men from the Fragile Families and Child Wellbeing Study who were unmarried and noncohabiting at the time of the child's birth. They found not only that risk and resilience factors had a direct effect on paternal engagement but also that their association with engagement was mediated by fathers' continued nonresidence and mother–father relationship quality. Men who leave trajectories of high risk behind during the transition to fatherhood and who have a trajectory characterized by resilience factors are more likely to experience better relationships with the mother of their children, more likely to establish subsequent coresidence with their children, and more likely to remain involved in their children's lives on a daily basis. Implications for policy and programs serving fathers and families are discussed.

Keywords: fragile families, nonresident fathers, father involvement, resilience, risk

Journal of Experimental Psychology:
Learning, Memory, and Cognition
2009, Vol. 35, No. 5, 1105–1122

Deficits in Cross-Race Face Learning:
Insights From Eye Movements and Pupillometry

Stephen D. Goldinger
Arizona State University

Yi He
Yale University

Megan H. Papesh
Arizona State University

The own-race bias (ORB) is a well-known finding wherein people are better able to recognize and discriminate own-race faces, relative to cross-race faces. In 2 experiments, participants viewed Asian and Caucasian faces, in preparation for recognition memory tests, while their eye movements and pupil diameters were continuously monitored. In Experiment 1 (with Caucasian participants), systematic differences emerged in both measures as a function of depicted race: While encoding cross-race faces, participants made fewer (and longer) fixations, they preferentially attended to different sets of features, and their pupils were more dilated, all relative to own-race faces. Also, in both measures, a pattern emerged wherein some participants reduced their apparent encoding effort to cross-race faces over trials. In Experiment 2 (with Asian participants), the authors observed the same patterns, although the ORB favored the opposite set of faces. Taken together, the results suggest that the ORB appears during initial perceptual encoding. Relative to own-race face encoding, cross-race encoding requires greater effort, which may reduce vigilance in some participants.

Keywords: face memory, own-race bias, eye movements, pupil dilation

Psychological Bulletin
2008. Vol. 134. No. 3. 460-476

The Role of the Media in Body Image Concerns Among Women: A Meta-Analysis of Experimental and Correlational Studies

Shelly Grabe
University of Wisconsin-Madison

L. Monique Ward
University of Michigan

Janet Shibley Hyde
University of Wisconsin-Madison

Research suggests that exposure to mass media depicting the thin-ideal body may be linked to body image disturbance in women. This meta-analysis examined experimental and correlational studies testing the links between media exposure to women's body dissatisfaction, internalization of the thin ideal, and eating behaviors and beliefs with a sample of 77 studies that yielded 141 effect sizes. The mean effect sizes were small to moderate ($ds = -.28, -.39,$ and $-.30$, respectively). Effects for some outcome variables were moderated by publication year and study design. The findings support the notion that exposure to media images depicting the thin-ideal body is related to body image concerns for women.

Keywords: body image, media, advertising, human females, meta-analysis

Journal of Experimental Psychology:
Animal Behavior Processes
2009, Vol. 35, No. 4, 447–472

The Dynamics of Conditioning and Extinction

Peter R. Killeen, Federico Sanabria, and Igor Dolgov
Arizona State University

Pigeons responded to intermittently reinforced classical conditioning trials with erratic bouts of responding to the conditioned stimulus. Responding depended on whether the prior trial contained a peck, food, or both. A linear persistence–learning model moved pigeons into and out of a response state, and a Weibull distribution for number of within-trial responses governed in-state pecking. Variations of trial and intertrial durations caused correlated changes in rate and probability of responding and in model parameters. A novel prediction—in the protracted absence of food, response rates can plateau above zero—was validated. The model predicted smooth acquisition functions when instantiated with the probability of food but a more accurate jagged learning curve when instantiated with trial-to-trial records of reinforcement. The Skinnerian parameter was dominant only when food could be accelerated or delayed by pecking. These experiments provide a framework for trial-by-trial accounts of conditioning and extinction that increases the information available from the data, permitting such accounts to comment more definitively on complex contemporary models of momentum and conditioning.

Keywords: autoshaping, behavioral momentum, classical conditioning, dynamic analyses, instrumental conditioning

Journal of Educational Psychology
2008, Vol. 100, No. 4, 741–753

Classroom Age Composition and Developmental Change in 70 Urban Preschool Classrooms

Arlen C. Moller
Children's Institute, Inc., and Gettysburg College

Emma Forbes-Jones and A. Dirk Hightower
Children's Institute, Inc., and University of Rochester

A multilevel modeling approach was used to investigate the influence of age composition in 70 urban preschool classrooms. A series of hierarchical linear models demonstrated that greater variance in classroom age composition was negatively related to development on the Child Observation Record (COR) Cognitive, Motor, and Social subscales. This was true when controlling for class size, general classroom quality, and socioeconomic status at the classroom level and for age, gender, and baseline ability at the child level. Additionally, to address possible concerns related to nonrandom assignment to classrooms, a series of models were run including variance in developmental age (i.e., baseline ability) at the classroom level and at the child level. The results were consistent for chronological age composition and developmental age composition at the classroom level; greater variance in classroom developmental age composition was negatively related to Time 2 scores on the COR Cognitive, Motor, and Social subscales. Furthermore, a cross-level interaction indicated that negative influence of greater variance in classroom developmental age composition was stronger for children older in developmental age. Implications for early childhood education policy are discussed.

Keywords: preschool, mixed age, single age, age composition, Child Observation Record

Health Psychology
2008, Vol. 27, No. 6, 799–810

Using the Internet to Assist Smoking Prevention and Cessation in Schools: A Randomized, Controlled Trial

Cameron D. Norman, Oonagh Maley, and Xiaoqiang Li
University of Toronto

Harvey A. Skinner
York University

Objective: To evaluate the impact of a classroom-based, web-assisted tobacco intervention addressing smoking prevention and cessation with adolescents. *Design:* A 2-group randomized control trial with 1,402 male and female students in Grades 9 through 11 from 14 secondary schools in Toronto, Canada. Participants were randomly assigned to a tailored web-assisted tobacco intervention or an interactive control condition task conducted during a single classroom session with e-mail follow-up. The cornerstone of the intervention was a 5-stage interactive website called the *Smoking Zine* (http://www.smokingzine.org) integrated into a program that included a paper-based journal, a small group form of motivational interviewing, and tailored e-mails. *Main Outcome Measure:* Resistance to smoking, behavioral intentions to smoke, and cigarette use were assessed at baseline, postintervention, and 3- and 6-month follow-up. Multilevel logistic growth modeling was used to assess the effect of the intervention on change overtime. *Results:* The integrated *Smoking Zine* program helped smokers significantly reduce the likelihood of having high intentions to smoke and increased their likelihood of high resistance to continued cigarette use at 6 months. The intervention also significantly reduced the likelihood of heavy cigarette use adoption by nonsmokers during the study period. *Conclusion:* The *Smoking Zine* intervention provided cessation motivation for smokers most resistant to quitting at baseline and prevented nonsmoking adolescents from becoming heavy smokers at 6 months. By providing an accessible and attractive method of engaging young people in smoking prevention and cessation, this interactive and integrated program provides a novel vehicle for school- and population-level health promotion.

Keywords: Internet, smoking prevention, smoking cessation, adolescents, school-based interventions

Journal of Occupational Health Psychology
2009, Vol. 14, No. 3, 318–333

Exploring Relationships Among Anger, Perceived Organizational Support, and Workplace Outcomes

Olivia A. O'Neill, Robert J. Vandenberg, David M. DeJoy, and Mark G. Wilson
University of Georgia

The present study examines anger within a perceived organizational support (POS) theory framework. Using structural equation modeling, the authors explored relationships among POS, anger, and workplace outcomes in a sample of 1,136 employees in 21 stores of a U.S. retail organization. At both individual and store levels, low POS was directly associated with greater anger. At the individual level, anger partially mediated relationships among low POS and turnover intentions, absences, and accidents on the job. Anger had direct and indirect effects on alcohol consumption and health-related risk taking. At the store level, anger had direct negative effects on inventory loss and turnover. The authors interpret these findings in light of social exchange theory and emotion regulation theory.

Keywords: anger, perceived organizational support, turnover, health, multilevel models

Journal of Personality and Social Psychology
2008, Vol. 95, No. 2, 293–307

Why People Are Reluctant to Tempt Fate

Jane L. Risen
University of Chicago

Thomas Gilovich
Cornell University

The present research explored the belief that it is bad luck to "tempt fate." Studies 1 and 2 demonstrated that people do indeed have the intuition that actions that tempt fate increase the likelihood of negative outcomes. Studies 3–6 examined our claim that the intuition is due, in large part, to the combination of the automatic tendencies to attend to negative prospects and to use accessibility as a cue when judging likelihood. Study 3 demonstrated that negative outcomes are more accessible following actions that tempt fate than following actions that do not tempt fate. Studies 4 and 5 demonstrated that the heightened accessibility of negative outcomes mediates the elevated perceptions of likelihood. Finally, Study 6 examined the automatic nature of the underlying processes. The types of actions that are thought to tempt fate as well as the role of society and culture in shaping this magical belief are discussed.

Keywords: tempt fate, magical thinking, accessibility, negativity

Psychology of Addictive Behaviors
2009, Vol. 23, No. 3, 491–499

© 2009 American Psychological Association
0893-164X/09/$12.00 http://dx.doi.org/10.1037/a0016632

Evidence for a Putative Biomarker for Substance Dependence

Jeanette Taylor and Lisa M. James
Florida State University

Electrodermal response modulation (ERM) reflects the reduction in skin conductance response to an aversive stimulus that is temporally predictable relative to when it is unpredictable. Poor ERM is associated with substance dependence (SD). It was hypothesized that ERM is a putative biomarker for SD rather than for externalizing disorders generally. Participants included 83 controls (no SD, antisocial personality disorder [PD] or borderline PD), 52 participants with SD only (SD and no PD), 12 with PD only (antisocial and/or borderline PD and no SD), and 35 comorbid (having SD and PD). Diagnoses at definite and probable certainty levels were used and were determined by semistructured clinical interviews. ERM was calculated from skin conductance responses to predictable and unpredictable 2-s 110-dB white noise blasts. As expected, the SD-only and comorbid groups had significantly lower ERM scores than the control group, which did not differ significantly from the PD-only group. Results provide preliminary evidence that ERM is a putative biomarker for SD. Future research should examine cognitive correlates of ERM in an effort to understand why it relates to SD.

Keywords: electrodermal response, substance dependence, antisocial personality disorder, borderline personality disorder, disinhibition

Rehabilitation Psychology
2009, Vol. 54, No. 3, 299–305

© 2009 American Psychological Association
0090-5550/09/$12.00 http://dx.doi.org/10.1037/a0016807

The Relationship Between Employment-Related Self-Efficacy and Quality of Life Following Traumatic Brain Injury

Theodore Tsaousides, Adam Warshowsky, Teresa A. Ashman, Joshua B. Cantor, Lisa Spielman, and Wayne A. Gordon
Mount Sinai School of Medicine

Objectives: This study examines the relative contribution of employment-related and general self-efficacy to perceptions of quality of life (QoL) for individuals with traumatic brain injury. *Design:* Correlational. *Setting:* Community-based research and training center. *Participants:* 427 individuals with self-reported TBI under the age of 65 were included in analysis. *Main Outcome Measure:* Employment-related self-efficacy, general self-efficacy, perceived quality of life (PQoL), unmet important needs (UIN). *Results:* Significant correlations were found between income, injury severity, age at injury, and employment and the QoL variables. In addition, employment-related and general self-efficacy correlated positively with both PQoL and UIN. Employment-related and general self-efficacy accounted for 16% of the variance in PQoL and 9.5% of the variance in UIN, over and above other variables traditionally associated with QoL. *Conclusions:* These findings highlight the importance of including subjective appraisals of employment, such as perceived self-efficacy at the workplace, in assessing QoL and successful return to work following TBI.

Keywords: traumatic brain injury, employment, self-efficacy, quality of life

Journal of Educational Psychology
2008, Vol. 100, No. 2, 272–290

Repeated Reading Intervention: Outcomes and Interactions With Readers' Skills and Classroom Instruction

Patricia F. Vadasy and Elizabeth A. Sanders
Washington Research Institute

This study examined effects of a repeated reading intervention, *Quick Reads*, with incidental word-level scaffolding instruction. Second- and 3rd-grade students with passage-reading fluency performance between the 10th and 60th percentiles were randomly assigned to dyads, which were in turn randomly assigned to treatment (paired tutoring, $n = 82$) or control (no tutoring, $n = 80$) conditions. Paraeducators tutored dyads for 30 min per day, 4 days per week, for 15 weeks (November–March). At midintervention, most teachers with students in the study were formally observed during their literacy blocks. Multilevel modeling was used to test for direct treatment effects on pretest–posttest gains as well as to test for unique treatment effects after classroom oral text reading time, 2 pretests, and corresponding interactions were accounted for. Model results revealed both direct and unique treatment effects on gains in word reading and fluency. Moreover, complex interactions between group, oral text reading time, and pretests were also detected, suggesting that pretest skills should be taken into account when considering repeated reading instruction for 2nd and 3rd graders with low to average passage-reading fluency.

Keywords: multilevel modeling, fluency, repeated reading, verbal efficiency, paraeducators

Psychotherapy Theory, Research, Practice, Training
2009, Vol. 46, No. 3, 362–375

Do Personality Problems Improve During Psychodynamic Supportive–Expressive Psychotherapy? Secondary Outcome Results From a Randomized Controlled Trial for Psychiatric Outpatients With Personality Disorders

Bo Vinnars and
Barbro Thormählen
Karolinska Institutet

Robert Gallop
West Chester University

Kristina Norén
Karolinska Institutet

Jacques P. Barber
University of Pennsylvania School
of Medicine

Studies involving patients with personality disorders (PDs) have not focused on improvement of core aspects of the PD. The authors examined changes in quality of object relations, interpersonal problems, psychological mindedness, and personality traits in a sample of 156 patients with *Diagnostic and Statistical Manual of Mental Disorders* (4th ed.; American Psychiatric Association, 1994) PD diagnoses being randomized to either manualized or nonmanualized dynamic psychotherapy. Effect sizes adjusted for symptomatic change and reliable change indices were calculated. The authors found that both treatments were equally effective at reducing personality pathology. Only in neuroticism did the nonmanualized group do better during the follow-up period. The largest improvement was found in quality of object relations. For the remaining variables, only small and clinically insignificant magnitudes of change were found.

Keywords: personality disorder, psychodynamic psychotherapy, psychotherapy outcome, personality problems

References

Adank, P., Evans, B. G., Stuart-Smith, J., & Scott, S. K. (2009). Comprehension of familiar and unfamiliar native accents under adverse listening conditions. *Journal of Experimental Psychology: Human Perception and Performance*, *35*, 520–529. http://dx.doi.org/10.1037/a0013552

Altman, D. G., Schulz, K. F., Moher, D., Egger, M., Davidoff, F., Elbourne, D., . . . Lang, T. (2001). The revised CONSORT statement for reporting randomized trials: Explanation and elaboration. *Annals of Internal Medicine*, *134*, 663–694. http://dx.doi.org/10.7326/0003-4819-134-8-200104170-00012

American Educational Research Association. (2006). Standards for reporting on empirical social science research in AERA publications. *Educational Researcher*, *35*(6), 33–40. http://dx.doi.org/10.3102/0013189X035006033

American Psychological Association. (2001). *Publication manual of the American Psychological Association* (5th ed.). Washington, DC: Author.

American Psychological Association. (2010). *Publication manual of the American Psychological Association* (6th ed.). Washington, DC: Author.

American Psychological Association. (2017). *Ethical principles of psychologists and code of conduct* (2002, Amended June 1, 2010 and January 1, 2017). Retrieved from http://www.apa.org/ethics/code/index.aspx

American Psychological Association, Council of Editors. (1952). Publication manual of the American Psychological Association. *Psychological Bulletin*, *49*(Suppl., Pt. 2), 389–449.

American Psychological Association, Presidential Task Force on Evidence-Based Practice. (2006). Evidence-based practice in psychology. *American Psychologist*, *61*, 271–285. http://dx.doi.org/10.1037/0003-066X.61.4.271

American Psychological Association Publications and Communications Board Working Group on Journal Article Reporting Standards. (2008). Reporting standards for research in psychology: Why do we need them? What might they be? *American Psychologist, 63,* 839–851. http://dx.doi.org/10.1037/0003-066X.63.9.839

Amir, N., Beard, C., Taylor, C. T., Klumpp, H., Elias, J., Burns, M., & Chen, X. (2009). Attention training in individuals with generalized social phobia: A randomized controlled trial. *Journal of Consulting and Clinical Psychology, 77,* 961–973. http://dx.doi.org/10.1037/a0016685

Appelbaum, M., Cooper, H., Kline, R. B., Mayo-Wilson, E., Nezu, A. M., & Rao, S. M. (2018). Journal article reporting standards for quantitative research in psychology: The APA Publications and Communications Board task force report. *American Psychologist, 73,* 3–25. http://dx.doi.org/10.1037/amp0000191

Atkinson, K. M., Koenka, A. C., Sanchez, C. E., Moshontz, H., & Cooper, H. (2015). Reporting standards for literature searches and report inclusion criteria: Making research syntheses more transparent and easy to replicate. *Research Synthesis Methods, 6,* 87–95. http://dx.doi.org/10.1002/jrsm.1127

Barlow, D. H., Nock, M. K., & Hersen, M. (2008). *Single case research design: Strategies for studying behavior change.* Boston, MA: Pearson.

Borenstein, M. (2009). Effect sizes for studies with continuous data. In H. Cooper, L. V. Hedges, & J. C. Valentine (Eds.), *The handbook of research synthesis and meta-analysis* (2nd ed., pp. 221–236). New York, NY: Russell Sage Foundation.

Borenstein, M., Hedges, L. V., Higgins, J. P. T., & Rothstein, H. R. (2009). *Introduction to meta-analysis.* West Sussex, England: Wiley. http://dx.doi.org/10.1002/9780470743386

Bowden, V. K., & Loft, S. (2016). Using memory for prior aircraft events to detect conflicts under conditions of proactive air traffic control and with concurrent task requirements. *Journal of Experimental Psychology: Applied, 22,* 211–224. http://dx.doi.org/10.1037/xap0000085

Bricker, J. B., Rajan, K. B., Zalewski, M., Andersen, M. R., Ramey, M., & Peterson, A. V. (2009). Psychological and social risk factors in adolescent smoking transitions: A population-based longitudinal study. *Health Psychology, 28,* 439–447. http://dx.doi.org/10.1037/a0014568

Burgmans, S., van Boxtel, M. P., Vuurman, E. F., Smeets, F., Gronenschild, E. H., Uylings, H. B., & Jolles, J. (2009). The prevalence of cortical gray matter atrophy may be overestimated in the healthy aging brain. *Neuropsychology, 23,* 541–550. http://dx.doi.org/10.1037/a0016161

Centers for Disease Control and Prevention. (2016). Transparent Reporting of Evaluations with Nonrandomized Designs (TREND). Retrieved from https://www.cdc.gov/trendstatement/index.html

Christensen, L. (2012). Types of designs using random assignment. In H. Cooper (Ed.), *APA handbook of research methods in psychology* (pp. 469–488). Washington, DC: American Psychological Association. http://dx.doi.org/10.1037/13620-025

Cohen, J. (1988). *Statistical power analysis for the behavioral sciences* (2nd ed.). New York, NY: Academic Press.

Collins, L. (1977). A name to conjure with. *European Journal of Marketing, 11,* 340–363.

Consolidated Standards of Reporting Trials. (2007). *CONSORT: Transparent reporting of trials*. Retrieved from http://www.consort-statement.org/

Cook, D. J., Sackett, D. L., & Spitzer, W. O. (1995). Methodologic guidelines for systematic reviews of randomized control trials in health care from the Potsdam Consultation on Meta-Analysis. *Journal of Clinical Epidemiology, 48,* 167–171. http://dx.doi.org/10.1016/0895-4356(94)00172-M

Cooper, H. (2006). Research questions and research designs. In P. A. Alexander, P. H. Winne, & G. Phye (Eds.), *Handbook of research in educational psychology* (2nd ed., pp. 849–877). Mahwah, NJ: Erlbaum.

Cooper, H. (2016). *Ethical choices in research: Managing data, writing reports, and publishing results in the social sciences*. Washington, DC: American Psychological Association. http://dx.doi.org/10.1037/14859-000

Cooper, H. (2017). *Research synthesis and meta-analysis: A step-by-step approach* (5th ed.). Thousand Oaks, CA: Sage.

Cooper, H., DeNeve, K., & Charlton, K. (1997). Finding the missing science: The fate of studies submitted for review by a human subjects committee. *Psychological Methods, 2,* 447–452. http://dx.doi.org/10.1037/1082-989X.2.4.447

Cooper, H., & Dent, A. (2011). Ethical issues in the conduct and reporting of meta-analysis. In A. T. Panter & S. Sterba (Eds.), *Handbook of ethics in quantitative methodology* (pp. 417–444). New York, NY: Routledge.

Cooper, H., Hedges, L. V., & Valentine, J. C. (Eds.). (2009). *The handbook of research synthesis and meta-analysis* (2nd ed.). New York, NY: Russell Sage Foundation.

Corbett, B. A. (2003). Video modeling: A window into the world of autism. *The Behavior Analyst Today, 4,* 367–377. http://dx.doi.org/10.1037/h0100025

Cummings, G. (2012). *Understanding the new statistics: Effect sizes, confidence intervals, and meta-analysis*. New York, NY: Routledge.

Davidson, K. W., Goldstein, M., Kaplan, R. M., Kaufmann, P. G., Knatterud, G. L., Orleans, C. T., . . . Whitlock, E. P. (2003). Evidence-based behavioral medicine: What is it and how do we achieve it? *Annals of Behavioral Medicine, 26,* 161–171. http://dx.doi.org/10.1207/S15324796ABM2603_01

Des Jarlais, D. C., Lyles, C., Crepaz, N., & the TREND Group. (2004). Improving the reporting quality of nonrandomized evaluations of behavioral and public health interventions: TREND statement. *American Journal of Public Health, 94,* 361–366. http://dx.doi.org/10.2105/AJPH.94.3.361

Dienes, Z. (2011). Bayesian versus orthodox statistics: Which side are you on? *Perspectives on Psychological Science, 6,* 274–290. http://dx.doi.org/10.1177/1745691611406920

Evers, W. J. G., Brouwers, A., & Tomic, W. (2006). A quasi-experimental study on management coaching effectiveness. *Consulting Psychology Journal: Practice and Research, 58,* 174–182. http://dx.doi.org/10.1037/1065-9293.58.3.174

Every Student Succeeds Act of 2015, Pub. L. No. 114-95, § 114 Stat. 1177 (2015–2016).

Fagan, J., Palkovitz, R., Roy, K., & Farrie, D. (2009). Pathways to paternal engagement: Longitudinal effects of risk and resilience on nonresident fathers. *Developmental Psychology, 45,* 1389–1405. http://dx.doi.org/10.1037/a0015210

Fleiss, J. L., & Berlin, J. A. (2009). Measures of effect size for categorical data. In H. Cooper, L. V. Hedges, & J. C. Valentine (Eds.), *The handbook of research synthesis and meta-analysis* (2nd ed., pp. 237–253). New York, NY: Russell Sage Foundation.

Geary, D. C., & vanMarle, K. (2016). Young children's core symbolic and nonsymbolic quantitative knowledge in the prediction of later mathematics achievement. *Developmental Psychology, 52,* 2130–2144. http://dx.doi.org/10.1037/dev0000214

Goldinger, S. D., He, Y., & Papesh, M. H. (2009). Deficits in cross-race face learning: Insights from eye movements and pupillometry. *Journal of Experimental Psychology: Learning, Memory, and Cognition, 35,* 1105–1122. http://dx.doi.org/10.1037/a0016548

Grabe, S., Ward, L. M., & Hyde, J. S. (2008). The role of the media in body image concerns among women: A meta-analysis of experimental and correlational studies. *Psychological Bulletin, 134,* 460–476. http://dx.doi.org/10.1037/0033-2909.134.3.460

Gurven, M., von Rueden, C., Massenkoff, M., Kaplan, H., & Lero Vie, M. (2013). How universal is the Big Five? Testing the five-factor model of personality variation among forager-farmers in the Bolivian Amazon. *Journal of Personality and Social Psychology, 104,* 354–370. http://dx.doi.org/10.1037/a0030841

Hedges, L. V., & Vevea, J. L. (1998). Fixed and random effects models in meta-analysis. *Psychological Methods, 3,* 486–504. http://dx.doi.org/10.1037/1082-989X.3.4.486

Hoyle, R. H. (2012). *Handbook of structural equation modeling.* New York, NY: Guilford Press.

International Committee of Medical Journal Editors. (2007). *ICMJE: International Committee of Medical Journal Editors.* Retrieved from http://www.icmje.org/#clin_trials

Jack, B. N., O'Shea, R. P., Cottrell, D., & Ritter, W. (2013). Does the ventriloquist illusion assist selective listening? *Journal of Experimental Psychology: Human Perception and Performance, 39,* 1496–1502. http://dx.doi.org/10.1037/a0033594

Jackman, S. (2009). *Bayesian analysis for the social sciences.* West Sussex, England: Wiley. http://dx.doi.org/10.1002/9780470686621

Kaplan, D. (2014). *Bayesian statistics for the social sciences.* New York, NY: Guilford Press.

Kazdin, A. E. (2011). *Single-case research design: Methods for clinical and applied setting.* Oxford, England: Oxford University Press.

Killeen, P. R., Sanabria, F., & Dolgov, I. (2009). The dynamics of conditioning and extinction. *Journal of Experimental Psychology: Animal Behavior Processes, 35,* 447–472. http://dx.doi.org/10.1037/a0015626

Kline, R. B. (2012). *Beyond significance testing.* Washington, DC: American Psychological Association.

Kline, R. B. (2016). *Principles and practice of structural equation modeling.* New York, NY: Guilford Press.

Kline, T. J. B. (2005). *Psychological testing: A practical approach to design and evaluation.* Thousand Oaks, CA: Sage.

Kohli, C. S., Harich, K. R., & Leuthesser, L. (2005). Creating brand identity: A study of evaluation of new brand names. *Journal of Business Research*, *58*, 1506–1515. http://dx.doi.org/10.1016/j.jbusres.2004.07.007

Kratochwill, T. R., & Levin, J. R. (Eds.). (2014). *Single case intervention research: Methodological and statistical advances*. Washington, DC: American Psychological Association. http://dx.doi.org/10.1037/14376-000

Lachin, J. M. (2005). A review of methods for futility stopping based on conditional power. *Statistics in Medicine*, *24*, 2747–2764. http://dx.doi.org/10.1002/sim.2151

Levitt, H. M. (in press). *Reporting qualitative research in psychology: How to meet APA Style Journal Article Reporting Standards*. Washington, DC: American Psychological Association.

Levitt, H. M., Bamberg, M., Creswell, J. W., Frost, D. M., Josselson, R., & Suárez-Orozco, C. (2018). Journal article reporting standards for qualitative primary, qualitative meta-analytic, and mixed methods research in psychology: The APA Publications and Communications Board task force report. *American Psychologist*, *73*, 26–46. http://dx.doi.org/10.1037/amp0000151

Lipsey, M. W., & Wilson, D. B. (1993). The efficacy of psychological, educational, and behavioral treatment: Confirmation from meta-analysis. *American Psychologist*, *48*, 1181–1209. http://dx.doi.org/10.1037/0003-066X.48.12.1181

Little, R. J., Long, Q., & Lin, X. (2009). A comparison of methods for estimating the causal effect of a treatment in randomized clinical trials subject to noncompliance. *Biometrics*, *65*, 640–649. http://dx.doi.org/10.1111/j.1541-0420.2008.01066.x

Little, R. J., & Rubin, D. B. (2002). *Statistical analysis with missing data* (2nd ed.). Hoboken, NJ: Wiley. http://dx.doi.org/10.1002/9781119013563

Luke, D. A. (2004). *Multilevel modeling*. Thousand Oaks, CA: Sage. http://dx.doi.org/10.4135/9781412985147

McLanahan, S., & Garfinkel, I. (2000). *The Fragile Families and Child Wellbeing Study: Questions, design, and a few preliminary results* (Center for Research on Child Wellbeing Working Paper No. 00-07). Retrieved from http://crcw.princeton.edu/workingpapers/WP00-07-FF-McLanahan.pdf

Menard, S. (2002). *Applied logistic regression analysis*. Thousand Oaks, CA: Sage. http://dx.doi.org/10.4135/9781412983433

Moher, D., Cook, D. J., Eastwood, S., Olkin, I., Rennie, D., & Stroup, D. (1999). Improving the quality of reporting of meta-analysis of randomised controlled trials: The QUOROM statement. *The Lancet*, *354*, 1896–1900. http://dx.doi.org/10.1016/S0140-6736(99)04149-5

Moher, D., Liberati, A., Tetzlaff, J., & Altman, D. G., & the PRISMA Group. (2009). Preferred reporting items for systematic reviews and meta-analyses: The PRISMA statement. *PLoS Medicine*, *6*, e1000097. http://dx.doi.org/10.1371/journal.pmed.1000097

Moher, D., Schulz, K. F., & Altman, D. G. (2001). The CONSORT statement: Revised recommendations for improving the quality of reports of parallel-group randomized trials. *Annals of Internal Medicine*, *134*, 657–662. http://dx.doi.org/10.7326/0003-4819-134-8-200104170-00011

Moller, A. C., Forbes-Jones, E., & Hightower, A. D. (2008). Classroom age composition and developmental change in 70 urban preschool classrooms. *Journal of Educational Psychology, 100*, 741–753. http://dx.doi.org/10.1037/a0013099

Muthén, L. K., & Muthén, B. O. (2007). *Mplus users' guide* (5th ed.). Los Angeles, CA: Author.

National Institutes of Health. (1998). *NIH policy for data and safety monitoring.* Retrieved from https://grants.nih.gov/grants/guide/notice-files/not98-084.html

No Child Left Behind Act of 2001, Pub. L. No. 107-110, 115 Stat. 1425 (2002).

Norman, C. D., Maley, O., Li, X., & Skinner, H. A. (2008). Using the Internet to assist smoking prevention and cessation in schools: A randomized, controlled trial. *Health Psychology, 27*, 799–810. http://dx.doi.org/10.1037/a0013105

O'Neill, O. A., Vandenberg, R. J., DeJoy, D. M., & Wilson, M. G. (2009). Exploring relationships among anger, perceived organizational support, and workplace outcomes. *Journal of Occupational Health Psychology, 14*, 318–333. http://dx.doi.org/10.1037/a0015852

Open Science Collaboration. (2015). Estimating the reproducibility of psychological science. *Science, 349*, aac4716. http://dx.doi.org/10.1126/science.aac4716

Ottaviani, C., Thayer, J. F., Verkuil, B., Lonigro, A., Medea, B., Couyoumdjian, A., & Brosschot, J. F. (2016). Physiological concomitants of perseverative cognition: A systematic review and meta-analysis. *Psychological Bulletin, 142*(3), 231–259. http://dx.doi.org/10.1037/bul0000036

Pocock, S. J. (1993). Statistical and ethical issues in monitoring clinical trials. *Statistics in Medicine, 12*, 1459–1469. http://dx.doi.org/10.1002/sim.4780121512

Risen, J. L., & Gilovich, T. (2008). Why people are reluctant to tempt fate. *Journal of Personality and Social Psychology, 95*, 293–307. http://dx.doi.org/10.1037/0022-3514.95.2.293

Sackett, D. L., Rosenberg, W. M. C., Gray, J. A. M., Haynes, R. B., & Richardson, W. S. (1996). Evidence based medicine: What it is and what it isn't. *British Medical Journal, 312*, 71–72. http://dx.doi.org/10.1136/bmj.312.7023.71

Shadish, W. R., Cook, T. D., & Campbell, D. T. (2002). *Experimental and quasi-experimental designs for generalized causal inference.* Boston, MA: Houghton Mifflin.

Spiegelhalter, D., & Rice, K. (2009). Bayesian statistics. *Scholarpedia, 4*(8), 5230., revision #91036. Retrieved from http://www.scholarpedia.org/article/Bayesian_statistics

Stroup, D. F., Berlin, J. A., Morton, S. C., Olkin, I., Williamson, G. D., Rennie, D., . . . Thacker, S. B. (2000). Meta-analysis of observational studies in epidemiology: A proposal for reporting. *JAMA, 283*, 2008–2012. http://dx.doi.org/10.1001/jama.283.15.2008

Tanner-Smith, E. E., & Tipton, E. (2014). Robust variance estimation with dependent effect sizes: Practical considerations including a software tutorial in Stata and SPSS. *Research Synthesis Methods, 5*(1), 13–30. http://dx.doi.org/10.1002/jrsm.1091

Taylor, J., & James, L. M. (2009). Evidence for a putative biomarker for substance dependence. *Psychology of Addictive Behaviors, 23*, 491–499. http://dx.doi.org/10.1037/a0016632

Tsaousides, T., Warshowsky, A., Ashman, T. A., Cantor, J. B., Spielman, L., & Gordon, W. A. (2009). The relationship between employment-related self-efficacy and quality of life following traumatic brain injury. *Rehabilitation Psychology, 54*, 299–305. http://dx.doi.org/10.1037/a0016807

Vadasy, P. F., & Sanders, E. A. (2008). Repeated reading intervention: Outcomes and interactions with readers' skills and classroom instruction. *Journal of Educational Psychology, 100*, 272–290. http://dx.doi.org/10.1037/0022-0663.100.2.272

Vandenbroucke, J. P., von Elm, E., Altman, D. G., Gøtzsche, P. C., Mulrow, C. D., Pocock, S. J., . . . Egger, M. (2014). Strengthening the Reporting of Observational Studies in Epidemiology (STROBE): Explanation and elaboration. *International Journal of Surgery, 12*, 1500–1524. http://dx.doi.org/10.1016/j.ijsu.2014.07.014

Verhagen, J., & Wagenmakers, E. J. (2014). Bayesian tests to quantify the result of a replication attempt. *Journal of Experimental Psychology: General, 143*, 1457–1475. http://dx.doi.org/10.1037/a0036731

Vinnars, B., Thormählen, B., Gallop, R., Norén, K., & Barber, J. P. (2009). Do personality problems improve during psychodynamic supportive–expressive psychotherapy? Secondary outcome results from a randomized controlled trial for psychiatric outpatients with personality disorders. *Psychotherapy: Theory, Research, Practice, Training, 46*, 362–375. http://dx.doi.org/10.1037/a0017002

Wheatley, K., & Clayton, D. (2003). Be skeptical about unexpected large apparent treatment effects: The case of an MRC AML12 randomization. *Controlled Clinical Trials, 24*, 66–70. http://dx.doi.org/10.1016/S0197-2456(02)00273-8

Wilkinson, L., & the Task Force on Statistical Inference. (1999). Statistical methods in psychology journals: Guidelines and explanations. *American Psychologist, 54*, 594–604. http://dx.doi.org/10.1037/0003-066X.54.8.594

Index

About the Author

Harris Cooper, PhD, is the Hugo L. Blomquist Distinguished Professor of Psychology and Neuroscience at Duke University. He is the author of several books, including *Research Synthesis and Meta-Analysis: A Step-by-Step Approach; Ethical Choices in Research: Managing Data, Writing Reports, and Publishing Results in the Social Sciences;* and *Critical Thinking About Research: Psychology and Related Fields* (second to Julian Meltzoff). He is a former editor of the journals *Psychological Bulletin* and *Archives of Scientific Psychology.* He served as chair of the psychology department at both Duke University and the University of Missouri–Columbia and as dean of the social sciences at Duke (2017–2018).